With best wishes

Christopher Frith

&

John Aston

BURGUNDY
VINES AND WINES

John Arlott
and
Christopher Fielden

BURGUNDY
VINES AND WINES

DAVIS-POYNTER LIMITED
LONDON

First published in 1976 by
Davis-Poynter Limited
20 Garrick Street London WC2E 9BJ

Copyright © 1976 by John Arlott and Christopher Fielden

All rights reserved. No part of this publication may be
reproduced, stored in a retrieval system, or transmitted,
in any form or by any means, electronic, mechanical,
photocopying, recording or otherwise without prior
permission of the publishers.

ISBN 0 7067 0197 6

Designed and maps drawn by Tony Cowell
Photographs by Patrick Eagar

Printed in Great Britain by
Hazell Watson & Viney Ltd,
Aylesbury, Bucks

To VALERIE *and* ANN, *who so selflessly helped with the tasting*

CONTENTS

Acknowledgements	page	xiii
Preface		xv
1 Prospect of Burgundy		1
2 *Appellation Contrôlée* in Burgundy		10
3 The Vineyards of Burgundy: Historical Survey		19
4 The Men of Burgundy and Their Work		31
5 The Generic Burgundies		53
6 The Beaujolais		67
7 The Mâconnais		88
8 Côte Chalonnaise: Région de Mercurey		99
9 Côte de Beaune		119
10 Côte de Nuits		179
11 Chablis and the Yonne		223
12 Apéritifs and Digestifs		238
13 Some Tasting Notes		243
Bibliography		251
Index		255

ILLUSTRATIONS
Photographs by Patrick Eagar

Between pages 46 *and* 47
The courtyard of the fifteenth-century Hôtel-Dieu, Beaune
The four major grapes of Burgundy
Drawing a sample of wine in a cellar in the Beaujolais
The Rock of Solutré, visible from all over Pouilly Fuissé

Between pages 78 *and* 79
'Le crieur' encouraging bidders at the Hospices de Beaune auction
Clos d'Arlot on the Côte de Nuits
Chablis, seen from the *grand cru* vineyard les Clos
The prestigious vineyards of Vosne-Romanée

Between pages 206 *and* 207
Beaune – the weekend of the Hospices wine sale
The vertical wooden grape press traditional in the Beaujolais
Radar equipment employed to give early warning of hail
One of the Air Alpes aircraft used to precipitate hail storms
Chénas, one of the nine named *crus* of the Beaujolais

Between pages 238 *and* 239
Meloisey in the Hautes-Côtes de Beaune
Égrappillage – collecting grapes missed by the pickers – at le Montrachet
Sampling new wines before the Hospices de Beaune wine sale
Clos de Vougeot, the heart of the Burgundy winefield

MAPS

1	France, showing the Burgundy wine-growing area	xviii
2	Villages of the Hautes-Côtes de Beaune	62
3	Villages of the Hautes-Côtes de Nuits	64
4	Beaujolais Villages	66
5	Beaujolais *Grands Crus*	80
6	Pouilly	96
7	The Côte Chalonnaise	100
8	Montagny	102
9	Givry	106
10	Mercurey	108
11	Rully	114
12	The Côte de Beaune	118
13	Santenay	122
14	Chassagne-Montrachet	126
15	Puligny-Montrachet	134
16	Meursault	136
17	Auxey-Duresses	140
18	Monthélie	144

MAPS

19	Volnay	146
20	Pommard	150
21	Beaune	154
22	Savigny-les-Beaune	166
23	Pernand-Vergelesses	169
24	Ladoix-Serrigny and Aloxe-Corton	174
25	The Côte de Nuits	178
26	Nuits Saint-Georges	182
27	Prémeaux	186
28	Vosne-Romanée	192
29	Vougeot and Flagey-Echézeaux	196
30	Chambolle-Musigny	202
31	Morey-Saint-Denis	208
32	Gevrey-Chambertin	216
33	Fixin and Brochon	220
34	The Yonne	224
35	Chablis *Grands Crus*	230
36	Chablis	234

ACKNOWLEDGEMENTS

We are deeply indebted to the many *vignerons, negociants, courtiers,* connoisseurs and simple drinkers, longer and wiser in knowledge of the wine than ourselves, who have helped us.

Our thanks are due, too, to M. Raby of the Yonne Maison de Tourisme; Messrs Canard, the Director, and Dufour of the Union Interprofessionnelle des Vins de Beaujolais; and – as ever – Mlle Catherine Manac'h of the 'Food from France' office in London for assistance in visits to the vineyards.

JOHN ARLOTT
CHRISTOPHER FIELDEN

PREFACE

This repeats our thanks to those many Burgundians and Burgundy enthusiasts who so generously shared their bottles and knowledge with us. Their names are too numerous to mention; and many of the most creditable are, by reason of that credit, lost in the roseate mists of vinous study. The books consulted are listed in the bibliography at page 251 and we would record our gratitude to their authors. Without them this book could never have been written; they share such merits as it may have; the errors and omissions are solely ours.

That eminent wine-historian of Burgundy, Pierre Forgeot, in the preface to his admirable *Pèlérinage aux Sources du Bourgogne*, says modestly that everything has already been said about the wines of Burgundy, and that it would prove difficult to find a new way of presenting it. The basic Poupon-Forgeot reference formula – colour, average production, area, alternative appellations – must be followed in any study of these wines. The justification for this book lies in the rapid developments in viticulture during the last twenty years. Advances in agriculture, chemistry, mechanization and vinification, new appellations and fresh emphases, have changed the aspect of wine-making everywhere, even in the most traditionalist vineyards of Burgundy.

There is, too, a new type of wine-student in the visitor, either by car – for whom the Route des Grand Crus, the two Routes du Beaujolais and the Route de Chablis have been planned and signposted – or on a 'package' vineyard tour.

We have dealt with the vineyards in simple geographic sequence, from south to north.

PREFACE

The average production cited for a vineyard or *appellation* is based on returns for the twelve years 1963–1974, except where * indicates that figures are not available for the entire period – generally because the *appellation* has not been in existence long enough.

Output is quoted in hectolitres (hl.); area in hectares (ha.).

Hectolitre = 100 litres
            21·9975 imperial gallons
            26·4171 U.S. gallons
            about 133 bottles

Hectare = 1 00 ares
          10,000 square metres
          2·47105 acres
          ·368 square miles

Are = 100 square metres
       120 square yards

Imperial gallon = 4·546 litres
                    8 pints
                    about 6 bottles

US gallon = 3·78531 litres
             about 5 bottles

Production of one hectolitre to the hectare is equivalent to 8·9 gallons (54 bottles) to the acre.

Ouvrée (Burgundian) = 428 square metres.

The following bottle-sizes are used for wines and spirits in Burgundy:

Half-bottle 37·50 cl. ⎫
Bottle   75·00 cl. ⎬ These are, specifically, bottle-sizes; the contents are, of course, less: thus, as shown on the label, the actual contents of a bottle will be 73 cl.
Magnum   1·50 litres ⎭

Pot (Beaujolais only) 50 cl.

The following are the traditional units of Burgundy cooperage:

Pièce (hogshead) 228 litres: 300 bottles
Feuillette (half *pièce*) 114 litres: 150 bottles
Quartaut (quarter *pièce*) 57 litres: 75 bottles
Beaujolais *pièce* (hogshead – Beaujolais only) 216 litres: 288 bottles
Beaujolais *feuillette* (half Beaujolais *pièce*) 108 litres: 144 bottles
Beaujolais *quartaut* (one quarter Beaujolais *pièce*) 54 litres: 72 bottles
Chablis *feuillette* (Chablis only) 132 litres: 175 bottles

The spelling of vineyard names in Burgundy varies considerably from grower to grower. Thus we find Savigny Dominode and Dominaude, Beaune Champs Pimonts and Champimonts, Mercurey Miglan and Myglands, and a host of other examples. This may account for apparent discrepancies in the text.

BURGUNDY
VINES AND WINES

FRANCE, SHOWING THE BURGUNDY WINE-GROWING AREA

1 PROSPECT OF BURGUNDY

Burgundy is a kingdom, a people, a tradition and a wine. Each is unique; all are interdependent. To understand the wine of Burgundy it is not enough to taste it, even at its best. You must know the terrain where the grapes are grown; which faces of its hills are tilted towards the sun; how the narrow vineyard strips of ancient inheritance lie across the slopes; how the soil feels when you rub it between your fingers. You must see and talk to the men who prune and train, spray and plough, grub up and plant again; who gather, press, nurse, fine and bottle. You must listen to them, and taste and discuss their wines, direct from cask and bottle in cool cellars; better still, appreciate them with the fine food of Burgundy, for on the doorstep are fish from the Saône and the Doubs, waterfowl from the Dombes, game from the Chatillonais, ham from the Morvan, beef from the Charollais and the finest chickens in the world from the Bresse. With *rigodon* and *jambon Persillé*, *quenelles de brochet* and *pochouse*, *farchuse* and *coq au Chambertin, marcassin à la lie, époisses* and *chevrotton de Mâcon*, the wines of Burgundy are at their best.

You must remember that the wine of Burgundy means not one but two of the greatest wines of the world, reds that are the equals – but not the rivals – of those from Bordeaux, and the finest of all dry white wines; that they are not simply many-sided, but many wines: even from neighbouring rows of vines, belonging to the same man, the wines are different. Their making is at once a science and a mystique, commerce and an ideal; both a technical and a human matter.

The wine of Burgundy is unique. Regardless of quality – or whether better wine is made elsewhere – this is a product which can only come from these specific grapes, grown in this specific way, in these specific – and differing – soils, and in this specific – and yearly different – climate. Gaston Roupnel – a native of Gevrey-Chambertin – in his expansive preface to Camille Rodier's monograph, *Clos de Vougeot*, wrote:

> This terrain took thousands of years to develop its genius and aptitude for producing these grapes and wines. The excellence of the product was only gradually revealed; and the due vocation of these vineyards was not made clear until they had been enriched by unending repetition of vegetable decay. This soil is the product of men and ages beyond reckoning. Over thousand-year periods the sap of centuries and the ancient potency of vegetation has been built up in this flank of the earth by the accumulation of the ruin of each year's crop.
>
> As with the vineyard, so with the wine. It is the creation of age. Only time brings the delicacy, the bouquet, the aroma and the velvet texture of a great vintage. Yet, however old it may be, the finest récolte has its beginnings far back beyond the year of its birth. The forces that shaped it were at work long before its vines were even planted; its excellence was already buried in the earth when it began to send down roots. Before it could start to be born, the earth that engendered it had to be ancient in labour; its cradle a tomb created by the ashes of years and the dust of centuries.

It must not be thought that Burgundy produces nothing but the greatest, most expensive wines. Within its boundaries are reared a host of more reasonably priced bottles. One of the main objects of this book is to present these wines, many of which are unknown to the general wine-consuming public. While the Chambertins and the Romanée-Contis may be the proud pennant on the tower, the wines of the Beaujolais and the Mâconnais are the warm body of the building with room for all.

Nowadays the province of Burgundy consists of the five French *départements* of the Yonne, Nièvre, Côte d'Or, Saône-et-Loire and Ain. The viticultural area of Burgundy, though, has different boundaries, since it includes also the vast area of the Beaujolais, which for governmental purposes comes in the Lyonnais. It excludes, however, the area which produces the charming wines of Bugey in the Ain *département,* which are classed with those of Savoie, and the better known white wines of Pouilly-sur-Loire.

To look first at its geography, the wine region of Burgundy broadly follows the A6 motorway from Paris to Lyon for a distance of about 250 kilometres; although at its broadest it is thirty kilometres across, at its narrowest it is less than 150 metres. It is not an unbroken succession of vineyards for the whole distance, but a series of different areas, each generally clearly separated from the next. Driving south from Paris, you come first, after about 150 kilometres, to the vineyards of the Yonne. Those on the left produce the great white wines of Chablis, those on the right the lesser known Irancy and Saint Bris. Planted on the chalky slopes of the valley of the Serein, the Chablis vineyards are more a continuation of those of Champagne than of those of Burgundy.

In another 120 kilometres to the south-east, you reach Dijon, for long the capital of the Dukes of Burgundy. For some time after that its importance declined and only with the coming of the railway did it re-establish itself as the chief town of the province. This is the gateway to the Côte d'Or, the Golden Slopes – in these times of highly priced wine, more aptly titled than ever before. Dijon, though, is rather like a port that has been deserted by the sea. The phylloxera plague among the vines and, latterly, the high price of building land, drove away the vineyards, for once the wine district of the Côte Dijonnaise stretched from Marsannay up to the north-west of the town. In 1935 Camille Rodier talked of the wines of Larrey, but they no longer exist: and those of Marsannay are now classified with those of the Côtes de Nuits. All that remains as witness of the past importance of the Dijon wines is the large oak wine-press, named after Margaret of Burgundy, which once belonged to a vineyard called Clos du Roi, formerly at Chenove.

While the importance of Dijon as a wine-town has diminished, it is still the base for certain shippers. Its gastronomic reputation rests more solidly now on its mustard, its gingerbread and its Crème de Cassis, the local blackcurrant liqueur. In November of each year there is a food fair, which attracts visitors from all over the world.

Dijon is a lively city, whose modern shops contrast with its ancient buildings. For those visitors who demand some life in the evenings, its fine hotels make it a better headquarters for Burgundy and its vineyards than the smaller, wine-steeped towns.

To the immediate south, the village of Marsannay-la-Côte marks the beginning of the most noble succession of wine-villages in the world, along the narrow sixty-kilometre strip that is the Côte d'Or. The first thirty kilometres are the Côte de Nuits, with the great red wines of Fixin, Gevrey-Chambertin, Morey-Saint-Denis, Chambolle-Musigny, Vougeot, Vosne-Romanée and Nuits Saint-Georges; then come the red and white wine villages of the Côte de Beaune – Aloxe-Corton, Savigny, Beaune, Pommard, Volnay, Meursault, Puligny-Montrachet, Chassagne-Montrachet and Santenay. Where the eastern-facing slopes of the Morvan catch the full warmth of the summer sun, are grown the *pinot noir* and *chardonnay,* producing wines of world reputation.

To the traveller in a hurry, Nuits Saint-Georges seems little more than a succession of traffic-lights and a series of traffic-jams. Apart from the thirteenth-century church of Saint Symphorien, there are few buildings of interest in the town, which was sacked by the Germans in 1578, the Swedes in 1636 and the Germans again in 1870. Beneath its narrow streets, though, lie the cellars of many of Burgundy's most important shippers and alongside them, two important fruit-juice factories.

Beaune is a far more impressive town, the medieval walls and towers originally built for its defence now provide cellars for much of the finest wine, and contribute to the feeling of antiquity and continuity. At the northern entrance to the town is the church of Saint Nicholas, dating from the thirteenth century, and a triumphal arch built in 1752. In the centre, within minutes' walk of each other are the fifteenth-century Hôtel-Dieu, the wine-museum housed in the former palace of the Dukes of Burgundy, the twelfth-century church of Notre Dame, which houses a valuable series of tapestries, and the seventeenth-century Hospice de la Charité. There can be few more agreeable cities in which to stroll at leisure, at every turn there are new surprises with glimpses of flowery courtyards from the middle ages and dusky cellars with row upon row of casks. Beaune is a town that is proud of its past, and its present, and is pleased to welcome visitors. The recently constructed motorways have brought new tourists for, while many hurry past on the way to the ski-slopes of Switzerland or the beaches of the Mediterranean, many others break their journey to sample the wine, food, culture and hospitality of Burgundy.

Behind the ridge of the Côte d'Or lies a pleasant hinterland of wooded hills, chalk cliffs, narrow gorges and sunlit valleys in which lie villages, often consisting of little more than a church, a bar and a jumble of houses. This is the land of the Arrière-Côtes, called euphemistically in the guide books 'the Switzerland of Burgundy'. The vineyards there produce many of the workhorse wines, which do justice to everyday fare, but have no pretensions to the high tables. In Nolay, with its covered market from the fourteenth century, a wine fair is held each spring. La Rochepot has a fairytale castle, and from the cliffs of Orches, on a clear day, you can see across the plain of the Saône to the distant Alps. There is an air of peace and calm, and the growers are happy to stop work and talk to anyone interested in their wines.

To the south, as you cross into the *département* of Saône et Loire, lies the Côte Chalonnaise, or – as it is more usually called nowadays – the Région de Mercurey. Off to the right of the N481, the main road from Chagny to the old monastic town of Cluny, lie the four villages of Mercurey, Rully, Givry and Montagny, which have long produced quality wines that are only now coming to be widely appreciated. Intermingled with the vineyards are fields of sleek cattle. Up on the slopes of the hills, though, the brush has been cleared and important areas of vines are being planted. Rully is also the centre of a flourishing sparkling wine business.

At Tournus begin the vineyards of the Mâconnais, which stretch to the south over a broad band for forty-five kilometres. In the fourteenth and fifteenth centuries the red wines of Tournus were so fine that Beaune had to take anti-dumping measures as protection against their competition. The best-known feature of Tournus today is the magnificent romanesque church of Saint Philibert. The other patron saint of the town, Saint Valérian, was martyred there at the end of the second century. As a Roman citizen, he was accorded the privilege of being executed by beheading; to show his contempt for the way he had been treated, he is said to have picked up his fallen head and walked away with it. The vineyards of the Mâconnais used to produce vast quantities of undistinguished red wine from the *gamay* grape, but there has been much replanting recently with the *chardonnay,* which produces there an agreeable, fresh, dry, white wine, largely sold through the great shippers of the town of Mâcon. At the southern end of the Mâconnais are the vineyards producing the well-known white wines of Pouilly-Fuisse, and its lesser known satellites, Loché and Vinzelles. The vines are dominated by the rock of Solutré, where human remains going back almost 20,000 years have been found. From a later date are the bones of 100,000 horses, apparently killed by our ancestors by being driven off the top of the rock.

The Mâcon shippers also handle much of the wine of the Beaujolais, the last wine area of Burgundy, but by far the most important in terms of quantity. As already mentioned, while the area is linked with Burgundy on wine-lists, the style of life there has a much more southern flavour. The villages, with their tall houses with red-tiled roofs – and the dusty squares where the most intrusive sounds are the clicking of *boules* and the clinking of glasses – could almost be in Provence. The spirit of Clochemerle still lives on and a large proportion of the wine not drunk on the spot goes south, to slake the never-failing thirst of the inhabitants of Lyons.

The vineyards of the Beaujolais cover an area of about forty-five kilometres by fifteen, an area of rounded hills of granite, sloping away in the east to the plain of the Saône, where the N6 marks the ultimate boundary of the vineyards. The area of Beaujolais Villages lies to the north of the region where it mingles with the fringes of the Mâconnais, and the nine best villages of all – Saint Amour, Juliénas, Chénas, Chiroubles, Moulin-à-Vent, Morgon, Fleurie, Brouilly (and Côte de Brouilly) – have the right to their name alone on the label. Whilst most Beaujolais should be drunk young, these can, in the best years, stand some age in bottle.

The vineyard areas of Burgundy are by no means compact and each has its own characteristics. Although these wines have achieved worldwide popularity, their average production is small; in a normal year about 1·3 million hectolitres or about 173 million bottles. To put this in perspective, Bordeaux produces between two-and-a-half and three times as much. Also, if the total production of Burgundy is considered as a single bottleful, less than a generous glassful would be from the finer wine areas of the Côte d'Or and Chablis. Since these two areas are not far from the northern limit of the vine, they are much at the mercy of the climate. This can cause wide variations, not just between the quality of the wine produced from year to year, but also of the quantity. This is well illustrated by the following table, which shows the declared production (in hectolitres) of quality wine from the four *départements* of Burgundy over the past few years:

	1974	1973	1972	1971	1961/70 (average)
Côte d'Or (Côte de Nuits, Côte de Beaune)	215,688	388,745	332,102	152,501	228,400
Yonne (Chablis)	78,364	81,139	53,187	35,419	50,000
Saône et Loire (Région de Mercurey, Mâconnais)	429,964	565,947	449,215	319,507	337,800
Rhône (Beaujolais)	1,019,539	800,424	719,396	700,037	711,400

It can be seen that, whilst there is little variation in the production of the Beaujolais, from year to year, this is not the case on the Côte d'Or and in Chablis. It should be noted that both 1972 and 1973 were exceptionally large crops.

The relatively small production has created special problems for Burgundy, for its wines have always been much in demand. As a result, wines which masquerade as Burgundies are produced in countries throughout the world. Whilst the Americans have now prohibited the importation of so-called Spanish Burgundy and Spanish Chablis, they are quite happy to sell Gallo's Hearty Burgundy from California and Pink Chablis (*sic*) from New York State. To make an even bigger mockery of the affair, there is often little attempt to produce a similar style wine. In Australia, many *vignerons* call a wine claret or burgundy, dependent on what orders there are outstanding and what bottles are available. One prestigious California Burgundy describes itself as being made from the Petit Syrah grape, a variety unknown in Burgundy itself. It is a pity that the local trade associations have not been as active as their colleagues in Reims and Jerez. It may be that the name Burgundy has been in the public domain for too long, but such recent encroachments as the production of Beaujolais in New Zealand should not go unchallenged.

More serious, however, is the deliberate stretching of the production of Burgundy. While most of the stories of tankers of Algerian wine arriving in Beaune, to be resold as Nuits Saint-Georges and Pommard are no doubt apocryphal, there can be little doubt that adulteration has taken place in some Burgundian cellars, as well as those of their clients overseas. This is now largely impossible because of the regulations of *'appellations d'origine contrôlées'* (A.C.) discussed in the following chapter.

More than any other part of France, Burgundy is the country of the small vineyard owner. On the Côte d'Or, the average holding is less than half a hectare and even smaller in the Yonne and Saône et Loire. This is an average and, since such Côte d'Or domains as those of Bouchard Père et Fils, J. Faiveley, Chanson Père et Fils, Clair-Däu, Louis Latour and the Hospices de Beaune are of forty or more hectares, it follows that many are extremely small. Current fluctuations in prices make it difficult to know how many vines are needed to make a living, particularly since it costs as much to make a hogshead of Bourgogne as a hogshead of Chambertin. A majority of Burgundy vineyard owners work among their vines in the evenings and at weekends, but make their basic living elsewhere during the week. Many holdings are split up into a series of small plots, scattered about, sometimes in more than one village. The only apparent advantage of this arrangement is that it affords some protection against hail damage, for hail-stones normally strike over a limited area and spreading the vines lessens the risk.

Such a multiplicity of small-holdings seems ideal for the setting up of an efficient network of cooperative cellars. This has happened in the Beaujolais and the Mâconnais, but the cooperative cellar is of little importance on the Côte d'Or. Burgundian independence means that each man seeks to make his own wine; each man has his own vats and his own cellars. Some even bottle their wine themselves. Most of the marketing is done, though, by the *négociants* or shippers, under their own labels.

This book seeks to show something of the production of the wines of Burgundy; where they come from and how they arrive on the table of the consumer; the vital roles of the wine men of the region; the growers and the work that they do during the year; the brokers and their function in the Burgundy trade; the cellarmen and, finally, the shippers. Its chief purpose, however, is to describe the vineyards and the wines they produce, for this is the heart of the matter. Nobody knows all Burgundy and its wines and this book is only one view of the subject. It is a happy and absorbing subject, but words cannot capture the life of the most cheerful of French regions. As one of the local drinking songs says,

> C'est nous les joyeux Bourgignons,
> Les francs buveurs, les gais lurons.

The Burgundian likes to show off his wines, to taste them, to talk about them, to sing about them with friend and stranger alike. He likes the pleasures of life; Beaune and *boules* are his beer and skittles. He has no pretensions. If the Mercedes has replaced the *Deux-Chevaux*, the driver, as like as not, will still be wearing a beret and faded blue dungarees. The owner of vines in Chambertin does not consider himself superior to the owner of vines in the Arrière-Côtes, for they both face the same problems. It is not a country of impressive viticultural châteaux, though there are some; it is the country of lunch round the kitchen table, of hearty welcomes, food and drink.

2 *APPELLATION CONTRÔLÉE* IN BURGUNDY

For all the quality vineyard areas of France there is strict control over:
1. The site of the vineyard
2. The grape varieties used
3. The quantity of wine produced per hectare
4. The minimum alcoholic strength of the wine
5. The method of planting, pruning and treating the vines
6. The vinification of the wine.

Of course the regulations vary in particulars between districts, but their original objective was to guarantee a fair price for a limited production of quality wine, thus protecting the growers in times of difficulty. Whilst the laws are more severe for the finest qualities of wine, there is often the possibility of the wine taking a lesser classification if it fails to meet all the requirements for the higher one.

We shall discuss each of the classified names later: for the moment it is sufficient to show the different degrees in the classification of Burgundy wine. At the bottom are the regional names of Bourgogne Grand Ordinaire, Bourgogne, Bourgogne Aligoté and Bourgogne Passetoutgrain. These wines can be produced anywhere in the viticultural area of Burgundy, so long as they fulfil the necessary conditions of their particular appellation. Basically speaking, Bourgogne Grand Ordinaire is the lowest quality *Appellation Contrôlée* – A.C. – wine produced in the region.

Next come the tighter area names of Côte de Beaune Villages and

'APPELLATION CONTRÔLÉE' IN BURGUNDY

Côte de Nuits Villages, Bourgogne Hautes Côtes de Beaune, and Hautes Côtes de Nuits, Beaujolais and Beaujolais Villages, Chablis and Petit Chablis. These generally have a higher degree of alcohol and a smaller production than the regional wines and are accordingly more expensive.

The following step on the ladder is that of the mass of village names; some well-known like Fleurie, Meursault, Gevrey-Chambertin and Nuits Saint-Georges, and some less often seen such as Saint Aubin, Chorey-les-Beaune and Ladoix-Serrigny. The range of qualities of wine and of prices within this classification can be considerable, and it is more likely that a wine from a village like Chorey-les-Beaune will be sold as Côte de Beaune Villages than under its own name. Although that seems like declassification, the wine sells more easily under its second name and at about the same price.

Finally, on a higher rung, come the single vineyards with their various levels of classification. A vineyard in Burgundy is a strictly delimited plot of land called a *climat* and marked on maps lodged at each town-hall. The vineyard name is itself an *appellation contrôlée* as opposed to the system in Bordeaux, where the most restrictive name is that of the village. Moreover, even the largest vineyards of Burgundy cannot rival those of Bordeaux for size. According to the latest figures available, Château Lafite has eighty hectares, Château Latour fifty-eight, Château Mouton Rothschild seventy and Château Margaux fifty-five, and while these are the most prestigious vineyards of the Médoc, they are not the largest. These figures may change, too, since nothing precludes the owners from increasing their area. On the Côte d'Or the largest vineyard is Clos de Vougeot with fifty hectares followed by les Echézeaux, Beaune Grèves and Santenay Clos des Tavannes, each with about thirty. Importantly, too, while in Bordeaux nearly all vineyards have one owner and produce one wine, in Burgundy that would be a rare exception. Clos de Vougeot, for example, has over eighty proprietors, each producing his own wine, which he may then sell under his own label or to a shipper. That situation falls within the historical survey which follows.

The classification of the vineyards is in some ways less rigid than in Bordeaux, though the system has grown up over the centuries and does not depend on a single decision made at a specific date; and it does change from time to time. Not long ago a complete classification of the wines of Burgundy was compiled, grading them into *grand*, first, second and third growths (*crus*); but the last two categories have all but disappeared and the wines of those qualities are generally now sold only under their village name. Often the classification of the vineyard is not mentioned on the label, yet, even if the name is unfamiliar, it is possible to distinguish between them.

A *grand cru* vineyard name appears alone, without the name of the village, thus:

CHAMBERTIN
Appellation Chambertin Contrôlée
or
ROMANÉE SAINT VIVANT
Appellation Contrôlée

For a *premier cru* vineyard, the name of the village and of the vineyard are in the same size type, so we might have:

GEVREY CHAMBERTIN LA PETITE CHAPELLE
Appellation Contrôlée
or
VOSNE ROMANÉE SUCHOTS
Appellation Vosne Romanée Suchots Contrôlée
or
BEAUNE CHAMPIMONTS
Appellation Beaune 1er Cru Contrôlée

or, if it is blended from two or more wines of the same classification, or comes from a little known vineyard, it might be seen as:

MEURSAULT 1er Cru
Appellation Meursault 1er Cru Contrôlée

For wines of lesser vineyards, the vineyard name must appear in letters not more than half the size of the village name; and the *appellation contrôlée* is simply that of the village:

MOREY SAINT DENIS Aux Chézaux
Appellation Morey Saint Denis Contrôlée

As to the grape varieties used in Burgundy, there are really only four, though certain lesser species are permitted in the Yonne *département*. For red wines, they are the *pinot noir* and the *gamay*; for the white, the *chardonnay* and the *aligoté*.

The *pinot noir* is used for all the fine wines of the Côte d'Or. It takes its name from the resemblance of its bunch to a pine cone. The grapes are small and form into tight bunches, which greatly increases the danger of *pourriture* or rot. The juice of the grape is colourless and it is the species used for much of the production of Champagne. The colour pigments are released from the skins only at the time of fermentation in the vats. Small proportions of certain sub-varieties such as the *pinot Liébault* and the *pinot gris*, or *beurot*, are sometimes used to add finesse to the wine.

Gamay is the name of a small wine village, by the side of the N6 Paris road, between Chassagne-Montrachet and Saint Aubin, and it has given its name to one of the world's most common grape-varieties. The finest wines it produces come from the weathered granite slopes of the Beaujolais. There it gives fresh wines with a full fruity bouquet, which are best when drunk young. On the Côte d'Or it produces a thin acid wine, without any distinction. When mixed with the *pinot* at the time of crushing in the proportion of two to one, it gives a wine called Bourgogne Passetoutgrain, which after a year or two's ageing can be most agreeable.

The *chardonnay* was for long confused with the *pinot blanc*, but is now recognized as a distinct variety. The *pinot blanc* is now virtually never seen in Burgundy, though there are extensive plantings of it in Alsace where it goes under the name of *Clevner*. The *chardonnay* grape is similar in size to the *pinot noir*, though the bunches are not so tightly formed. All the great white wines of Burgundy – of the Côte d'Or, the Mercurey region, the Mâconnais and Chablis – are produced from it, though in the last area it is called the *Beaunois*. The *chardonnay* variety has succeeded in many other countries: California has produced some outstanding wines from it.

The last of the four grape varieties is the *aligoté*, which gives a large production of average quality wine, generally sold under the name of Bourgogne Aligoté. When young, it has an agreeable fresh acidity and makes the perfect white carafe wine. It is mainly planted in the Arrière-Côtes; and certain villages, such as Bouze-les-Beaune, have created a reputation for their *aligotés*. Due to its low price, though, it is being increasingly replaced by the *chardonnay* and the *pinot noir*. Not long ago, however, such great vineyards as Corton Charlemagne were legally planted in part with the *aligoté*.

From the 1974 vintage the laws controlling the production of A.C. wines have been changed but it is important to consider what happened until then. Limitations of maximum production per hectare and the minimum degree of alcohol were – and still are – prescribed for every classification of Burgundy, though the quantity figure could be amended from year to year dependent on the crop. Thus, in 1973, most of the village appellations of the Côte d'Or were allowed to increase their maximum production from thirty-five hectolitres to the hectare to forty-five. That, though, was a record vintage in terms of quantity produced.

The system had one considerable weakness, however, and the regulations have been altered to correct it. While the maximum amount of wine produced under any *appellation* was controlled, the declassification method allowed for further quantities to be made so long as they took a lower classification. Thus the restriction did not improve the quality of the wine, but merely restricted the quantity for sale at the highest levels, and maintained price-levels. Unfortunately this meant that, although certain vineyard owners concentrated on producing limited quantities of quality wine, others sought to make the maximum possible under the full range of declassification. Perhaps this is best illustrated by the table of declassification of the *grand cru* vineyard Chambertin Clos de Bèze.

Appellation of wine	Minimum degree of alcohol	Maximum production per hectare (in hectolitres)	Balance per hectare over superior classification (in hectolitres)
Chambertin Clos de Bèze	11·5°	30	—
Gevrey-Chambertin 1er Cru	11°	35	5
Gevrey-Chambertin	10·5°	35	—
Bourgogne	10°	50	15
Bourgogne Ordinaire	9°	50	—

Thus it can be seen that, in this case, the grower could produce, quite legally, more than 50 per cent over the maximum quantity decreed for the best *appellation* of his vineyard. Until recently much of this surplus used to be sold in England under the optimum name. Naturally this led to abuses since one had to trust the shipper, when he said that the wine he sold under the appellation Bourgogne came in fact from the Chambertin Clos de Bèze vineyard. Important stocks of such wines still exist and it is well to beware of wine labels that make no mention of the words *Appellation Contrôlée,* or that carry such incongruities as:

CHAMBERTIN CLOS DE BÈZE
Appellation Bourgogne Contrôlée

Some British shippers undoubtedly bought good and honest wines under the declassification system, but they were few and were greatly outnumbered by those who sought to exploit a loophole in the legal system. To illustrate the dangers more graphically, the quantity of the 1971 Burgundy vintage was so small that no wine was declassified. Yet some merchants bought, in good faith, wines with the *appellation* Bourgogne, reputedly coming from greater vineyards. This deception was made easier because the *acquit vert* – the A.C. certificate – only guaranteed the source of the wine, not the vintage.

As this evidence shows, nothing is simple in Burgundy. The form of declassification varied from area to area, and even in some cases, from village to village. On the next page are two more examples of the old system: one from the Beaujolais and the other from Chablis.

The new – 1974 – legislation should go far to guarantee the quality of the wines of Burgundy for it gives the authorities more power to demand samples of any wine in a shipper's or grower's stock at any time, and records of all blending carried out must always be held available for inspection. Within five years it will be compulsory for samples of all wines to be submitted for tasting and analysis before a wine is granted A.C. status. This sampling is to be carried out before the wine leaves the growers' cellars – much to their disgust. They claim, perhaps with some justification, that to give judgement on a wine, possibly when it is only a month or two old, is a task beyond the capability of any inspector. To back their claim they point out that at the Concours Agricole in Paris, perhaps the most prestigious annual open wine competition in France, the wines of Burgundy were always judged in the second year of their life, whereas those of all other regions were assessed in their first year. The shippers, on the other hand, argue that it would

BURGUNDY

Appellation of wine	Minimum degree of alcohol	Maximum production per hectare (in hectolitres)	Balance per hectare over superior classification (in hectolitres)
Juliénas les Capitans	11°	40	—
Juliénas	10°	40	—
Beaujolais Villages	10°	45	5
Bourgogne (this declassification is only allowed in the Beaujolais for the nine village *crus*) or	10°	50	5
Beaujolais Supérieur	10°	50	—
Beaujolais	9°	50	—
or Bourgogne Grand Ordinaire	9°	50	—
Chablis les Clos	11°	35	—
Chablis 1er cru	10·5°	40	5
Chablis	10°	40	—
Bourgogne	10·5°	50	10
Bourgogne Grand Ordinaire	9·5°	50	—

be unfair if they were to buy a wine in all good faith as, say, a Pommard, only to have the sample rejected by inspectors after it reached their cellars. Despite protest marches by the growers, the shippers gained the day.

The most important change, however, is that declassification '*en cascade*' is now forbidden. Each year a base production figure for each *appellation* will be announced by the authorities after consultation with the local growers' association. Each grower then is entitled to so much wine per hectare with the *appellation*. If he produces up to 20 per cent over the base figure, he can still have the full appellation if he submits samples for tasting and analysis, and they are approved. If the samples are rejected, his entire production is refused the *appellation* and must either be distilled or turned into vinegar. If the grower has little confidence in the quality of his wine he can declare it in a lesser *appellation* where the quantity he can produce is greater and no sample has to be submitted. His production from one vineyard, however, can only be declared under one *appellation*.

To illustrate this let us take, as a hypothetical case, a grower in the

'APPELLATION CONTRÔLÉE' IN BURGUNDY

vineyard of Chambertin Clos de Bèze where the authorities have decreed for this vintage the following base production figures:

    Chambertin Clos de Bèze 30 hectolitres per hectare
    Gevrey-Chambertin   35   ,,
    Bourgogne   50   ,,

The following chart shows the different options open to the grower, dependent upon the size of his crop.

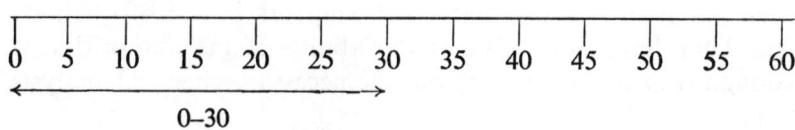

```
0    5   10   15   20   25   30   35   40   45   50   55   60
←─────────────────────→
        0–30
 Chambertin Clos de Bèze
 without submission of sample

                              ←────→
                              30–36
                       Chambertin Clos de Bèze
                          after approval of sample

                              ←────→
                              30–35
                          Gevrey-Chambertin
                       without submission of sample

                                    ←──────→
                                    35–42
                                Gevrey-Chambertin
                              after approval of sample

                                    ←──────────→
                                      35–50
                                    Bourgogne
                            without submission of sample

                                                ←──────→
                                                50–60
                                              Bourgogne
                                        after approval of sample

                                                        ──→
                                                        60–
                                                      Wine for
                                                     distillation
```

17

If a grower or shipper wants to do so he may, at a later date, declassify his wine to an inferior *appellation*. Thus, although he may have, for example, declared his crop as les Echézeaux for commercial reasons it may be easier for him to sell his wine as Vosne-Romanée 1er cru; or, as in the past, the majority of the red wine of a village like Chorey-les-Beaune will be sold as Côte de Beaune Villages.

The success or failure of the new regulations must depend on the efficiency of the organization responsible for their 'policing'. The initial reaction on the part of the growers and shippers is one of qualified scepticism. They have doubts as to the ability of the authorities to recruit enough technicians to carry out the necessary chemical analysis and tasting.

3 THE VINEYARDS OF BURGUNDY: HISTORICAL SURVEY

Burgundians, or their ancestors, have been drinking wine from the earliest times, though it is largely speculation on the part of Gaston Roupnel, when he suggests that the vine was introduced there from Switzerland during the sixth century BC. Indeed it is likely that the vine was growing wild in Gaul even earlier than that. The first known traces of wine in Burgundy were found in the grave of a Celtic prince, discovered in 1953 at Chatillon-sur-Seine, northwest of Dijon. The tomb dates from about 500 BC and amongst funeral trophies were a triumphal chariot, a solid gold diadem, various bracelets, an Etruscan wine-jug and a complete Greek wine-service. Perhaps the most interesting find was a crater or vessel used for mixing wine and water. This stood almost five feet high, had a maximum diameter of four feet and held 250 gallons.

How, then, did the Gauls obtain their wine? It is unlikely that, at that time, they had vineyards of their own. The most likely theory is that it was supplied by the Etruscan and Phoenician merchants, passing through the area, on their way to England for tin from the mines of Cornwall. If they came from Italy their trade route lay by the Alto Adige and the Brenner Pass by the shore of Lake Neuchâtel: to the Saône and across to the Seine; if from the Mediterranean, up the Valley of the Rhône to the Saône. It cannot be doubted that the merchants came through Burgundy, since ingots of Cornish tin from this period have been found in the bed of the Saône at Châlon.

The most difficult part of the route lay across the foothills of the

Morvan from Beaune, on the plain of the Saône, to Vix on the Seine: and it is certain that the merchants relied on local manpower to help them with their porterage. There was too, a large Gallic camp overlooking the Seine at Vix and it is likely that toll was levied on travellers and that it was often paid in the form of Italian or Greek wine.

There is plenty of evidence that the Gauls enjoyed wine: that fact is quoted by such reliable sources as Livy, Pliny the Elder and Plutarch as one of the main reasons for their invasion of the north of Italy about 400 BC. In all, about 300,000 Celts crossed the Alps, and the Aedui, who came from Burgundy, settled on the plain between the southern end of Lake Como and the site where they founded the city of Milan. This was already an area of reputable vineyards and the invaders soon gave up their nomadic ways and settled down to tend the vines. Viticulture was even then a well-developed science among the Italians and their techniques of vine-selection, plantation, grafting and pruning were well-established.

The Gauls stayed in Italy for about 250 years. In that period they sent expeditionary forces to Greece, which met with considerable success there until they reached Delphi, where, after sacking the city, they were defeated. The army returned to Italy, small parties drifted back to Gaul and it was not long before the Romans began to regain the upper hand. It would be unreal to suppose that they returned home without supplies of vine shoots and the knowledge of how to cultivate them.

Pierre Forgeot, in his *Origines du Vignoble Bourguignon*, examines their return logically, suggesting that the earliest cultivation of the vine in Burgundy occurred in the first half of the second century BC and that it is likely to have taken place on the slopes behind Meursault, where the present-day vineyards of Monthélie, Auxey-Duresses and Saint Romain stand. In the first instance they were probably planted with the Italian vines, but then it would not be long before cuttings from the native vines would be used.

The Aedui were one of the last tribes to hold out against Julius Caesar and their defeat with the Arverni, under the command of Vercingetorix at Alésia, after a lengthy siege, marked the end of Gallic resistance. The arrival, occupation and the civilization of the Romans had a profound effect on Burgundy and its wines. Autun was named Augustodunum in honour of the Emperor and raised to the position of a Roman city. It was surrounded by extensive fortifications with a total of sixty-two towers. The pride of the city was the Maenian Schools, staffed by professors from Athens and Rome, containing a map of the whole universe as it was then known. Such towns as Auxerre, Dijon and Beaune were founded as Roman camps and, in Beaune, the outline of the *castrum* can still be traced by streets in the town centre.

The vineyards belonged to the principal nobles and their area spread rapidly. Columella in his *Treatise on Agriculture* talks at length of the vineyards of Gaul and describes the different varieties of grapes grown. From his description, one may well have been the present-day *pinot*. In 93 AD, the Emperor Domitian, worried about over-production of wine and a shortage of grain, decreed that there should be no fresh planting in Italy and that half the vineyards in other provinces should be grubbed up. In fact, it is very doubtful that this edict was ever put into effect, and even less likely in Burgundy, where the vineyards were planted on the slopes, in soil quite unsuitable for the cultivation of cereals. Some writers have maintained that until 281 AD, when the measure was repealed by Probus, viticulture was in decline in Burgundy. A document, dated 312 AD, however, refers to vines 'of which no-one knows the age' and which are 'an object of admiration', so such a decrease would seem to be improbable. Probus did encourage his garrisons to spend their time in agriculture, rather than become bored and discontented on foreign duty; and this may have inspired an extension of the area under vines.

The sack of Rome by Alaric in 409, and the overthrow of the western Roman Empire, meant the end of the Gallo-Roman landlord, interested in the cultivation of the vine himself and, during the coming centuries, more and more land passed into the hands of the Church. Regrettably, the monks, interested in leading a life of luxury, were content more often than not to leave the cultivation of their vineyards to others.

The first mention of a king of the Burgundians dates from the early sixth century and the region soon passed into the dominion of the Frankish king, Clovis, who married a local princess, Clothilde. His sons ruled the kingdom of Burgundy, which was to remain an independent monarchy until the early eighth century, and an autonomous duchy until the end of the fifteenth. Among the kings of Burgundy can be noted 'le bon roi Dagobert' who travelled faithfully round his kingdom to dispense justice. He had the reputation of being accessible to all his subjects. (Perhaps he is better known, though, for the French nursery rhyme, which imputes to him the uncomfortable habit of wearing his underpants back to front.) The establishment of his kingdom led to the formation of a local body of land-owning nobles, who soon rivalled the church in the extent of their vineyard holdings.

The Emperor Charlemagne, King of the Franks, planted vineyards at Aloxe-Corton, reputedly with both red and white grapes. In 775, he presented them to the Collegiate Church of Saint Andoche at Saulieu, in whose possession they remained until the time of the French Revolution. Since the Emperor was only thirty-three at the time – and was to live for another thirty-nine years – it seems a particularly generous gift.

In 910, the Benedictine order founded the Abbey of Cluny, which soon relied on vineyards for a considerable proportion of its income and was responsible for planting many areas with grapes for the first time, particularly in the district now known as the Mâconnais. The lax acceptance of monastic principles at Cluny led to three monks, Robert, Alberic and an Englishman, Stephen Harding, setting up a stricter order at Citeaux, near Nuits Saint-Georges in 1098. At first they regarded with disfavour the vineyards given by their benefactors, but they soon concentrated their efforts on their domain at Vougeot, where they built a press-house. They became involved in a series of disputes with the neighbouring monastery of Saint Vivant but in 1162 Duke Eudes II of Burgundy gave them his support and two years later they came under the protection of Pope Alexander III. Thus in the favour of both their temporal and spiritual masters, they and their vineyards prospered.

In the Middle Ages the vineyards of Burgundy increased considerably and there were continual protests from those who owned vines on the Côte itself about the *vignerons* of the plain. As Camille Rodier says, 'From that time began the struggle between the noble plant, the *pinot*, and the treacherous *gamay*; between the production of wine worthy of the reputation of Burgundy and the unlimited production of wines of inferior quality; and for some time the result was in doubt.' In 1395 the famous decree of Philippe le Hardi commanded that all plantations of the *gamay* should be grubbed up as it was 'most harmful to every human creature; to such a point that many who have used it in the past have suffered from serious illnesses'. However severe this decree may seem, it can only have had limited effect as it had to be renewed in 1441, and the same complaints were repeated regularly over the next three centuries.

Inferior plants were not the only problems the growers faced. For the forty or more years after 1460 the roots of the vine were attacked by a plague of insects. The problem proved so intense that the Bishop of Dijon called for a general confession. The power of the Church seems to have had only a limited effect, for, apart from a small plot at Pommard, all the vines had to be torn up and new ones, from as far away as the Crimea, were planted in their place.

At this time the wines of Burgundy were largely appreciated in ecclesiastical and royal circles. The guests at the coronation of Philippe de Valois, at Reims in 1325, drank 300 hogsheads of wine of which most came from Beaune. Just eight years later, the Papal Court at Avignon gave as one of the reasons for their unwillingness to return to Italy, the fact that there they would be deprived of the wines of Burgundy. Their monotheism must have been in doubt when they described them as being the 'nectar of the gods'. In 1370 Jean de Bussières, Abbot of Citeaux, sent several hogsheads of wine to Gregory XI on his accession and must have been pleased, if not surprised, shortly after when he was awarded a cardinal's hat.

As a result of the marriage of Philippe le Hardi, Duke of Burgundy, to Marguerite of Flanders, in 1369, a large part of the Low Countries was attached to the Duchy of Burgundy and, for a long time, Flanders was Burgundy's only true export market for wine. Those wines were not Burgundies as we know them now. They were much lighter in colour and we would probably describe them as '*œil de perdrix*'. It was not until the eighteenth century that they became deeply coloured, full bodied and better able to travel. The revocation of the Edict of Nantes in 1685, with the expulsion of the Protestants from France, provided an opportunity for sales abroad. There had been quite a considerable Huguenot congregation at Beaune; and those at Volnay had built their own church. They emigrated to Switzerland, Holland and Germany and immediately began to order the wines of their native region. Within ten years, the price of a cask of Beaune had risen from 60 francs to 200 francs, and some fifty years later to 328 francs.

The beginning of the eighteenth century saw a rapid rise in the popularity of Burgundy, largely through the success of the surgeon Fagon in curing his royal patient, Louis XIV, of a fistula, by dosing him with Romanée Saint-Vivant. This was not, however, the first recognition of the therapeutic value of the wines. At the end of the fifteenth century, Innocent VIII had been taking Beaune for an unspecified complaint and was so satisfied that he wrote to the Duc de Bourbon, asking him to send a few more casks of the same medicine. In 1665 the medical school of the Sorbonne had accepted the thesis of one Dr. Arbinet, who had proved by the means of syllogisms that '*Vinum Belnense esse potum, suavissimum et saluberrimum*'. Perhaps it is only fair to observe that 250 years later, an aunt of Professor Saintsbury took Richebourg to restore her failing eyesight!

The beginning of the eighteenth century saw the foundation of many of the houses of the great *négociants* or shippers we know today, with Champy Père et Fils in 1720, Bouchard Père et Fils in 1731, Poulet Père et Fils in 1747, Bouchard Ainé et Fils and Chanson Père et Fils in 1750. Originally the Belgian merchants, particularly those of Liège, used to come to Beaune after the vintage, when they would visit the various cellars with brokers from Beaune or Nuits. These brokers soon realized the limits of their profession and began to visit the markets of the north of France and Belgium on their own account. The rise of the *négociant* meant the first systematic prospecting of markets both in France and abroad. Some of the sales ledgers from the period are still preserved and they afford a precise view of the trade as it was at that time. That of Chanson Père et Fils – called Gaboreau et Verry at that time – for the decade from 1770 shows customers throughout France, particularly in the north-east of the country, Switzerland, the Rhineland and the Low Countries. There is an entry for 'Milord le Viscomte de Montagu à Londre', and another for Voltaire, then in self-imposed exile at Ferney. Members of the clergy accounted for a large proportion of the entries and there were also many purchases from regiments fighting on the Rhine. This ledger also includes purchases made by the company and it is interesting to see entries for Clos Vougeot, purchased from the Abbott of Citeaux; Richebourg, from the Croonenbourg family who had at one time owned Romanée-Conti (the fact that they used to send their gardener to collect the money is also recorded);

THE VINEYARDS OF BURGUNDY: HISTORICAL SURVEY

Hugues Bétault, whose name remains as one of the Cuvées of the Hospices de Beaune, and such families as the Glantenays, who are still vineyard owners at Volnay. The sales book of Affre Lavirotte for the years 1771–1813, includes one customer in England, one in Spain, one in Italy, two in Austria and several in Alsace, Germany and Switzerland. Labaume Ainé, between 1794 and 1799, sold almost all their wine in Germany.

The French Revolution had a profound effect on the vineyards of Burgundy, since both the Church and the nobles were dispossessed of their lands. Thus the great estates were broken up and the individual vineyards sold to private people: Clos de Vougeot to Citizen Focard, a wood-merchant from Paris, for F643,710; Romanée Saint-Vivant to the Marey family of Nuits for F91,000; Clos de Tart to M. Charles Dumagner, also of Nuits, for F68,200; and Corton Charlemagne to M. François Ray of Pernand, for F10,800. Under the French laws of inheritance, which lay down that 70 per cent of a man's estate must be shared equally between his children, these vineyards soon had to be split up, a process that has continued ever since. Moreover, some of the new owners were unable to maintain the properties that they had bought so cheaply. Thus in the hundred years following its purchase by Citizen Focard, Clos de Vougeot changed hands no less than five times until, finally, in 1889 a property dealer bought it for F600,000 and immediately split it up into fifteen parcels which he sold off to various local vineyard owners.

Until the Revolution, Beaune had a considerable religious population: the property of the monasteries and nunneries, like that of the aristocracy, passed into private hands. Thus, in a short period, both the vineyards and the premises where their wines were lodged came into the market. A short study of the shippers of Beaune shows how important the ecclesiastical cellarage must have been. Within a single small area it is still possible to visit the (now secular) cellars of the Bastion de l'Oratoire, the Abbey of Saint Martin, the Batistines and the Visitandines.

The Revolution also produced a profound change on the French market, for church dignitaries had been the most important customers for many *négociants*. The fact that Napoleon used to drink little but Chambertin (and cognac?) led to the wines of the whole region becoming immensely popular and caused much abuse, and blending with inferior wine became widespread. Unfortunately, Burgundy still suffers from this reputation.

Further advances were made and individual vineyards became better known in the early nineteenth century. Jullien, in his *Topographie des Vignobles*, lists the best red wines in Burgundy as – Clos de Vougeot, Romanée, Chambertin, Richebourg, Clos des Fèves, Saint Georges, Corton, Vosnes, Nuits, Clos du Roi, Santenot-Volnay, Volnay, Pommard, Beaune, Savigny and Santenay: and the white; le Montrachet, Meursault and Chablis. This was a fair reflection of the values of the wines at the time, as is confirmed by price-lists of only twenty years later. The table showing comparative prices (in francs) of wines offered by a Beaune shipper over a period a century ago demonstrates that rapid increases are not simply a phenomenon of recent years:

	Monthélie	Santenot-Volnay	Clos du Roi (Beaune)	Saint Georges	Richebourg	Fèves (Beaune)	Romanée and Chambertin
April 1853	240	350	390	440	440	—	460
Nov. 1853	300	420	420	550	550	—	600
Dec. 1860	—	—	730	—	1130	—	1230
Nov. 1862	500	—	780	—	1200	—	1300
Oct. 1866	380	520	520	750	850	850	1000
March 1871	360	480	480	700	780	780	900
Dec. 1878	—	540	540	800	850	850	950
May 1881	—	750	750	1000	1100	1100	1200

These price-lists are significant in several directions. The last figures mark the beginning of the price increases caused by the onset of the phylloxera plague, which will engage us later. Wines from the new vintage were offered in the November or December immediately after. It was not uncommon for four different vintages to be offered in cask – which would suppose a style of Burgundy different from that drunk now – as well as two further vintages in bottle.

The same company in 1853 also issued its first price-list specifically for the English market. The wines could be purchased through Mr. Edward Rawcliffe of 71, Mark Lane, in the City of London. Shipments to England increased strikingly in consequence of the liberal policies of William Gladstone, between 1860 and 1876. Indeed, from 1860 to 1868, clearances of French wine from bond quadrupled. Those of

THE VINEYARDS OF BURGUNDY: HISTORICAL SURVEY

Bordeaux showed the greatest rise, but there can be no doubt that the Burgundy shippers also profited from this boom. In 1877, Septimus Beardmore, the gastronomic correspondent of the *Quarterly Review*, strongly recommended the wines of Burgundy. He qualified his praise, however, with the comment, 'Nowhere is Burgundy to be obtained in such perfection as in the Walloon district of Belgium, comprising Liège, Namur, Spa, Dinant and etc. At little hostelries in remote districts in the Ardennes, you will get Burgundy that would be of value at great banquets in London. For some reason the climate and cellars of that district suit the wine; and the people have the sense to lay down enough of it.' That observation remains valid today.

In 1818, Jules Lausseure, a Nuits Saint-Georges shipper, initiated the commercial production of Sparkling Burgundy. Observing the continuing shortage of Champagne in world markets, he concluded that competitive wines could be produced in Burgundy. Indeed, he suggested that sparkling local wines could be superior to Champagne, by virtue of their greater body and bouquet. For more than twenty years he experimented with a variety of wines before he found a harmonious formula for a wine directed specifically at the English market. London shippers, in fact, used to import a full range of Sparkling Burgundies, including such novelties as Sparkling Chambertin and Sparkling Clos de Vougeot. Such wines seem also to have been popular in the United States at the beginning of this century. Current sales of Sparkling Red Burgundy are almost solely restricted to that country and the north of England. They must once have had some attraction for the French, however, since in a presentation of Burgundies to the Emperor Napoleon III in 1860 were included parcels of Romanée and Nuits Mousseux.

In the middle of the nineteenth century, there arrived from the United States, by way of Britain, the two plagues oïdium and phylloxera. The former, a form of microscopic fungus, was first noted in Margate in 1845 and it arrived in Bordeaux soon after 1850. Fortunately, by the time it reached Burgundy a treatment had already been discovered: sulphur spray was – and still is – effective. *Phylloxera vastatrix*, however, proved a far more serious problem. It completely changed viticulture, not simply in Burgundy or in France, but throughout the world. Phylloxera is a louse that feeds on the sap of vines and other plants. In the United States it confines its attention mainly to leaves, but in France the roots proved more attractive. Its first, and unlikely, appearance in Europe was in a greenhouse in Hammersmith in 1863. In the same year it arrived in the Gard *département* of southern France. It spread slowly, being first noted in the Bordeaux area in 1866; in the Beaujolais in 1874; and, finally, on the Côte d'Or, at Meursault, in 1878. By this time several treatments had been tried in other areas with only limited success. In Bordeaux, carbon bi-sulphide was injected between the vines with a marginally greater chance of saving them than of killing the person applying the mixture, which was not only highly poisonous, but also highly inflammable – and expensive. It is interesting that the most satisfactory treatment had already been proposed, as early as 1869, at the Viticultural Congress in Beaune. That was – and is – the grafting of French cuttings on to native American rootstock, which is either impervious – or unattractive – to phylloxera. Unhappily this solution was not permitted in the Côte d'Or until 1886. In the meantime the vineyards of Burgundy underwent a profound change. On the eve of the plague, 75,280 acres of the Côte d'Or were planted with vines. Today the area is no more than 25,000 acres, of which, in 1970, only 15,300 consisted of *appellation contrôlée* vineyards. To demonstrate the immediate result more graphically, in the years 1870 to 1880, the average annual total production of wine in France amounted to 51,800,000 hectolitres: in the following decade it had fallen to 29,700,000 hectolitres.

Before phylloxera there were vast plantings of vines around Auxerre. Semur, Seurre and Is-sur-Tille; areas where now the vine is almost unknown. The district to suffer most seriously was Chablis. Before phylloxera there were 96,000 acres under vines in the *département* of the Yonne; in 1970 there were less than 7,000 of which no more than 2,600 were in *appellation contrôlée*. Since then fresh planting has been stimulated by investment by local growers, and capital not only from Beaune but from Paris investors, and the planted area is now growing steadily.

Another result of phylloxera, which is less generally appreciated, is the completely changed aspect of the vineyards. Until they were replanted with American stock, all regeneration had been by the system of *provignage*. That is to say when a vine reached the end of its useful life, the body of it was buried in a shallow trench and a shoot from it became the new vine. This meant that there was no real order to the vineyards: often there were as many as 10,000 plants to the acre, each supported by a stake. Nowadays they are planted in neat rows, which makes for easier cultivation, since they can be trained on wires and have a density of less than 4,200 plants to the acre. This also favours the penetration of the sun and the circulation of air. Despite the considerably smaller number of plants, production – also calculated to the acre – is nevertheless doubled by comparison with the pre-phylloxera era.

The two most important developments in Burgundy in this century have been the introduction of the *appellation contrôlée* and the dramatic expansion of export markets. Regulations and decrees to control the production and the quality of the wines of the area have existed since the earliest times. These were fully developed and polished, however, during the period of 1930–1939 when it was difficult to sell wine. Laws passed in 1919 had sought to ensure that the wine in the bottle should be the wine on the label, but they proved unsatisfactory. The owners of the Chambertin vineyard, for example, were so worried about outsiders passing off alien wine under their name that they formed a 'Syndicat de Défense de l'Appellation Chambertin'. At their request the civil court of Dijon laid down, in February 1931 and July 1932, what wines could be sold with the *appellations* Chambertin and Chambertin Clos de Bèze. In 1935 controls of this kind were introduced on a national scale. Alexis Lichine, in his *Wines of France*, talks of the work involved in drawing up these laws. Perhaps it is unfortunate that they were designed by vineyard owners, largely for their own protection, with the result that the interests of the merchants, who were to sell most of the wine, or the consumers, were scarcely taken into account. Overall the system was fair, but the independence of the Burgundian meant that, in this viticultural region particularly, there was a surfeit of *appellations*.

The last twenty years have seen spectacular increases both in the production and export of the wines of Burgundy. Though recently there has been a succession of successful vintages, they cannot be attributed solely to the weather. An average increase of 50 per cent in annual production over a period of ten years is largely due to modern viticultural techniques, since most diseases of the vine can now be treated swiftly and effectively. Spraying is done by helicopter. Potential hail-storms can be broken up before they happen by sowing the clouds. The increase in production, however, has scarcely kept pace with the demand, particularly from abroad. Even in the last ten years export sales have trebled and, from the standpoint of quality, it is encouraging that the increases have come in Burgundy-bottled wines. The fact that supply has not kept pace with demand has resulted in substantial rises in prices, which have brought in their train unfavourable reaction from the consumer. The problem for the immediate future would seem to be for producers and shippers to find the correct price-level for the wines they offer. This problem is not peculiar to Burgundy. Indeed, other wine regions throughout the world are finding an even greater task in achieving that kind of stability. For Burgundy, an area of small production of quality wines, the future should be bright.

4 THE MEN OF BURGUNDY AND THEIR WORK

A fine wine can only be made from correctly chosen grapes grown in the right soil and in an ideal weather-sequence. Even given those ingredients, though, the quality of the final product depends on the human element at every stage. Wine is a living thing and as such it is vulnerable to ill treatment. From the selection and planting of the vine shoots to the ultimate stage of drinking and enjoying a mature bottle, a whole chain of people – *vigneron*, broker, merchant, cellarman, retailer or wine waiter – have their separate responsibilities for its welfare.

The wines of Burgundy, more than any others of comparable eminence, are individual creations. The vast majority of the vineyards where they are made are family concerns. A man, his wife and son – or perhaps father or daughter – are quite capable of tending the average vineyard of the region. Some of the larger *domaines* have their own labour forces, but that is exceptional. In the past all the work had to be done by hand and horse. Now, as labour becomes more costly, an increasing amount of mechanization has been introduced, the tractor has replaced the horse almost everywhere, while the helicopter and even the aeroplane can be summoned at need. No machine, however, can replace the human skills demanded for pruning the vines. Machine picking of grapes is common in California, Australia and even the Cognac area: but the slopes of Burgundy are at many points too steep for it and, even more conclusively, the *vignerons* regard their fruit as far too precious to be subjected to such risks. For the better wines too, a loss of 12 per cent of the grapes, the accepted norm for a machine, is too costly.

The vineyards of the Côte d'Or are at their most beautiful, a rolling sea of russets, reds and golds, immediately after the vintage, when work in the vines is only just beginning – for next year's harvest. As the last grapes are gathered in, fertilizers of nitrogen and potassium are spread to fortify the vines against the stresses of the winter. (While horses were still in general use their manure was one of the most useful by-products; if only for that reason the tractor can never be a complete replacement.) At this time, too, the land that has been lying fallow and is due to be replanted must be deeply ploughed.

The vine in Burgundy can have a useful life of fifty or more years, but as it grows older, it suffers from the law of diminishing returns. Although the wine it produces improves in quality, the yield decreases from year to year. So they are generally uprooted after about thirty years. The land is then planted with a different crop for three years, before it is replanted with vines. It is then another three years before the grapes can be picked for *appellation contrôlée* wine. In Chablis, because of the poor nature of the soil, the land was sometimes allowed to lie fallow for fifteen or more years; but probably during the depressed times for the wines of that area, the growers did not think it financially worthwhile to replant quickly. Nowadays (can it simply be due to the efficacy of recently developed fertilizers?) the Chablis vineyards are replanted more promptly. In any case, throughout Burgundy, the intelligent grower rotates his replanting so that he never has too large a proportion of his vineyard non-productive.

In November and December a preliminary pruning takes place to remove dead twigs, which may be burnt on the spot or taken home for kindling. One of the most attractive sights of early winter in the region is of thin columns of grey smoke rising to the sky from the braziers in the middle of the vines. Before the frosts arrive, the fertilizers must be dug in and the roots protected by earth piled up around them.

During the months of winter there is little to do and, apart from a certain amount of maintenance work, the grower can take his rest. On 22 January, each vineyard village celebrates the feast of Saint Vincent, the patron saint of the vine grower. On the following Saturday, under the patronage of the Confrérie des Chevaliers du Tastevin, the Saint

THE MEN OF BURGUNDY AND THEIR WORK

Vincent Tournante is celebrated – each year in a different village of the Côte-d'Or or the Région de Mercurey. Every village – and there are fifty or more of them – sends its representatives with their statue of Saint Vincent, to join in the procession, which is enlivened by all the best brass bands of the region. Afterwards the Confrérie, in their robes of scarlet and yellow, attend a solemn mass of thanksgiving, honour those who have worked long and well in the vines, and then retire to Clos Vougeot for a traditional banquet.

The main pruning is begun towards the middle of February. The shape into which the vines are pruned, and thus grow, varies from area to area, even within Burgundy. The main determining factor is the grape variety. In cooler vineyard areas they generally prefer a form of pruning that gives a low plant which will benefit in full during the night from the heat stored in the soil during the day. One disadvantage of this form, though, is that it increases the risk of damage by spring frosts. So far as the *gamay* grape is concerned, all the buds on the shoot are productive, so it can be pruned severely. On the other hand, in the case of the *pinot*, the buds closest to the trunk are less productive, so the pruning is less rigorous.

In the Beaujolais, the vines grow separately and are pruned '*à gobelet*', each with its individual stake. In the Mâconnais, the traditional method is the '*taille à queue*', where the producing branch is bent over in a semicircle. On the Côte d'Or, the '*taille guyot*' is general: the main branch is trained along a wire about a foot from the ground, with a double wire above it to hold the shoots in place, and then a final, single wire above that. The vines are planted a metre apart, with a metre between the rows.

On certain places on the Côte d'Or, you can also see plantings following the Austrian *Lenz Moser* system. This is allowed, on an experimental basis, for the lesser *appellations*. The rows of vines are planted considerably further apart than is general in France and they are allowed to grow to a height of six or seven feet. This makes for ease of cultivation and for better aeration of the bunches of grapes. (It also makes for much less suffering on the part of grape-pickers.) The number of such plantings is strictly limited, and one old grower said, 'They will carry out tests for fifty years or so and then forbid it.'

Pruning is a very specialized job and the good *vigneron* knows every vine and how it should be treated. He will be familiar with its production over past years and will adapt the pruning to its potential and its limitations. The purposes of pruning are to assure the fruitfulness of the vine, to increase the production of best quality grapes and to give the plant a regular, planned form.

At the end of the winter and the beginning of spring, the earth that was piled round the roots for protection is dug up and spread out. At this time, too, selected shoots are grafted on to American rootstock. The selection of both the shoots and the rootstock is of the greatest importance. Immediately after phylloxera, the most common phylloxera-resistant stock used was pure *riparia*, but now there is an increasing preference for *riparia* × *rupestris* no. 3309 and *riparia* × *berlandieri* no. 161.49, both of which have a success rate of approximately 70 per cent in grafting. The shoots are chosen from individual vines with successful production records.

The more important domains have their own nurseries, where the young vines are kept for a year in sterile conditions, to protect them from danger of disease during infancy. As phylloxera arrived in France by way of England, it is perhaps fitting that the method of grafting usually used is the '*greffe anglaise*', which matches the stock to the French shoot in z-shaped cuts.

In April the vines begin to grow and the young shoots have to be trained along the wires. If the weather has been fine and dry, the vines can be attacked at this moment by the red spider, a comparatively recent addition to the problems of the French *vigneron*, released by newly-developed insecticides killing off those insects that used to prey upon them. The spider, which is often invisible to the naked eye, feeds on the green parts of the vine. As a result, development is slowed up, or possibly stopped. The spider is impervious to DDT, and even sprays developed specifically to deal with it have had only limited success.

Other pests that develop at this time are the grubs of three insects: *Pyralis*, *Eudemis* and *Cochylis*. All three have different life-cycles: *Pyralis* has one generation during the season; *Cochylis* (whose grub is called the *ver rouge* on the Côte d'Or and the *ver coquin* in the Beaujolais) has two; and *Eudemis* three. In common, they all feed upon the leaves and, later in the year, upon the grapes themselves. Certain treatments carried out during the winter have had limited success in destroying the chrysalids, but spraying with DDT and Parathion during the spring is more general.

At the beginning of May each year, the Service de la Protection des Végétaux offers a prize of F50 to the first person who brings them vine-leaves suffering from mildew. This appears in hot, humid weather and causes the leaves to dry up and fall. As a result the grapes cannot receive the nourishment they need from the leaves, so some of them wither or rot and give an unpleasant taste to the wine. As the mildew fungus exists in the tissue of the vine, no treatment can eradicate it, but can only restrict its effect. The usual treatment is by spraying with Bordeaux mixture (two kilos of copper sulphate and one kilo of lime dissolved in 100 litres of water). This is normally sprayed on by tractor, but if the vineyards are too muddy for convenient working, a helicopter can be called in. The slopes are spread with signs in blue, yellow and white to show the pilot where to spray.

The end of April and the first week of May are also the time when frost can cause the most damage. This is particularly the case if there has been a mild spring and the vines are far advanced. Generally frost strikes just before dawn and the grower will set his alarm to be up in time to take protective measures. It is not unknown, though, for frost to strike in the middle of the night and it can attack just a patch of vines, leaving a band of damage, where one row might be affected and the next not. In Chablis, where the problem is most real, some vineyards have propane heaters installed or even a system for spraying the vines with water, so that they are protected by a layer of ice. On the Côte d'Or, smudge pots or burning tyres are more generally used to safeguard the vines with a cloud of smoke. On rare occasions industrial fan-heaters can be seen in the vines. Vineyards on the plain and in hollows, though, are most likely to suffer from frost and thus the great *climats* of the Côte d'Or are rarely affected. If there has not been frost damage by 15 May – Sainte Denise's day – the danger is considered to be past.

At the beginning of June the vines flower, and the vintage is traditionally taken to be a hundred days from that day. The weather at this time is important, because, if it is cold or wet, either the flowers or the grapes might abort and not mature. The former problem is called *coulure*, the latter *millérandage*. Whilst the grower can do nothing to prevent the bad weather that causes these, there are other dangers he should foresee. The *chardonnay* is particularly liable to *coulure* and when he grafts this plant the *vigneron* should take special care to choose his shoots from vines that have not suffered from it. Over-use of nitrogenous fertilisers and any contact whatsoever with hormone weed-killers are also potential sources of damage. Perhaps the most serious cause of *coulure*, however, is the virus disease *court-noué*, for which there is no other treatment but the complete rooting up of the vine, cleansing of the soil and replanting with completely healthy vines.

As well as treatment against mildew during June and July, the grower must be on his guard in warm, damp weather, against another fungal disease, oïdium. The leaves and grapes take on blackish scabs and develop a mouldy smell. The recommended preventive treatment is three sprayings with powdered sulphur, one before flowering, the second at the time of flowering and the third two or three weeks before the grapes change colour. The most effective cure, once oïdium has attacked, is spraying with a solution of potassium permanganate.

During the summer days of July and August, the tops of the vines are trimmed back, so that the grapes derive maximum benefit from the food brought up through the roots. Whilst sun is always welcome, rain, too, is needed from time to time, to swell out the grapes. Too much sun can present almost as many problems as too much rain, since the grapes can shrivel up for lack of moisture. That happened in 1973 when, just a week before the vintage, about twenty-four hours' rain was needed to fill out the grapes. The rains came but, unfortunately, they continued for a week. All the moisture was thirstily absorbed. As a result, in a matter of hours, what might have been one of the best vintages of the century, with an important quantity of wine, became one of only average quality, but with the largest crop since records began.

Hailstorms in the summer are another grave threat. Although they generally cause damage over only a limited area, within those limits it can be total. From the eighteenth century until the First World War, the fashionable preventative was the *canon grélifuge*, which looked rather like a vertical foghorn of up to fifteen feet in height. The makers claimed that firing this at the hail-clouds caused enough turbulence in the air to protect an area of up to sixty acres. When this weapon became unfashionable, vineyard owners turned to prayer – and insurance. More recently rockets have been developed to explode at a height of four or more thousand feet, in the cumulo-nimbus clouds where the hail forms, causing the stones to liquefy and fall as rain.

For the last three years the growers of the Côte d'Or and the Mercurey region have joined together to take apparently even more successful steps against hail. During the summer two or more aircraft of Air Alpes are based in the area, at Châlon-sur-Saône. These can take off at a moment's notice to seed the storm clouds so that just rain falls. From radar detection of cloud formations they can be alerted in time to reach the clouds whilst they are still over the Morvan and break them up before they reach the vineyard areas. It is too early yet to say how effective this watch is, but in 1973 when the climatic conditions would normally have made for a considerable incidence of hailstorms, the damage was minimal. Only a few miles away in the valley of the Saône, on the other hand, there was considerable damage to crops. In 1974, however, an August hailstorm caused considerable damage in certain villages of the Côte de Beaune, and to another in the southern Beaujolais. In the Beaujolais, there is at least one plane on hail alert; it is based at the Seagram property, Château de Pizay, at Morgon.

Vineyards that have suffered from hail damage produce wines with an unmistakable smoky taste which can be detected, for example, in some wines of the 1971 vintage from Pommard, a village that suffered particularly in that year. A violent hailstorm can have even more enduring effects, damaging the vines so severely that their production can suffer the following year.

September sees the final preparation for the vintage, which normally begins towards the end of the month and continues for a fortnight. All the materials and equipment for the pickers are prepared. The vat-house is thoroughly cleaned out; the oak vats scrubbed and filled with water to swell the wood; and all metalwork is repainted.

The vintage in Burgundy is not such a glamorous affair as in Bordeaux. As the majority of the vineyard holdings are small, the picking is generally done by the family and friends. Unfortunately, in 1973, some government official decided that picking grapes was not suitable work for young children, so the work force, which used to be swelled on school holidays, has suffered. No longer do swarms of gipsies descend from the Morvan, singing, according to Camille Rodier,

> Let's be off to the vintage
> To earn five sous,
> Sleep in the barns
> And gather some fleas.

There are few places now where pickers come in from outside and eat and lodge together. The former team-feeling may have been impaired as a result of each *vendangeur* nursing his stiff back alone in the evening. Nevertheless, every year many visitors from other non-wine-growing countries come to Burgundy for the experience of a grape harvest.

In early times the day for the beginning of the vintage was declared by the feudal lord or, later, by the commune; and there were severe punishments, such as the confiscation of their crop, for those who began picking too early or who sought to recruit their work-force before the due date. Nowadays sample bunches of grapes are analyzed to establish the sugar content and when this is at the optimum, picking may begin – each grower starting when he feels so inclined. Sometimes the date may be brought forward if the weather breaks and there is a danger of the crop being ruined. This is the age-old dilemma of the grower. Shall he leave the grapes on the vines in the hope that they will get more sunshine and thus produce better wine – and, if he does, will they be damaged by rain or hail?

Since many *domaines* have vineyards scattered along the Côte d'Or, the grapes in some cases have to be transported several miles to the press-house – yet each load must be accompanied by a government certificate – even at this stage the system of *appellation contrôlée* has begun.

Most vineyard owners in Burgundy vinify their grapes themselves, though, as has already been mentioned, the co-operative cellars have an important role to play in the Beaujolais, the Mâconnais and to a lesser extent in Chablis. On the Côte de Nuits, particularly, it is not uncommon for a grower to sell his grapes directly to a *négociant*, who will then vinify them himself. In exceptional vintages, like 1972 and 1973, this is even more common, for the grower might find himself short of both vat-space in which to vinify and cellar-space in which to store the wine. In 1972, when the price of young wine rose considerably during the following year, many extremely profitable deals were made by those who purchased grapes cheaply at vintage time. (In Alsace, where the purchase of grapes is more widespread, the growers insist on a clause in the contract of sale, which allows for additional compensatory payments to be made during the following year, in the event of the price of the wine rising. No doubt this will come in Burgundy, though it is unlikely that growers would be prepared to make a reimbursement if the value of the wine fell.)

When the grapes arrive at the press-house, the juice is tested for its sugar content, for this will give the ultimate alcoholic degree of the wine. (In co-operative cellars, the grapes are also weighed, for payment is generally made on the kilo-degree; that is to say, on the combination of the quantity of grapes and the strength of the wine they will produce.) Before the grapes are de-stalked they are sprinkled with sulphur dioxide, which acts as an antiseptic, killing off harmful bacteria.

On arrival at the press-house the tubs of fruit are tipped into the *fouloir-égrappoir,* which looks like a large mangle with ridged rollers. This machine crushes the grapes and separates them from their stalks. It is important, though, that the operation is not so violent as to crush the pips since that would release oils which give an unpleasant astringency to the wine.

The question of the proportion of stalks to be put in the fermenting vats to add tannin is much discussed in Burgundy. One thing is certain, the term '*méthode ancienne*', used by some shippers to describe a long first fermentation, with a high percentage of stalks, is misleading. It is, in truth, by no means traditional and seems to have come into fashion only at the end of the last century. This may have come about because Burgundy was difficult to sell at the time and therefore had to be able to support a longer period before it was consumed. One thing is certain, the traditional way of making Burgundy is with a short fermentation of five or so days. Each grower and shipper tries consistently to produce a style of wine of which he is proud. These styles can vary considerably, yet each, in its own way, is correct. It is a peculiarly British (and perhaps Danish) fallacy to consider that Burgundy should have the consistency, and colour, of an unfortified ruby port. Some growers make such wines (often to please their customers) but others produce wines lighter in colour, yet which have more finesse and in no way lack such depth and keeping qualities as there might be in their deeply coloured brethren. Depth of colour should not be equated with the potential of a wine. It may be true that, because of increasing demand, some growers vinify to produce wines that mature more quickly and are therefore more rapidly marketed. This situation is not peculiar to Burgundy, but one that occurs equally in Bordeaux. It is regrettable that over 80 per cent of Côte d'Or wine shipped to the United States, presumably for immediate consumption, is three years old or less. Thus the chances of a wine from such a great vintage as 1971 being drunk at its best – with years of bottle-age – must be rated as negligible.

From the de-stalker, the juice and pulp is pumped to the fermenting vat. Traditionally this is of oak with an open top, but more and more it is replaced by a closed, enamel-lined tank, which is easier to maintain, and which can be used during the rest of the year, if needed, for storage purposes. The depth to which the vat is filled is of primary importance, as in certain vintages, such as 1972, the fermentation can be so violent that there is a risk of the must overflowing.

On the skin of the grape there is a dusty bloom which contains the natural yeasts that will precipitate the fermentation. On the extremely rare occasions when the process does not start spontaneously, strains of local yeasts may be added to the must, or, more commonly, the must is slightly heated to set off the ferments.

The length of time that the fermentation takes depends on the grower, but it is important that each vat is carefully tended. The temperature must be taken at regular intervals, as fermentation takes place most comfortably between 22°C and 30°C (72°F and 86°F). If it falls below the lower figure, there is a danger that the fermentation will stop – and it is difficult to restart it – so part of the must is heated, generally by passing it over pipes containing hot water, and then returned to the vat. If the must becomes too hot – usually because of too active a fermentation – it must be cooled down, either by passing it over pipes containing cold water, or by circulating it in contact with the air. Each vat will also have its individual graph, which shows two lines apart from the temperature; one is the decreasing amount of sugar in the must and the other the increasing amount of alcohol. Since, in all the wines of Burgundy, the sugar is fermented out completely, when the first line reaches – or approaches – zero the first fermentation is considered to have finished.

Whilst the must is fermenting in the vat the oenologist has to decide whether the resultant wine will be sound and balanced, and, if not, what treatment is necessary. As Burgundy is near the northern limit of the vine, it may happen that there is not sufficient sugar in the grapes to produce a stable wine, therefore the process called chaptalization is permitted for every vintage. Basically this gives the producer the possibility of adding sugar to the must so as to increase the strength of the wine by a maximum of 2°. (In Bordeaux, chaptalization is only permitted in exceptional circumstances, and then after an official decree. In the Midi it is completely forbidden.)

Whilst, officially, chaptalization can only be carried out after notice has been given to the necessary authorities, and only strictly limited amounts of sugar can be purchased to carry it out (200 kilos per hectare of vines is the maximum), there is no doubt that the process is open to abuse. The good wine-chemist will never chaptalize beyond the necessary limit; and in some years, when the grapes are rich in sugar, he will not chaptalize at all. Each vat, each wine, must be considered as a separate case and the correct amount of sugar must be added. Some growers, who consider that a high strength is the only criterion for a wine will, therefore, sugar to the maximum. They even go beyond the maximum in some cases, for it is not difficult to buy an extra pound or two of sugar for the family every week; nor is there any control over the distribution of the officially permitted allowance between vats. In any case, the allowance is not granted on how much you produce, but on how much you might produce.

The question as to whether chaptalization should be permitted has long been debated in Burgundy. The idea was originally proposed at the beginning of the nineteenth century, as a means of using up the excess production of beet sugar. Even as early as 1845, though, a congress of vine growers in Dijon passed a resolution condemning it as being a harmful practice. 'It cannot be disputed,' they said, 'that sugaring denatures wines, taking away from them that which is most precious to them; that incomparable bouquet and delicacy that is their true mark.'

Whilst some over-chaptalized wines taste 'exaggerated' on the palate, it is generally only by analysis that it can be traced. Even having over-chaptalized wines in one's cellar is a serious offence in France, punishable by heavy fines and prison sentences. With the introduction of the Common Market regulations, a decision was apparently taken to make an example of some offenders. As a result one or two prosecutions were launched against those who had in their cellars over-sugared Beaujolais of the 1973 vintage.

Other problems, such as lack of acidity, tannin or colour in the wine can also be rectified to some extent whilst the fermentation is taking place. The addition of unripe grapes to the must will increase acidity; a higher proportion of stalks will add to the tannin. To make the colour deeper, some of the must, together with the skins, is heated, which releases the pigments.

During the fermentation, all the solid matter is thrust up to the top of the wine, where it forms a thick crust, or *'chapeau'*. Some growers consider that this crust should be regularly broken up and immersed in the must; and in traditional cellars teams of men clamber into the vats to trample it in. The term for this operation is *pigeage*. Nowadays, gym-shorts are the dress for the event, but formerly it was generally carried out in the nude and, as witness, a photograph in the wine museum at Beaune shows a line-up that would not disgrace *Oh! Calcutta*. Other growers will twice a day pump over a proportion of the must to break up the crust – this is the process of *remontage*.

After five or six days, or longer as desired, the juice is drawn off from the bottom of the vat and the *marc* (or mass of pulp) is shovelled into a horizontal press. In Burgundy the *marc* is pressed just once and the resultant juice (the *vin de presse*) is added to that which has already been drawn off (the *vin de goutte*). The resultant blend is put into oak casks to continue its development. During the coming six or more months, the wine undergoes a secondary fermentation, known as the malo-lactic. During this time, the bacterium *gracile* converts the natural malic acid (the acidity of apples) in the wine into lactic acid (the acidity of milk). It is not difficult to judge that the second acid is much less prominent than the first. This secondary fermentation also liberates a certain amount of carbon dioxide, which gives a prickle to a wine if it is bottled before the process has ended. (In certain circumstances if the wine is bottled too cold it might also have the same prickle, for, although the fermentation has been completed, the gas has remained in suspension and has not been liberated. A simple warming of the glass in the hand will make the prickle disappear.)

Whilst the malo-lactic fermentation traditionally took place in oak casks, certain growers now return the wine to the metal fermenting vats and let it take place there in bulk. The thought behind this is that the process occurs rather more quickly in large quantities and that there is less likelihood of any problems in an enamel-lined vessel. It has yet to be seen whether the character of the wine is altered in any way – or whether it will be shorter lived, for not having absorbed the six months' tannin from the cask.

So far, we have studied only the vinification of red wines – for the white it is different. As soon as they arrive at the press-house, the grapes are crushed and immediately put into the press with the stalks, where they are usually pressed twice. The *jus de presse* and the *jus de goutte* are then blended together and put straight into casks. These are not filled completely, nor are the bungs hammered home, since the fermentation takes place slowly during the winter months in the grower's cellars. It is important, though, that the fermentation should be continuous, so often it is necessary to light a stove in the cellar to keep it warm enough to maintain the activity of the ferments.

The amount of time the wine spends in cask again depends on the grower, or, more often, the *négociant*, who is more generally responsible for the *élevage*, or upbringing, of the wine. The average length of time in cask for a Côte d'Or wine is between twelve and eighteen months, though some shippers think it wrong to bottle great wines under two years old. For wines from the Beaujolais and the Mâconnais, a period of three to nine months in cask is generally considered adequate.

After the wine has spent six months in wood it is fined to remove any impurities resting in suspension. When the finings have dropped to the bottom of the cask, the first racking takes place; that is, the bright wine is drawn off its deposit and placed into a clean cask. As the level in the old cask drops, it is gently tilted forward and the cellarman continually studies the clarity of the wine in his silver *tastevin*, or tasting cup. As soon as there is any trace of cloudiness, the tap in the cask-head is closed. This racking takes place every six months while the wine is in cask, though an extra one or two may be necessary if the wine has some foreign taste which might disappear on exposure to the air. To avoid oxidisation, white wines are normally racked without coming into contact with the air. In all cases, the receiving cask has always either had a sulphur candle burnt in it, or has been rinsed out with a sulphur solution as an antiseptic measure.

The lees, or deposit, are either sold for distillation into Fine Bourgogne or else sent to one of the great restaurants in the region or in Paris for use in preparing such local specialities as *jambon à la lie*.

To avoid oxidisation, every two weeks or so the cellarman carries out the operation of *ouillage*, or topping up. To do it he uses a vessel like a watering-can with a long spout, which turns down at the end. Also at the end a holder is fitted to take a candle to light up the bungholes in the casks, which may be stacked three or four high.

Before bottling, a sample of each cask is analysed to see that the malo-lactic fermentation is finished and the wine is generally filtered, though some traditionalists prefer to bottle directly from the cask-head. After bottling, the vintage should spend some months resting, to overcome the shock, before it is consumed. Certain shippers pasteurize their wines to minimize possible problems once it is in bottle. Some feel that this caponizes the wine and prevents it developing naturally; others argue that it preserves the wine at the peak of its condition. Certainly pasteurization is an artificial process which must destroy some of the natural attributes of a wine.

Although the grower is a considerable man of Burgundy, however, he actually bottles and sells only a small proportion of the production of the region. Over 80 per cent of the wine sold outside the area passes through the hands of the *négociants*. Before it reaches them, though, the *courtier* or broker plays his considerable part. He is the important middleman between the grower and the merchant. It is his job to introduce the wines of the vast number of growers to the small number of shippers.

Generally speaking, each merchant works through a limited number of brokers; perhaps one for wines of the Côte de Nuits, two for those of the Côte de Beaune and one each for the Mâconnais and the Beaujolais. Each broker knows what style of wine his customer is looking for and the price he is prepared to pay for it. He will know what stocks the growers have available for sale, and what price they are seeking.

THE MEN OF BURGUNDY AND THEIR WORK

He will submit small samples of those wines he thinks suitable to the *négociants*, with the quantity on offer, the price and the name of the grower. If the price is too high, it is his job to negotiate on behalf of the merchant, without letting the grower know the name of the potential purchaser. Thus, whilst the shipper might buy from the same producer year after year, he has an interest in working through a broker, so that he may maintain a certain anonymity in his bargaining. The *courtier* is responsible also for fixing terms of payment, arranging the transport of the wine from the grower to the merchant, and overseeing the racking of the wine into the merchant's casks. Formerly, for his services, he was paid a fixed sum per cask, but now he generally works on a percentage commission on the sale price. Generally this is 2 per cent, paid by the purchaser, though it is not uncommon for the seller also to pay a commission.

The profession of *courtier de campagne* is both skilful and honourable. Unfortunately, the 'wine explosion' of recent years has attracted some to the profession who consider it an easy way of making money. By peddling useless sample after useless sample round the merchants and failing to accept the full responsibilities of the job, they bring not just themselves, but the whole profession into disrepute. In a time of increasing prices and demand for wine, a good broker can make a handsome living. However, the wine-trade moves like a pendulum and the good years may have to support many lean years in the future.

Increasing awareness of the wines of Burgundy overseas has produced a new style of broker: he deals directly with the foreign customer. By cutting out the *négociant*, there are certain savings to be made, but these bring with them certain risks. Naturally such a broker is frowned upon by much of the traditional trade, even though he may have spent many years studying the wines of the region. More dangerous is the outsider who attempts to exploit the situation.

In Burgundy, the grower and the shipper tend to live in different worlds, for they each have different problems and requirements. The good broker is a valuable bridge between them: he keeps them informed of the condition of the market; he is their eye upon the world. In many ways, he, of all the men of Burgundy, should be the best instructed.

Why is the *négociant* so important in Burgundy? We have shown that his original role was that of salesman for the wines of the area in the more distant corners of France and abroad. That is still true today, though it is only one aspect of his function. Where there exists such a multitude of producers, many of whom do not make enough wine to commercialize individually, it is the function of the merchant to blend their output so that he can offer reasonable quantities of any given wine on the market. It is important to realize that Burgundy is a blended wine, and that this, so far from being a disadvantage, is its strength.

For example, the shipper might buy Gevrey-Chambertin from ten different growers; from some, just one cask or two, from others six or even more. Some of this wine will have been purchased immediately after the vintage, perhaps even as grapes; some may have been bought a year or eighteen months later. All the time he is striving to produce a Gevrey-Chambertin in the style of his company, one that will do credit to his label. Weaknesses in some of the wines he has bought will be cancelled out by excesses in others, but he seeks perfection of the ultimate blend. Buying wine is not the simple matter it may seem. A grower's price may vary considerably during the year, dependent on his bank balance, the weather, and the space that he has in his cellar for the coming crop. The buyer, for his part, must consider, when he plans his purchases, what he expects his sales to be in three or four year's time. A good shipper may list as many as sixty different *appellations* in perhaps two or three vintages. Since future sales in any country are dependent on circumstances beyond the control of either shipper or grower, it is by no means simple to plan even a short time ahead. Lamentably, in many countries, wine is considered as a luxury and is accordingly put far down on the list of priorities where imports are concerned. Governments have, too, the unhappy habit of imposing punitive taxes overnight. For the wine trade of Burgundy this is a particularly grave matter, since it is an area that depends on exports. It sends twice as great a proportion of its production abroad as Bordeaux does: and it is not uncommon for three-quarters of a shipper's turnover to be earned on foreign markets.

The roles and methods of the merchants of the Beaujolais and of the Côte d'Or are different. The financial problems of the former are much slighter since he sells a wine that is to be drunk young and he should turn his stock over more than once a year. He is ready to sell the new vintage, as Beaujolais Nouveau, within a matter of weeks of

The courtyard of the fifteenth-century Hôtel-Dieu, which is the centre of Beaune, the mercantile centre of Burgundy. It is a charitable institution subsidized by its holdings in the Beaune vineyards whose wines are auctioned at the annual sale. With its great van der Weiden altarpiece, tapestries, preserved medieval ward and pharmacy, it is a tourist attraction in its own right.

Drawing a sample of the wine in the longest cellar (110 metres) of Burgundy, at Château la Chaize, Odénas, the biggest vineyard (150 hectares), in the largest *grand cru* (Brouilly) of the Beaujolais.

The four major grapes of Burgundy:
    a) *Aligoté*, used for the lesser white wine entitled to the *appellations* Bourgogne Aligoté and Bourgogne Grand Ordinaire.
    b) *Gamay*, the red wine grape which achieves its greatest eminence when grown on the granitic soil of Beaujolais.
    c) *Pinot noir*, the grape grown with no outstanding results elsewhere but which reaches its peak of distinction in the great red wines of Burgundy.
    d) *Chardonnay*, the grape grown all over the world but at its greatest in the finest of all dry white wines, those of Burgundy, like le Montrachet, Corton Charlemagne, Meursault and Chablis.

The Rock of Solutré, the landmark visible from all over Pouilly Fuissé; surrounded by vineyards, and an absorbing subject to archaeologists from all over the world.

the vintage. His commitments are thus limited, since he can often buy his wine when he has already found a customer for it. Moreover, the bulk of the wines of the Beaujolais and the Mâconnais are kept in vats so the total storage space needed is less in proportion to the quantity sold.

On the other hand, a Côte d'Or *négociant* must carry in his cellars a fortune in wine, much of which he probably will not sell until it has been in stock for two or three years. (The sale of wine *en primeur* shortly after the vintage is almost unknown on the Côte d'Or and, due to the fragmented vineyard ownership, there is no system of selling by 'slices' as in Bordeaux.) The increasing amount of capital needed to finance these stocks in a period of expensive borrowing has proved too much for some merchants. As a result, during the past few years, much outside capital has come into Burgundy; and companies both in Beaujolais and the Côte d'Or have come under foreign control.

Recently, too, there has been much consolidation within the trade itself and several well-established names have been taken under the wings of their brethren. Thus, whilst the Beaune telephone directory lists almost 140 different wine shippers' names, it is doubtful whether as many as thirty of them are truly independent: the rest are trading names and *sous-marques*.

It is not surprising that many of the more financially successful shippers are those who have considerable vineyard holdings, for each year they have a good proportion of their needs in stock at basic prices. Of the major shippers it is unlikely, however, that any account for much more than 10 per cent of their turnover in output from their own vineyards.

Of the seven largest *domaines* on the Côte d'Or, five belong to shipping houses; Bouchard Père et Fils, J. Faiveley, Chanson Père et Fils, Louis Latour and the Société d'Élèvage et de Diffusion des Grands Vins (SEDVG) – or as it is more generally known, La Reine Pédauque. Of these, Louis Latour enjoys perhaps the best success in the auction room (the most reliable barometer of fashionable acceptance at present). The offices are in the aptly named rue des Tonneliers in Beaune and they own a remarkable press-house (listed by the French government as being of national interest) in Aloxe-Corton. It is set in a quarry in the middle of the vineyard Corton Perrières, and has floor after floor of cellars cut into the rock. At the top level is a traditional *cuverie* that is well worth a visit. Across the road is the Latour family home of Château Corton Grancey, which gives its name to an outstanding blend of wines from the Latour *domaine* with the *appellation* Corton. The *domaine* also includes a considerable portion of the Corton Charlemagne vineyard. The style of these wines is generally full-bodied, deeply coloured and rich in alcohol, giving them the ability to support long years in bottle. Demand for such wines always seems to be greater than supply, and customers often find themselves strictly rationed.

With eighty hectares, Bouchard Père et Fils have the largest viticultural *domaine* on the Côte d'Or. Their main cellars are in the Château de Beaune, which was built at the end of the fifteenth century in the form of a regular pentagon, with a large tower at each corner; the two facing outwards were over 150 feet in diameter. At the end of the seventeenth century Henri IV ordered the destruction of the château but fortunately his instruction was never completely carried out and a century later it was admired as a masterpiece by Vauban, France's greatest military architect.

The most valuable vines in the *domaine* of Bouchard Père et Fils must be those in the vineyard of le Montrachet, but the best known may well be those in that part of the Beaune Grèves vineyard, known as Vigne de l'Enfant Jésus. Up to the time of the French revolution, it belonged to the Carmelite sisters of Beaune, who gave it that name. The wine it produces has been described as having 'an exquisite finesse, a taste that is both warm but delicate, which carries on, leaving after it a sweet and perfumed breath'. Warner Allen rated the 1906 vintage of the wine, opened in 1933, the most noteworthy wine from Beaune he ever tasted.

Another company to rely on the fortifications of Beaune for their cellar space, is Chanson Père et Fils, which purchased the Boulevard (the original name for the great towers or bastions) des Filles or de l'Oratoire in 1794, for 1,980 francs, the value at that time of six hogsheads of wine from Beaune. With walls twenty-six feet thick at ground level, it makes ideal cellars for wine, having a constant temperature of 12°C (52°F). The young wines are unloaded at the higher levels by lorries which drive up on to the town walls. As the wines age, they go down to the lower floors. Chanson own a remarkable collection of old wines, including some more than a hundred years old. The Chanson *domaine* of forty-five hectares is spread over the *premier crus* of Beaune, Savigny and Pernand-Vergelesses, but the one of which they are most proud is Beaune Clos des Fèves, which is named in documents of as long ago as 1307.

Chanson wines tend to have a style of their own, often rather light in colour, but with a deceptive fullness and great delicacy of flavour. They are honest wines which support ageing without problem. To say that the wines of a merchant have a certain style by no means implies that they all taste the same and this can well be demonstrated by comparing wines of the same vintage from a grower such as Chanson. Even when one tastes together their wines of Beaune Clos des Marconnets, Beaune Clos du Roi and Beaune Blanchefleurs, three vineyards which lie next to each other, one is surprised by the differences between them, though they all have a family resemblance.

The cellars of Joseph Drouhin are in the picturesquely named rue d'Enfer, within yards of the Wine Museum. These were once the royal cellars of the Dukes of Burgundy and the Kings of France. Some traces of the crypt of the former church of Saint Baudèle, which dates from the eighth century, can still be seen there. The Drouhin cellars welcome visitors throughout the week. Their *domaine* includes holdings in Clos Vougeot, le Musigny, le Chambertin and Corton, but they also produce an interesting white wine from the Clos des Mouches in Beaune. The Hospices de Beaune have recently named a *cuvée* after Maurice Drouhin, the father of the present owner, who was one of their major benefactors.

The Nuits Saint-Georges house of J. Faiveley claims to have the largest vineyard holding in Burgundy, with many vines in Nuits itself and in Mercurey in the Saône et Loire *département* and elsewhere, particularly on the Côte de Nuits. Two wines often seen with the Faiveley label are Nuits Clos de la Maréchale and Mercurey Clos des Myglands.

It is interesting how certain shippers are particularly well placed on certain export markets. For example, Albert Bichot, who own the important *domaine* of Clos Frantin at Vosne-Romanée and are currently the most important exporters in Burgundy, are very strong on the British market. Bouchard Ainé et Fils have a large proportion of the Canadian sales, and the label of Louis Jadot is as likely to be seen in the United States as anywhere in the world. Perhaps unfortunately, Burgundy, unlike Champagne and whisky, is not a product that can be sold with ease throughout the world. Switzerland is the largest export market – though it takes largely Beaujolais – followed by the United States, Britain, Germany and Belgium. Japan has not yet made a significant impression as a consuming customer.

Some *domaines* sell directly to customers either in France or overseas under their own label; certain others still sell under their own label, though through the shippers. Thus Calvet had the exclusivity of the two important *domaines* of Prieur, with holdings, amongst others, in le Musigny and Clos Vougeot, and of Poupon. Joseph Drouhin distributes the Montrachet of the Marquis de Laguiche; Piat, the Gevrey-Chambertins of General Rebourseau. The interest for the grower in such an arrangement is considerable, as he has a guaranteed outlet for his production and someone else is bearing the cost of publicizing it. The whole question of supply contracts with vineyard owners is a sensitive one. In a period of expanding sales and increasing prices, it can be useful for the shipper to have a guaranteed source of supply. In a period of falling demand and prices, however, there is every interest in having complete liberty in choosing one's source.

The notion of *domaine* bottling, as opposed to '*vin de négoce*' is one that was actively fostered by Alexis Lichine in *The Wines of France* and one must wonder whether he was not, in part, inspired by commercial motives as his own company, selling in the United States, specialized in such wines. According to him there were substantial incentives for the *négociants* to debase the wines in their cellars and thus defraud the customers. The only way you could be certain of buying a bottle of genuine wine was to buy it bottled at the *domaine*.

The result is that there has been some increase in bottling by the growers. There have been such developments as mobile bottling lines coming over from Bordeaux. Wine has even been taken away and cared for in central cellars, to be returned to the grower for bottling, so that it can bear on the label the magic words, 'Domaine Bottled'.

The basic truth of the matter is that the majority of the growers are simply that; they know how to cultivate their vineyards to produce a good crop and then how to make a wine. Once the wine has been made, their knowledge of oenology is sometimes rudimentary. White wines, particularly, need constant attention and the shipper, who generally employs his own wine-chemist, has better facilities for the full range of treatments.

There is no reason why a grower should be more honest than a shipper, though it may be argued that the latter, with larger stocks of wine at his disposal, has more room for manipulation. It is unfortunate that, due to biased conditioning, so many people now think in Orwellian terms, 'Four legs good! Two legs bad!' *Domaine*-bottled wine good; merchants' wine bad. Such thinking must confuse, when one considers the wines of a shipper who has his own vineyards. Is one to take the wines from his own vines as being honest, whilst the rest are fraudulent? Indeed one *négociant*, with extensive vineyard holdings, refuses to label any of his wines as being 'Domaine Bottled', because that might suggest that they are in some way superior to the other wines that he sells.

There is one French word that sums up the whole situation – '*sérieux*'. This does not exactly mean serious, but rather conscientious. A wine from a '*maison sérieuse*' will be sound and honest – as will be a wine from a '*domaine sérieux*'. However, you are more likely to get a sound wine from even the most dishonest shipper, which is more than can often be said of a careless *domaine*. It would be ignoring the facts, if one said that there are no dishonest shippers, but there is dishonesty in every trade and the trade in Burgundy has been largely cleaned up. In itself the words 'Domaine Bottled' are considerably less convincing guarantee than the label of a serious shipper – or a serious *domaine*.

The shipper and the grower must depend on each other for their existence, for even those *domaines* that try to sell their wine direct, rarely do it for their total production. They realize that the American market, which is in most cases their largest customer, is particularly sensitive and can change overnight. Every grower seeks to maintain good relations with the *négociants* who are his insurance policy in the case of a difficult market.

The future of the good shipper is assured for he alone offers wine in quantities acceptable to the larger customers. The amounts the *domaines* can offer are so limited that it is often difficult to put an intensive effort behind their sale. Moreover, for the foreign buyer, it is more convenient to buy a full range of the wines of Burgundy from one source than to have to group together a number of small parcels of wine; to correspond in the language of his choice (or almost) and to have the full commercial knowledge of documentation and labelling at his disposal.

Whilst there has been much talk of the *domaines*, what are the labels one is most likely to see? The best known is that of the Domaine de la Romanée-Conti at Vosne-Romanée, which, with its sister *domaine* of Marey-Monge, has the monopoly of Romanée-Conti and la Tâche, as well as holdings in Richebourg, Romanée Saint-Vivant, Grands Echézeaux and le Montrachet. These are the most prestigious, and expensive, wines of Burgundy. The prices that they fetch at auction even rival those of the great wines of Bordeaux.

The Côte de Nuits has a string of well-known *domaines*, beginning geographically, as well as in size with that of Clair-Däu at Marsannay la Côte, which extends over forty hectares and even includes vines at Santenay at the far end of the Côte de Beaune. Among the other well-known names are those of Rousseau of Gevrey-Chambertin, Roumier of Chambolle-Musigny, Bertagna of Vougeot and Henri Gouges of Nuits Saint-Georges.

On the Côte de Beaune the largest *domaines* are in the hands of the shippers, though those of the Marquis d'Angerville and the Pousse d'Or at Volnay, and of the Duc de Magenta at Chassagne Montrachet are well-known. Another important *domaine* is that of Roland Thévenin, the mayor of Saint Romain, who is also a shipper. He owns a portion of le Montrachet, the Château of Puligny-Montrachet and vines at Saint Romain and Auxey-Duresses.

5 THE GENERIC BURGUNDIES

To the average Englishman, Burgundy may mean Nuits Saint-Georges and Gevrey-Chambertin; to the average American, Pommard and Pouilly-Fuissé; but these are not the characteristic wines of the area. The reputation of any viticultural region must depend on its lowest common denominator and, while the wines of the Beaujolais are widely known, they do not come under this heading. The base – regional – wines are called Bourgogne Ordinaire, or Bourgogne Grand Ordinaire. The two names are interchangeable, though the latter seems more popular: perhaps it has a grander ring to it. Above this come two wines for which there are restrictions on the grape varieties used. Bourgogne Aligoté, which is white, and Bourgogne Passetoutgrains which is red, or occasionally rosé. The final regional wine is Bourgogne, with its three subsidiary *appellations*.

These are the wines by which all Burgundy must prosper. In a period of rising prices and tighter purse-strings, people will not hesitate to buy other wines if Burgundy cannot provide the quality they seek at the price they are prepared to pay. The lesser wines of Burgundy are often sadly underestimated outside the area: they have had little success by comparison, for example, with Bordeaux and Bordeaux Supérieur. Perhaps there should be some reorganization in the naming of these lesser wines of Burgundy. The fact that 'Ordinaire' is tacked on to the end of a name hardly suggests fine quality, even if it has 'Grand' added as well. The word Bourgogne, by itself, suggests that it is the lowest wine of the area and it is often difficult to persuade customers that they should pay a higher price for the quality of the wine. When the laws of

Appellation Contrôlée did not apply in Britain, such wines were sold there, without complaints, under the greatest names of Burgundy, at high prices. Now it is often difficult to sell the same wines, sailing under their true colours, for half the price.

Unfortunately even the regional wines of Burgundy labour under the same disadvantage as their more eminent brothers – simple shortage of production. This applies almost as much to the cheapest wines as to the most expensive. The lowest priced red wine of the area, Bourgogne Grand Ordinaire, in an average year, has a crop about twice that of a village like Gevrey-Chambertin, or less than the village of Saint Julien in Bordeaux. This chapter, however, will list the generic *appellations* of Burgundy, which can be produced in any of the basic areas.

Bourgogne Grand Ordinaire or Bourgogne Ordinaire
Colour: red, white or rosé
Average production: red: 21,227 hl.   white: 10,364 hl.
Minimum degree: red and rosé: 9°; white: 9·5°

It is interesting that the cheapest of all the *appellation contrôlée* wines of Burgundy should be amongst the most difficult to find in the trade. There are two reasons for this; firstly, the production is limited, and, secondly, the quality, particularly among the red wines, is variable. It is produced largely from the *gamay*, which on the Côte d'Or produces acid wines without distinction. Most of the Bourgogne Grand Ordinaire made is probably sold by the glass over the bar counters of the region.

Whilst the *gamay* is generally used for the red wines, the *pinot* can also be used; so can the *césar* and the *tressot* in the Yonne department. Since these varieties, apart from the *gamay*, can generally produce wines of higher *appellation*, they are not often used for wines of this level, except in bad years when they are low in sugar. One BGO (as it is often called), made from the *gamay* that is often most agreeable is the rosé wine grown at Orches in the Hautes-Côtes de Beaune. Whilst there are a few independent *vignerons* there, most of the wine is vinified at the Cave Coopérative des Hautes Côtes. When young, this wine is most enjoyable, but after a couple of years it tends to lose the freshness that is its main attraction.

For the white wines the permitted varieties are the *pinot blanc*, the *chardonnay*, the *melon de Bourgogne* (the same variety that is used for producing Muscadet) and, in the Yonne, the *sacy*. The *melon* is an interesting grape in that the wine it makes is one of the very few to produce a truly white sauce, and it was traditionally used for the fish stew of Burgundy – the *pochouse*. One co-operative cellar that regularly produces award-winning wines with the *appellation* of Bourgogne Grand Ordinaire is that of Buxy on the Côte Chalonnaise. It is not often listed by *négociants*, though Patriarche Père et Fils sell some under brand-names.

Bourgogne Aligoté
Colour: white
Average production: 52,344 hl.
Minimum degree: 9·5°

Of the lesser wines of Burgundy, Bourgogne Aligoté has the most regular following, for, at a reasonable price, it offers a dry white wine that is typically Burgundian. Without pretensions, it nevertheless shows that it comes from a noble family. It is generally grown in those villages of the Côte which are withdrawn from the front 'rank' geographically, such as Savigny and Pernand-Vergelesses, and also on the higher vineyards of the Arrière-Côtes and the Côte Chalonnaise. As it is a late-ripening grape there is often a danger of losing the crop and Hugh Johnson, in his *World Atlas of Wine*, calculated that the owner with his vineyards planted in *aligoté* makes a net loss over the year. Whilst the price obtained for the wine has increased recently, it is doubtful whether it has kept up with the rising overheads; and many vineyards formerly planted in *aligoté* have been replanted with *pinot* or *chardonnay*.

In good years an Aligoté is a wine with an agreeable amount of acidity, which goes well with the coarse fish from the local rivers. In some years – as happened particularly with some badly-made wines of the 1972 vintage – the acidity can be excessive and the wine difficult to drink. In such a case, it makes a superb Kir, the Burgundian apéritif: a glass of Aligoté with a dash of blackcurrant liqueur. Canon Kir, from whom it takes its name, was a noted resistance hero and for many years Mayor of Dijon. Now some prefabricated Kirs are being introduced on the market, not even made with the wine of Burgundy. It seems a pity that anyone should seek to take advantage of only part of Burgundy's heritage.

Bourgogne Aligoté is best drunk young and some Burgundian restaurants serve it the spring after the vintage, drawn straight from the cask into pitchers. It will maintain its freshness for two to four years, though H. Warner Allen recalls having enjoyed a bottle over twenty years old – which sounds like carrying the Englishman's love for old white Burgundy to the extreme. It is, though, permitted to add *chardonnay* grapes to those of the *aligoté* and still keep the *appellation,* so it is possible that he came across a wine with a high proportion of *chardonnay* in it, which would give it better keeping powers.

Some of the finest Bourgogne Aligotés come from the village of Pernand-Vergelesses and it is always worth trying a bottle, if you come across one. Since, however, it is illegal to join the name of the producing village to the *appellation*, you must study the grower's address carefully. Another interesting Aligoté is produced at Marey-les-Fussey by the *domaine* Thévenot-le Brun, which they describe as *perlant*. This, like some of the wines of the Muscadet, is bottled '*sur lie*'; that is to say that it is bottled directly from the cask, being drawn straight off the lees, without filtration. This gives a wine with rather more body and freshness and from which a series of lazy bubbles bead the glass.

Possible declassification: Bourgogne Grand Ordinaire.

Bourgogne Passetoutgrain
Colour: red or rosé
Average production: 28,449 hl.
Minimum degree: 9·5°

This wine is produced on the Côte d'Or and in the Région de Mercurey from mixing *gamay* and *pinot noir* grapes in the vat, the latter accounting for at least a third of the total. In a leaflet produced by the growers of Saône et Loire, the wine is described as follows: 'It is not a marriage of convenience, but a real love match, and the child is beautiful and good, as one would expect!' This is perhaps not entirely true, for the wine certainly was produced originally as a 'marriage of convenience'. The translation of the name literally means 'treat all the grapes' and this was because many of the smaller growers, who had plots of both *gamay* and *pinot*, did not have the facilities to ferment the two varieties separately.

Bourgogne Passetoutgrain is a wine of contrasts; when it is young, the *gamay* predominates (and *gamay* wines produced on the Côte d'Or are considerably less appealing than their brothers from the Beaujolais). The wine tends then to be acid, and has a curious unbalanced taste. As it ages the finesse of the *pinot* begins to impose itself and it gains greatly with maturity.

One of the problems with Bourgogne PTG (as it is commonly called) is that it is often drunk too young. It is not a wine to be drunk '*en primeur*'. Because it is cheap there is a tendency to put it quickly on the market. This has happened particularly in England, where sales of the wine have increased considerably, because, following the introduction of *Appellation Contrôlée*, it is still one of the few examples of a genuine, labelled, bottle of Burgundy at a reasonable price. As a general rule of thumb, Passetoutgrain should not be drunk under two years old; and, in a good vintage, it will continue improving over a period of twelve years or more. In an exceptional year it is a worthwhile investment to buy some bottles, put them away in your cellar and forget about them. Patience will be rewarded. Occasionally Passetoutgrain is vinified as a rosé wine and in that case it should be drunk young.

As much of the Passetoutgrain is produced in the Hautes-Côtes de Beaune and de Nuits, which are now allowed to make wines of superior classifications – which gain higher prices – from the *pinot noir* grape, there is little replanting in *gamay*; and it is possible that over a period of several years the *appellation* will disappear. (On the other hand, it is also worth noting that less Bourgogne Grand Ordinaire is being made as the first plantings are made of *pinot*: this is leading to a transitional time when more Bourgogne Passetoutgrain is made.)

Possible declassification: Bourgogne Grand Ordinaire.

Bourgogne
Colour: red, white or rosé
Average production: red: 53,798 hl.   white: 11,812 hl.
Minimum degree: red and rosé 10°; white 10·5°

BURGUNDY

One of the greatest difficulties for those trying to sell the wines of Burgundy both in France and abroad, is to persuade the customer to realize that the *appellation* 'Bourgogne' is already a superior level. The reasons for this are not difficult to find. The name of Burgundy has been so devalued by Spanish, Australian, Californian and a host of other so-called Burgundies, that there is a feeling that Bourgogne is on a similar level. This impression is strengthened if the consumer compares with the wines of France's other great viticultural region, where Bordeaux is the lowest of the *appellations*.

Bourgogne Rouge can never be a cheap wine as it has to be produced from the best grape varieties, the *pinot noir*, or, in the Yonne, the *césar* and *tressot*. The *gamay* can only be used if it is planted in one of the nine great *crus* of the Beaujolais (Saint Amour, Juliénas, Chénas, Moulin-à-Vent, Fleurie, Chiroubles, Morgon, Brouilly and Côte de Brouilly). The difference between a wine sold as Bourgogne produced from the *pinot* and one produced from the *gamay* will be considerable, but in either case it will be a wine of a certain quality.

Bourgogne Blanc is produced either from the *chardonnay* or the *pinot blanc*; in no case from the *aligoté* or any other lesser variety. In practice a large proportion of the Bourgogne Blanc sold comes from the *chardonnays* of the Mâconnais. (One interesting Bourgogne Blanc is that produced by Guillemard-Dupont at Meloisey in the Hautes-Côtes de Beaune entirely from the *pinot beurot*).

Burgundy is not known for its rosé wines, but there is a certain amount of Bourgogne Rosé, or *clairet*, produced from the same grape-varieties as the red wines. Bourgogne is the highest *appellation* that any rosé from Burgundy can aspire to. For example, a Gevrey-Chambertin or Beaune vinified as a rosé would immediately lose all rights to the village *appellation*. The rosés of the village of Marsannay, just to the south of Dijon, however, have created such a reputation for themselves that they have the right to tack the village name on to the word Bourgogne, thus creating a *sub-appellation*. Another village known for its rosé is Irancy in the Yonne.

In certain areas the best wines produced have Bourgogne as their maximum *appellation*; all along the Côte d'Or, on the plain, below the vineyards having the right to the village or better names, are vineyards producing Bourgogne. Even in the middle of Beaune there are two

THE GENERIC BURGUNDIES

vineyards which cannot call the wine they produce Beaune, but only Bourgogne. To the west of Dijon, towards Sombernon, there are some vines, poor survivors of the Côte Dijonnaise; in the Yonne there are certain pockets of vines outside the Chablis area; in the Saône et Loire, to the west and south of those villages that have their own *appellations*; each of these areas produces no wines of a higher quality than Bourgogne. To find a vineyard wine with just this *appellation* is rare, but one that is much appreciated is the Clos des Topes-Bizot of the Beaune shipping house Louis Max.

Apart from these vines which produce Bourgogne, and nothing better, there was also a large quantity made in abundant years through the system of declassification. As has been described in the first chapter, all the greatest wines of Burgundy could be declassified: and on the Côte d'Or, in the best villages, about 800 bottles to the acre over the village *appellation* could be produced as Bourgogne. Thus in some years it was possible to buy Bourgogne from the Chambertin vineyard which had been vinified in the same way and at the same time as a wine probably six times the price. Unfortunately, the label could give no indication of the provenance of the wine other than the *appellation* and the address of the grower. Of course it is only logical that if this grower, in an abundant year, was forced to sell le Chambertin, Gevrey-Chambertin and Bourgogne from the same vineyard, he would have used his best *cuvées* for the most expensive wines. In those years, though, that produce the greatest wines there is usually a small crop and little or no wine was declassified. However, in a vintage like 1972 with a limited amount of deduction and a certain amount of guesswork, it should be possible to buy at reasonable prices some great wines which have been declassified into Bourgogne. It should be borne in mind, though, in years when there are large crops, it sometimes happens that the maximum production per hectare for each *appellation* is increased.

Since it is hard for a shipper to sell a wine with the plain *appellation* Bourgogne, his best way to overcome the difficulty generally is to create a brand-name which will personalize the wine and, with luck, tie the customer to that shipper. Amongst such wines to be found with the *appellation* Bourgogne are:

      la Vignée – Bouchard Père et Fils
      la Chèvre Noire – Boisseaux Estivant

Cuvée Voltaire – Chanson Père et Fils
Cuvée Elizabeth – Patriarche Père et Fils

but there are many others.

Possible declassification: Bourgogne Grand Ordinaire.

As the *Appellation Contrôlée* system in Burgundy has developed, so has it tended to fragment and, as a result, Bourgogne has spawned three *sub-appellations* on a slightly superior level: Bourgogne (or Bourgogne rosé)-Marsannay, Bourgogne Hautes-Côtes de Beaune and Bourgogne Hautes-Côtes de Nuits.

Bourgogne-Marsannay or Bourgogne Rosé-Marsannay
Colour: rosé
Average production: 1,997 hl.
Minimum degree: 10°

Marsannay is an undistinguished village that has managed precariously to hold out against the urban sprawl of Dijon and it seems an unlikely place for the distinguished restaurant it boasts (Restaurant des Gourmets). Until recently the last viticultural bastion of the Côte Dijonnaise, it has only lately allied itself to the Côte de Nuits. There are records from as far back as the seventh century of wines having been produced in Marsannay, but it has always suffered from its proximity to Dijon, for in times of transport difficulties it has been necessary to purchase one's *vin ordinaire* from as close a source as possible. As the *gamay* wines from Marsannay used to fetch as much, or more, in Dijon as the wines they produced from the *pinot*, there was little incentive to plant noble grapes. The situation became so bad that, even in the middle of the nineteenth century, there was not enough *pinot* grown in the village to make one vat of wine. Surprisingly, this sad situation lasted until after the First World War, when the economic situation made it imperative that a start should be made in planting the finer grape varieties. Further incentive was given by the fact that, in 1919, a cooperative cellar was founded in the village. This cellar differs from almost every other in that it produces only rosé wines.

Decrees of 1960 and 1965 gave the villages of Marsannay and Couchey the right to their own *appellation* by adding Marsannay to

THE GENERIC BURGUNDIES

the generic *appellation* of Bourgogne. In 1973, however, the villages were given the right to sell their wines as Côtes de Nuits Villages, a superior *appellation*. This led to a storm of protest from the growers in the villages which already had the right to the *appellation*, and although the decree was signed by the minister it has been 'temporarily' withdrawn. Ultimately it is therefore likely that, except in rainy years, less wine will be vinified as rosé and rather more in red. So, sadly, Burgundy's best rosé may disappear over the next few years.

Apart from the co-operative cellar, other fine wine of Marsannay is produced by the Clair-Däu *domaine*. The wines are best drunk young and cool; they have an agreeable fruit and freshness with a wonderful nose. The wines are sold under the village name alone, and such vineyard names as aux Favières, aux Crais and Fer-Meulin, which had a certain reputation in the past, are no longer seen.

Possible declassification: Bourgogne Grand Ordinaire.

Bourgogne Hautes-Côtes de Beaune
Colour: red and white
Average production: red 3,751 hl.   white 56 hl.
Minimum degree: red 10°; white 10·5°

Villages having the right to this *appellation* are: in the Côte d'Or – Baubigny, Bouze-les-Beaune, Cirey-les-Nolay, Cormot, Echevronne, Fussey, la Rochepot, Magny-les-Villers, Mavilly-Mandelot, Meloisey, Nantoux, Nolay and Vauchignon. In Saône-et-Loire – Change, Créot, Epertully, Paris-l'Hôpital and part of the villages of Cheilly-les-Maranges, Dézizes-les-Maranges and Sampigny-les-Maranges.

The vineyards of the Arrière-Côtes are but a fraction of what they were before phylloxera, and most of the area that has been replanted is in *aligoté* and *gamay*. Unfortunately there has been a considerable drift of population away from these country villages to the towns of Dijon, Beaune and Chalon, and efforts are being made to rehabilitate the area. One direction they have taken is in extensive plantings of the noble varieties, *pinot* and *chardonnay*. One major advantage of the two *appellations* of the Hautes-Côtes is there are considerable possibilities of extending the vineyard area; and it is likely that these wines will become much better known in the future. The main obstacle lies in the

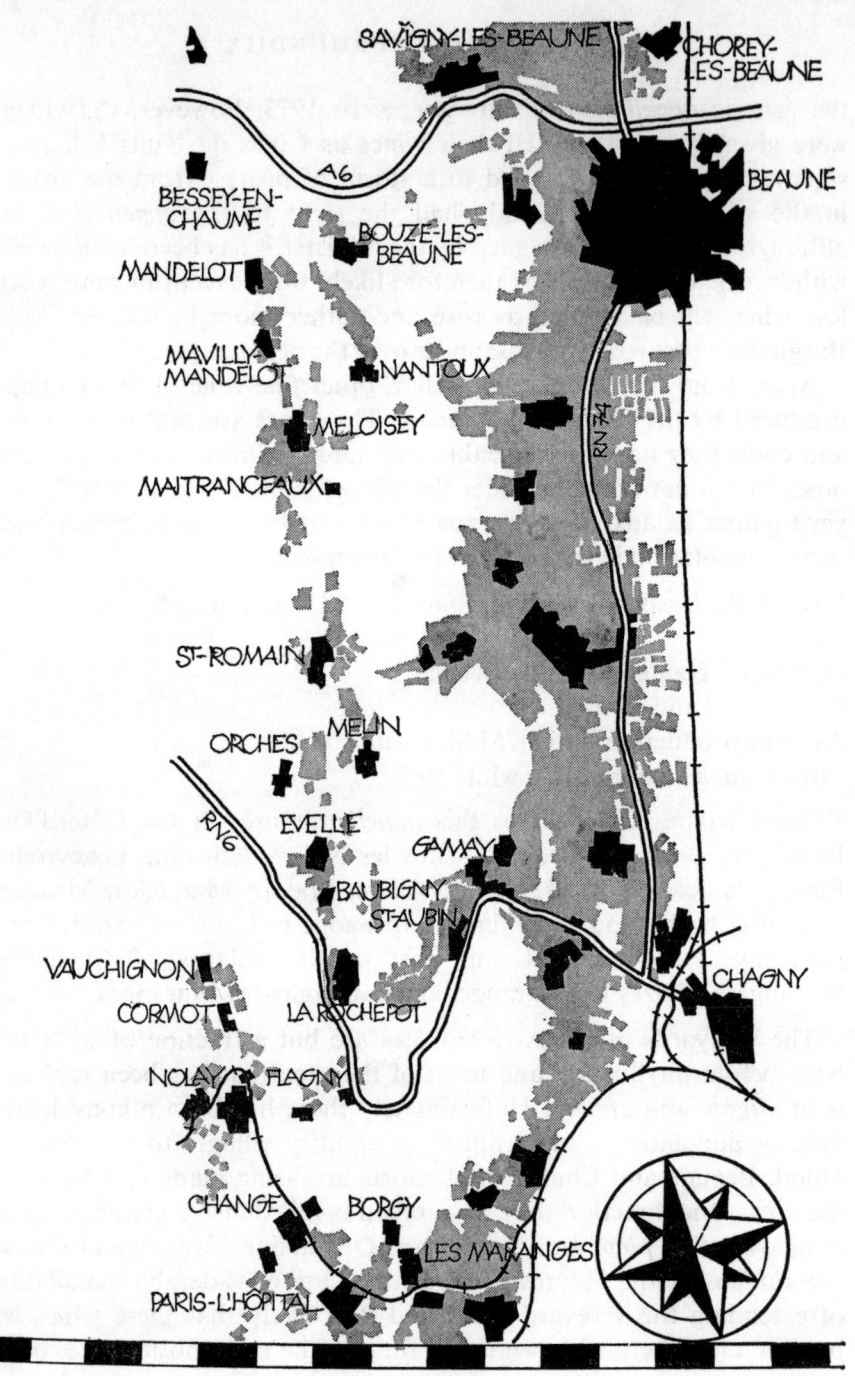

THE HAUTES-CÔTES DE BEAUNE

fact that, in many cases, the angle of the vineyards to the sun is not ideal, so that the grapes ripen as much as ten days later than those on the main Côte. Even if the wines produced meet the requirements for the minimum degree, maximum production, and are from the correct grape-varieties, they will not automatically qualify for the *appellation*. Samples of each wine have to be submitted to a tasting panel for approval and, while this gives an extra guarantee of the quality of the wine, it is an added trial for the growers.

This is not just a region of vineyards; there are fields of cattle pasture, corn and important plantings of soft fruits: red- and blackcurrants, strawberries and raspberries. Each village has its own character. The capital, Nolay, is a quiet market-town; la Rochepot is dominated by its fairy-tale château; Nantoux lies at the foot of what must be the steepest vineyards in the Côte d'Or; Mavilly-Mandelot is overlooked by the rocky crest of the Pas Saint Martin, off which the saint is reputed to have jumped on his horse, to escape from the devil; and Meloisey, with its church, part of which dates from the thirteenth century.

Much of the wine is made at the Cave Coopérative des Hautes-Côtes, at Beaune, and most of it is sold through the Savigny shipping firm of Henri de Villamont. A number of *vignerons* vinify for themselves, though most of their wine is sold in cask to the shippers. Nevertheless, certain growers, amongst them Louis Jacob of Echévronne, have managed to create a reputation for their own-bottled wines, and Beaune shippers Bouchard Père et Fils have the exclusivity of the production of the Château de Mandelot.

In good years red wines from the Hautes-Côtes can rival their more august cousins from the Côte de Beaune and make admirable *vins de garde*, lacking nothing in fruit, but perhaps a little in finesse. The production of white Hautes-Côtes de Beaune is limited and most of it is consumed in the local village restaurants.

Possible declassification: Bourgogne Grand Ordinaire.

Bourgogne Hautes-Côtes de Nuits
Colour: red and white
Average production: red 802 hl.   white 68 hl.
Minimum degree: red 10°; white 10·5°

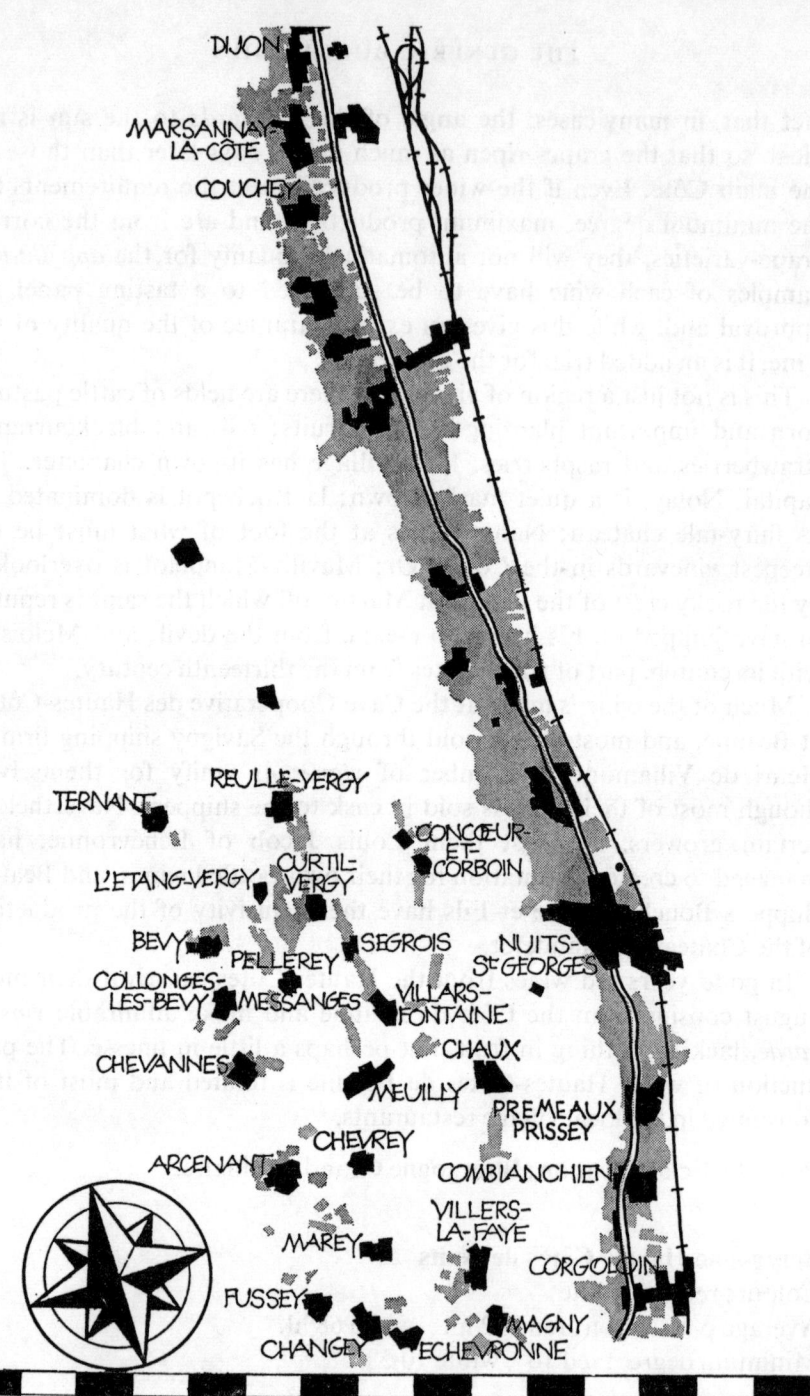

THE HAUTES-CÔTES DE NUITS

Villages having right to the *appellation*: Arcénant, Bévy, Chaux, Chévannes, Collonges-les-Bévy, Curtil-Vérgy, l'Etang-Vérgy, Magny-les-Villers, Marey-les-Fussey, Messanges, Meuilley, Reule-Vérgy, Villars-Fontaine, Villers-la-Faye.

The area under vines in the Hautes-Côtes de Nuits is considerably less than that of the Hautes-Côtes de Beaune, and the production is severely limited, but the wine is of similar style. Again, much of the wine is made by the co-operative cellar at Beaune.

In order to promote the wines of the Arrière-Côtes, a Maison des Hautes-Côtes was opened at the beginning of 1974 at Marey-les-Fussey, overlooking the valley of the Meuzin. There it is possible to taste a full range of wines from the area; not only those wines with the Hautes-Côtes *appellations*, but also Aligotés and Passetoutgrain, rosés from the *gamay* and the *pinot* and Crémant de Bourgogne made from local *aligoté* wines. Light meals of local specialities are on sale and the house is a genuine and popular tourist resort.

Marey-les-Fussey has another of the few vineyards in the Arrière-Côtes to sell wine under its own name. This is Clos Vignon, a twenty-acre plot that used to belong to the Abbey of Lieu-Dieu des Champs. founded in 1140 by Robert de Vérgy of the Cistercian order.

Possible declassification: Bourgogne Grand Ordinaire.

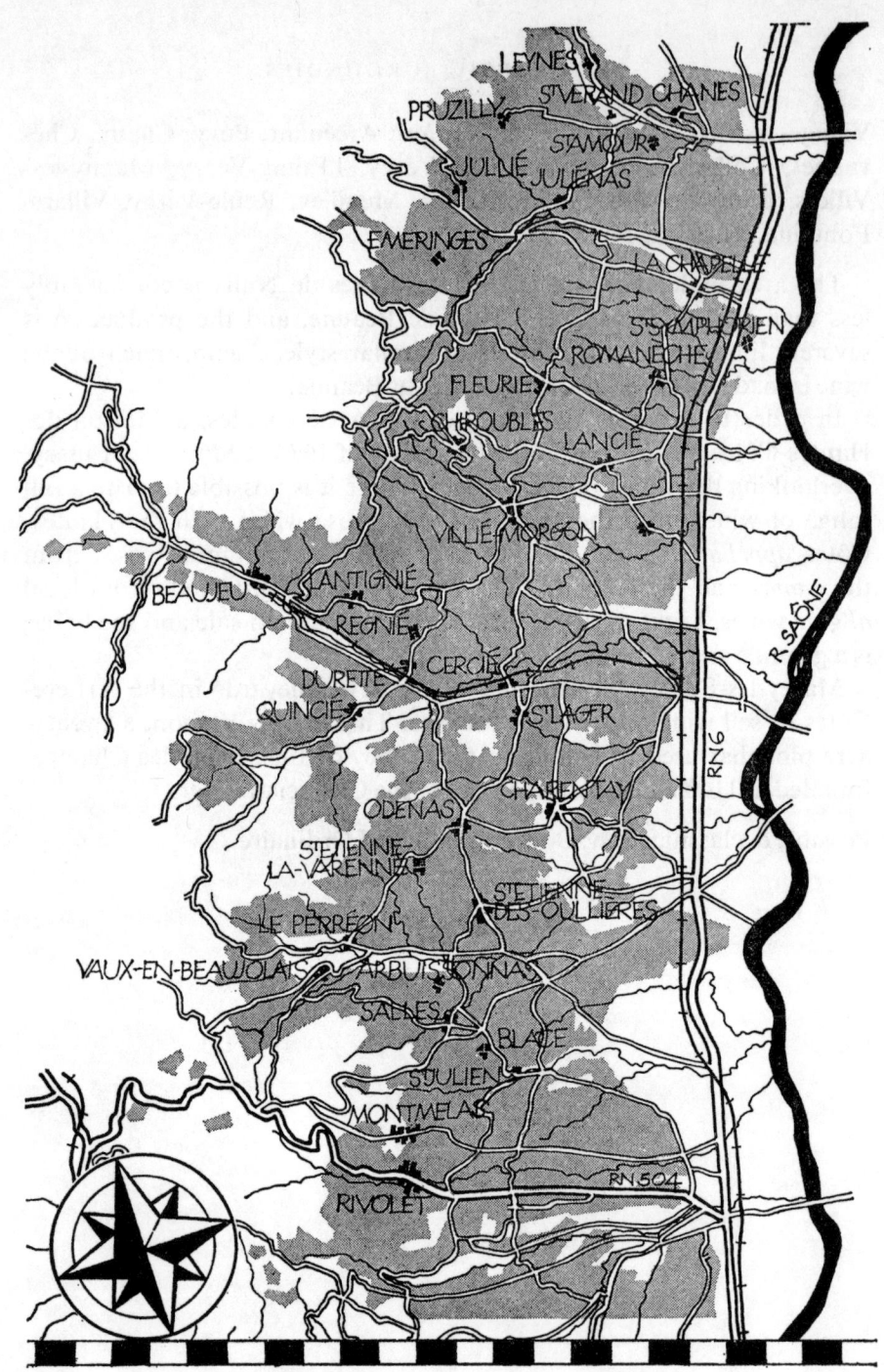

BEAUJOLAIS VILLAGES
Communes named are entitled to the *appellation* Beaujolais Villages.

6 THE BEAUJOLAIS

Except in the Beaujolais, wine-lists invariably include Beaujolais under the heading of Burgundy. That custom is so firmly established that it is followed here, since most people will expect to find it dealt with in a book on the wines of Burgundy. In fact the Beaujolais is so clearly physically distinct as to be geographically a separate region. The traveller coming down from the Mâconnais is conscious of entering the south. The houses are more generously spaced; the roofs, of the strong, semi-circular, red tiles, are flatter; and hardly a house but has its balcony – for building here is based on an assumption of the sun. Yet in many years, not long after the *vendage*, the snow lies on the tops of the hills above the vines.

It is historically and viticulturally – as well as geographically and architecturally – surprising, too, that Beaujolais should be considered part of Burgundy. The area never came under the Dukes of Burgundy; and its wine is of a different style, produced from a different grape variety, on different soil and by different methods – by people of a different character.

Nevertheless, many people's first introduction to 'Burgundy' is through Beaujolais, for over 110,000,000 bottles – more than two-thirds of the total red wine production of the Burgundy region – come from the vast rolling vineyards in the *arrondissement* of Villefranche in the Rhône *département*, and a few in the south of Saône-et-Loire.

Recently, too, Beaujolais has made a separate reputation. As late as the early days of this century it was still the wine of the country people who made it and – as they had done for centuries – drank all that was not traded out. It was the local wine of Lyons a few miles away, but it was hardly known farther than that from its native soil until the nineteen-twenties, when a number of Paris cafés began to adopt it as a carafe wine. It was in 1929 that Leon Foillard, poet of the Beaujolais and *négociant*, whose son has succeeded him in the family business at Saint Georges de Reneins, collaborated with Tony David in *Le Pays et le Vin Beaujolais*, an evocative study of the wine of that district with an 'anthologie Bacchique'.

Latterly the Beaujolais Nouveau – at a few weeks old – has become a fashionably smart drink in Britain and even the United States.

Apart from its obvious merits – of colour, scent and taste, lightness and freshness – Beaujolais has probably become popular outside France for its very 'Frenchness', as a symbol of French wine, vineyards, rural France itself. More than any other red wine it should be drunk cellar-cool, when all its youth and gaiety become apparent. In its versatility it makes a happy partner for almost any meat, poultry, cheese, pasta or egg dish. Yet it is so eminently drinkable that it has the reputation of being, above all, a wine for swigging. Indeed, it is reputed to be the only wine that truly quenches thirst. The Beaujolais is the mighty drinking region of France; with its eternal *boule* players, their berets tugged forward into peaks, faces brick-red and lined by the weather – and the wine – quaffing hugely from their heavy glasses. There is talk there of men who drink fourteen litres a day – a figure which assumes at least a couple of bottles with breakfast.

It was not by accident, but the divination of the novelist, that Gabriel Chevallier – himself a Parisian – set his splendidly broad, bawdy, boozy novel, *Clochemerle*, in the Beaujolais. The French people who knew the district recognized the larger-than-life accuracy of the picture; many more, as readers, simply felt its quality of perception. *Clochemerle* was written in the nineteen-thirties when Beaujolais was still a relatively remote rural area. Even as late as 1948 many of its roads were not metalled; the villages remained quiet, places of the people who lived there. Now, at weekends and in summer, the narrow country roads of the 'Route de Beaujolais' – two versions, one *touristique*, one rapid – are crowded with the cars of trippers. Many of the true country people of the Beaujolais were at first suspicious and resentful of the invasion, but it is a commercially backward village indeed which does not now set out its stall – the Cave de Dégustation, wine bar, café and bottle-sales – and take an extra living from the visitors.

Out of the holiday season and on weekdays it reverts – almost – to normal. The *boule* players can go undisturbed about their grave business.

To a greater degree than any other part of France, the Beaujolais is true wine country, almost all its people involved in it; all cheerfully proud of it. It remains contentedly and prosperously so because, although – especially in the north – it produces some fine bottles, it has enough daily wine for its own folk, and plenty that ordinary people can understand and enjoy, at prices they can afford.

Although there is no written evidence of vineyards in the Beaujolais until the eighth century, there can be little doubt that the Romans planted vines there. They had extensive vineyards in the Côtes du Rhône, where, as in the Beaujolais, the *taille à gobelet* method of pruning, the direct descendant of the Roman *capitum jugatio*, is still employed. Moreover several of the patois words of the Beaujolais *vigneron* are derived directly from Latin and owe nothing to French. Lugdunum, or Lyons, was the most influential trading centre in Gaul, and had its own wine port. The history of Beaujolais wines has always been tied to that of Lyons, a city said to be watered by three rivers – the Rhône, the Saône and the Beaujolais – though not necessarily in that order of importance. In the words of Louis Orizet, 'It is only after two thousand years of loyal and devoted service to Lugdunum, that our victor . . . has left to conquer Paris.'

So it is only during this century that the wines of the Beaujolais have come to be appreciated outside their own country. Professor Saintsbury had a little Chénas in his cellar, but he grouped it with wines from the Côte d'Or. Jullien, however, classifies the wines of Romanèche-Thorins, Moulin-à-Vent, Fleurie, La Chapelle de Guinchay, Juliénas and Morgon. It may be indicative of the relative unimportance of the wines of Beaujolais in Britain at the time that, when Stephen Gwynn was preparing his book on Burgundy, published in 1934, he considered it sufficient to study those vineyards from his railway carriage.

Beaujolais takes its name from the barony of Beaujeu, which has its own stormy history of independence. It seems to have been founded towards the end of the tenth century by a certain Béraud, who built a castle on the site of present-day Beaujeu, to protect the locality from the predatory masters of Tourvéon, who constantly made plundering expeditions into the plain of the Saône.

The property of the barony was extended by a series of judicious marriages and by playing off the Counts of Lyons and Mâcon against each other. Unfortunately for Edward II of Beaujeu, he had to surrender the title and land to the Bourbon family in 1400, as the alternative to being executed after an unsavoury series of events involving the abduction of a minor and the killing of an officer of the peace. Although it was soon succeeded by Villefranche as the capital of the area, Beaujeu for a long time retained a certain measure of autonomy, granted by a charter of Guichard IV of Beaujeu, in 1260. These rights included freedom from local taxes, liberty for a serf after living in the town for a year and a day, and the opportunity for a man to strike his wife with impunity – unless she died as a result of it. The wives of neighbouring Anse were more fortunate: in 1340 the Chapter of Lyons granted them exemption from punishment for adultery committed during fairs and market-days. In Villefranche, those caught in the act of adultery had either to run down the main street naked, or pay a heavy fine.

The vineyards of the Beaujolais run westwards from the main Paris-Marseilles railway line, rising to a height of 1,600 feet in the foothills of the Massif Central; above them, the woods, below, fields of maize, and beyond, the rich plain of Bresse stretches away across the Saône. Thus the vineyards enjoy plenty of sun and are sheltered by the high hills of the Arrière-Beaujolais from the prevailing rain-bearing westerly winds. In the south of the area the soil has a chalky base, but in the north, where the best wines are produced, it is of schist and granite. This is the country of the *gamay noir à jus blanc*; on the Côte d'Or a poor relation, but here giving wines of quality.

The more ordinary vines of the Beaujolais are pruned either by the *guyot* method – as used on the Côte d'Or, where the shoots are trained along wires – or the *taille courte*, where the vine grows like a bush, the shoots trained out like a fan, or bent over in a goblet shape. (An advantage of this latter method is that it affords more protection against wind.) In the nine great *crus*, only the *taille courte* is permitted.

Production methods differ, too, from the Côte d'Or, particularly in that co-operative cellars play an important role. There are eighteen of them in the Beaujolais and they are responsible for the vinification of about 30 per cent of the total wine produced.

While the Beaujolais has some large *domaines*, most of the vineyard area is split up into family holdings of about ten acres. In many cases these occupy the sites of the country villas built by the Roman nobility of Lyons. If the rolling English drunkard made the rolling English road, whoever planned those of the Beaujolais can have been no stranger to the local wines.

Some owners do not cultivate their vineyards but let them out to vineyard-workers, under a system dating back to the sixteenth century called *vigneronnage*. Generally, in this relationship, the owner provides a house, vinification equipment, the new vine-plants and fertilizers; whilst the *vigneron* supplies the labour and the equipment used in the vineyard. Then the two share equally the profit on the wine.

To extend and emphasize the difference from the rest of Burgundy, Beaujolais has its own cask: the Beaujolais *pièce* holds only forty-seven gallons, whilst that of the Côte d'Or holds fifty. Also special to the area is the *pot*, or bottle of fifty centilitres, claimed by some writers to be the ideal size for two people – though, by the standards of the Beaujolais, they would be an abnormally abstemious couple.

The role of the broker here differs from that of his more northerly counterpart. Rather than be a *courtier*, putting the seller in contact with the buyer and taking a commission on the deal, he is often a *commissionaire*, buying wine on his own account and invoicing it himself to the purchaser, taking a profit on the transaction.

The wines of the Beaujolais are sold by all the great shippers of Beaune and Nuits Saint-Georges, but many shippers specialize in the local wines. Amongst those that are best known, or who have a good reputation, are Mommessin, of La Grange Saint-Pierre, just outside Mâcon; Georges Duboeuf, of Romanèche-Thorins; Piat of Mâcon (now largely owned by a British hotel and brewing group); Chevalier (who are also large producers of sparkling wine); and Thorin, of Pontaneveux, who offer an important range of single-vineyard wines from the *crus* of the Beaujolais.

As we have noted, the Beaujolais shippers stand in a situation different from those of the Côte d'Or; much of the wine they sell leaves their cellars in the year after the vintage. Also they can draw on large stocks lying in the area at the co-operative cellars. For the tourist who has visited cellars in Beaune, those of the growers and shippers of the Beaujolais and the Mâconnais must often seem a disappointment. For the majority of these wines, ageing in cask is no advantage; their charm lies in their freshness and fruit. Thus the wines are stored in row after row of glass-lined, concrete vats. On the other hand, much of the equipment is more sophisticated than that used on the Côte d'Or, with pasteurization and chilling plants, centrifuges and bottling lines, capable of turning out vast quantities of wine. To guarantee the stability of so much young wine for world distribution presents considerable difficulties and all the most modern, technological methods are employed. The export demand for these wines – and particularly for young wines as drunk in France – has been so explosive that the local shippers have had to invest considerable capital in the most sophisticated equipment.

Though the wines of the Beaujolais have found favour in France for some time, they also have their devotees abroad. The fact that Switzerland is the largest export customer for the wines of Burgundy is little related to the quality of the great wines of the Côte d'Or, but almost entirely to the attractions of Beaujolais. The Swiss like nothing better than to drive the short distance to select their wines on the spot and appreciate the good cooking of the area. Germany, too, is an important market, though one has the impression that there quality is less important than price. The Americans buy vast quantities of the wine and modern vinification techniques enable them to appreciate the fruitiness loved by the French. Sales of Beaujolais are also increasing rapidly in Britain, though there the wines are traditionally appreciated rather older: and it is by no means rare to find a bottle of ordinary Beaujolais three or four years old.

Whilst the Englishman might appreciate his Beaujolais with some age, this is considered heresy by the French drinker. For him, pleasure in a Beaujolais is to drink it cool, while it has all its fresh fruitiness and charm. This is no wine to rhapsodize over, but one that he takes to quench his thirst. It is a wine to gulp down with pleasure, not one to sip and treat as a mystique. To the Frenchman, it is the equivalent of the Englishman's beer.

The Beaujolais is traditionally divided into two areas, the Bas-Beaujolais and the Haut-Beaujolais. The former, which begins at l'Arbresle, some ten miles to the north-west of Lyons and continues as far as Villefranche sur Saône, produces the bulk of the wine consumed in vast quantities in every bar of Lyons and Paris. This is the *vin de comptoir par excellence*: most of it will never see a bottle, it is sold from the barrel by the carafe or glass. The Haut-Beaujolais is the region of the Beaujolais Villages, the finer wines on which the reputation of the Beaujolais has been so firmly founded. This is also the area of the nine *crus* which sell under their own village names, the nearest things to *vins de garde* that one can find in the Beaujolais.

Beaujolais
Colour: red, white or rosé
Average production: red 323,526 hl.   white 4,063 hl.
Minimum degree: red 9°; white 9·5°
Area: 17,000 ha. approx.

Wines from any part of the Beaujolais may be sold under this *appellation* but the bulk of it with the label is produced from the Bas-Beaujolais, the vineyards to the south of Villefranche. In order to upgrade their image, the forty-one villages of the area have joined together to promote their tourist attractions and wines under the regional name of Les Pierres Dorées – the Golden Stones. They say, 'It is useless to dismiss the name Bas-Beaujolais, even if for long the wines did not deserve much in the way of compliments! Now, by strict selection of plants, the complete elimination of hybrids and a radical transformation in methods of vinification, the Beaujolais of the Pierres Dorées has become one of the most flattering to the palate.' The capital of the area is Le Bois d'Oingt, which never belonged to the barons of Beaujeu, but traditionally came under the Seneschal of Lyons. Little remains of the thirteenth-century castle, but for those interested, the vaults and windows of its chapel can be seen in Nice. More imposing is the Château of Châtillon d'Azergues whose ruins have been well restored. Parts of it date from the twelfth century and it is built on the site of a Roman camp. For tourists the nearby Ville sur Jarnioux might be worth a detour. There one can see the spring of Saint Abraham, who finds husbands for girls who drink from it; and shrines dedicated to Saint Roch, for those suffering from the bubonic plague, and to Saint Clair for those with eye-trouble. For the less matrimonially and medically minded, the area of the Pierres Dorées has eleven co-operative cellars and ten tasting-rooms, where the wines of the local growers can be appreciated. One worth a visit is the Châlet de Saint-Jean-des-Vignes, which overlooks vineyards and the valley of the Azergues.

Azergues produces wines which mature quickly and it is the source of much of the Beaujolais Nouveau, the wine which can be sold from 15 November following the vintage. (This applies to wines with the *appellations* Beaujolais, Beaujolais Supérieur and Beaujolais Villages. Wines from the nine *crus* cannot be sold until 15 December.) Once a taste appreciated by a few specialists in Lyons and Paris, it has now become nothing less than a craze in Amsterdam, London and New York as well. It has become a challenge to have the first new Beaujolais on each market. Unfortunately, the quality of the wine has now become a secondary consideration. Until 1973, the wines could not be moved from the growers to the shippers until twenty-four hours before the opening date. Fortunately, from that vintage, the wine could be moved to the shippers a fortnight before and thus could be better prepared to face the rigours of transportation and rapid commercialization. In many years Beaujolais has a distinct charm, even at such an early date; however, in a late vintage, like 1972, it is difficult to find wine in any way ready for shipment. Unfortunately, in such a case, the date is not postponed although in much of the wine the malo-lactic fermentation is still in progress or has been artificially stopped. So the vintage is given bad publicity, because of its high acidity. Although samples have to be submitted to the authorities before shipment, some bad wines always seem to slip through the net.

Commercially, at all levels, the idea of selling Beaujolais Nouveau is most attractive – the retailer, the wholesaler, the importer and the shipper all have firm orders for the wine before they need buy. It also gives valuable publicity to the wines of the area and of the various shippers because comparative tastings are popular and discussed on the radio and in the press. The situation is tending, however, to become artificial. Fortunately the bad publicity for the new Beaujolais of 1972 was cancelled out by the wines of 1973, for many of that vintage were at their best during the first months of their life. One disadvantage for the serious wine company, and restaurateur, in France, is that for a period of a month or more customers tend to order nothing but the new Beaujolais with their meals. As a result the sales of greater Burgundies suffer; and, in consequence, some restaurants refuse to stock the Beaujolais Nouveau.

If imitation is a form of flattery, the growers of the Beaujolais must be proud, for now competition has arrived from the wines of the Côtes du Rhône and even from Bordeaux. Certainly, so far as these two *primeur* wines are concerned, vinification techniques alien to the traditional styles of the regions have been introduced. For the wines of the Beaujolais it is a different matter – they have always been drunk young.

Is Beaujolais Nouveau simply a gimmick? The answer is that an original idea has been exploited and in the process has been at least partly lost. If aircraft are to be chartered to fly cargoes of wine across the Atlantic, dates must be known well in advance. This now seems to be more important than whether the wines are drinkable or not. If the competitive angle of the Beaujolais race were stressed less, shippers would be more likely to wait until the wines were showing well before releasing them on to the market. There is nothing more enjoyable in its class than a good, young Beaujolais: and the reputation of many *zincs* in Paris stands or falls on the quality of the Beaujolais that they sell in the year after the vintage. It may be that the English drink their Beaujolais either too young or too old. Perhaps the drinking of wine at only five or six weeks is popular only because it is fashionable. Fashions change, and in time the vogue for ultra-young Beaujolais may disappear.

Rarely seen, though it does have certain enthusiasts, particularly in the United States, is white Beaujolais. The production is about a hundredth of that of the red and it comes mainly from the very north of the Haut-Beaujolais, where it overlaps and intermingles with the Mâconnais. Indeed, the output is less than it used to be, because in 1971, a new *appellation*, Saint Véran, was created for white wines of this area. Unfortunately this has not been successful so that the main result has been a noteworthy increase in the price of Beaujolais Blanc, due to its rarity. The wine is made from the *chardonnay* grape and resembles one of the better wines from the Mâconnais, or even a lesser Pouilly-Fuissé. Two examples one might come across are Château de Chatelard and Château de Loyse.

BURGUNDY

In common with most of the viticultural areas of France, the Beaujolais has its wine brotherhood. Founded in July 1949, the Compagnons du Beaujolais, junior in Burgundy only to the Confrérie des Chevaliers du Tastevin, have their headquarters in the fifteenth-century press-house of the Château de Montauzan at Lacenas.

Beaujolais Supérieur

Colour: red. (White and rosé are possible, but, in practice, never found.)
Average production: red 26,929 hl.
Minimum degree: red $10°$; (white $10·5°$)

The only difference between this *appellation* and the previous one is the alcoholic degree of the wine; it must have at least $1°$ more. However, as Alexis Bespaloff has pointed out, much of the wine that could be sold with this *appellation* is declassified and sold as Beaujolais, which is the name everybody knows and the difference in the price that could be justified is marginal, for the wine is similar. In any case it is unlikely that any shipper would send overseas a Beaujolais of less than $10°$, since there is more danger of its arriving out of condition. Alcoholic strength is not the most valid criterion for judging a wine, but it is a contributing factor to the quality.

Possible declassification: Beaujolais *or* Bourgogne Grand Ordinaire.

Beaujolais Villages

Colour: red (white and rosé are possible but rarely found)
Average production: red 211,641 hl.   white 622* hl.
Minimum degree: red $10°$; white $10·5°$

Villages having the right to the *appellation*: in Saône-et-Loire – Chanes, la Chapelle de Guinchay, Leynes, Pruzilly, Romanèche-Thorins, Saint Amour-Bellevue, Saint Syphorien d'Ancelles, Saint Vérand. In Rhône: Arbuissonnas, Beaujeu, Blacé, Cercié, Charentay, Chénas, Chiroubles, Denicé, Durette, Emeringes, Fleurie, Juliénas, Jullié, Lancié, Lantignié, Montmélas, Odénas, le Perréon, Quincié, Regnié, Rivolet, Saint Étienne d'Ouillères, Saint Étienne la Varenne, Saint Julien, Saint-Lager, Salles, Vaux, Villié-Morgon.

THE BEAUJOLAIS

This is the area of the Beaujolais aristocracy, for within its borders lie the nine great *crus* of the region and in some of the northern villages the growers can also produce the white wine Saint Véran. As opposed to the ordinary wines of the Beaujolais, those of the villages have more finesse and character and are no longer counter-, but table-wines. Two writers from the region, David and Foillard, even went so far as to classify the wines of all the Beaujolais, with basically ten different zones of villages:

> Zone Juliénas: stout, full-bodied wines, to be kept.
> Zone Moulin-à-Vent: delicate wines, with a fine bouquet, rich and aromatic.
> Zone Fleurie: strong and smooth, with much breeding.
> Zone Morgon: stout, well rounded wines, for long keeping.
> Zone Brouilly: full, fruity wines, with distinct class.
> Zone Quincié: generally lively wines with breeding.
> Zone Saint Étienne: fruity and soft, quick-developing wines.
> Zone Saint Julien: wines full of colour and body, often rather hard.
> Zone Anse – Lachassagne: full wines, lively and long-lived, generally well-coloured.
> Zone Theize – le Bois d'Oingt: generally lighter wines than those of the preceding group.

As an alternative to the *appellation* Beaujolais Villages, one sometimes sees the name of the village tacked on to the word Beaujolais. Thus one can find such wines as Beaujolais-Chanes, Beaujolais-Lancié or Beaujolais-Vaux. These are of interest as they show the style of the wine of a particular village. At the time of the vintage the grower has to decide whether to declare his crop with the particular village, or a more general *appellation*, and usually he plays safe by choosing the more widely sold name.

Not only are the wines from each village different, but the villages themselves have their distinct characteristics. The most famous place-name of the Beaujolais, Clochemerle – Vaux-en-Beaujolais is the alias under which it appears on the maps – attracts thousands of tourists every year. (Perhaps it was to preserve its anonymity that the television series of Gabriel Chevallier's novel was filmed in the neighbouring – and rival – village of Saint-Lager.) The charms of the women may have faded and the spring, made famous in Clochemerle-les-Bains, has dried to a trickle. It no longer cures everything from anaemia to venereal disease, by way of scabies and jaundice. So those seeking the vino-aqueous treatment, propounded by Doctor Suffock, will have to rely on the first half of the cure, rather than the second. Nevertheless, the author is honoured in the naming of Rue Gabriel Chevallier: the wines of the village can be appreciated at the Cave de Clochemerle, which is decorated with drawings by Pierre Dufour of scenes from the novel, and is the headquarters of an appropriately named Bacchic brotherhood, les Compagnons du Gosier Sec – the Companions of the Parched Gullet.

Beaujeu, the capital of the area, is built on the banks of the Ardières, the stream once the southern frontier of the territory of the Aedui, the Gallic tribe that was probably the first to introduce the cultivation of the vine into Burgundy, and one of the last to hold out against Julius Caesar (whose presence in the area is remembered in the names Jullié and Juliénas). The town has a Hospice, financed like that of Beaune by vineyard holdings. In all it has a *domaine* of sixty hectares, mainly in Beaujolais Villages, but the best wine produced is a Brouilly Pisse-Vieille. The *cuverie* and the lodgings of their vineyard workers is at the Grange Chartron at Regnié, which is an interesting early example of planned workers' accommodation. Largely as a result of its limited transport facilities Beaujeu has lost any commercial dominance of the area's wine trade to the larger and better situated Villefranche. Its name, that of the old greeting 'have a good time', Beaujeu is now a slightly run-down town of one long street, picturesquely set in a deep valley. It has an interesting folk museum and a tasting cellar called the Temple of Bacchus.

Rather less attractive is the reputed origin of the village of Létra. It appears that in the mists of time, an un-named giant was filling in his time clearing the bed of the Saône and creating many of the hills in the area by emptying the baskets full of soil and rocks. No doubt, he had enjoyed to the full the food and wine of the area, since he found it necessary to drop his breeches and relieve himself. The result was the foundation of the village, whose inhabitants for many centuries suffered from an unsavoury nickname.

At Montmerle, near Saint Georges de Reneins, is the Chapelle des Minimes, with a black statue of the Virgin, known as Notre-Dame du Ver Coquin, because of her successful record of intercession after

M. Deschamps – '*le crieur*' – encouraging bidders at the wine auction of the Hospices de Beaune, held in the Market Hall annually on the third Sunday of November. On his right the traditional candle, which marks the length of each bidding, burns in front of M. Masson, factor for the vineyards of the Hospices: on his right is M. Rappenau, the auctioneer.

Chablis, seen from les Clos, the largest of its seven *grand cru* vineyards, all of which lie on the slope to the north-east of the town; looking across to the *premier cru* vines of Vaillons.

Clos d'Arlot (no relation?) on the Côtes de Nuits, the narrowest point of the entire Côte d'Or vineyards. From its two different types of soil – the division marked by the old stone quarry – it produces both red and white wines from an area of no more than eight hectares.

The most valuable agricultural land in the world. The prestigious vineyards of Vosne Romanée – Romanée Conti, la Romanée and Richebourg – climb the hill behind the stone cross of Romanée Conti.

prayers against the pyralis grub. Lay treatment for this problem was discovered in 1829, by Bernard Raclet, whose house in Romanèche-Thorins is now a museum. His name is immortalized in the Fête Raclet, an exhibition of the new wines of the Beaujolais and the Mâconnais, which takes place every year at the end of October.

Anyone who wants a comparative tasting of the nine *crus* of the Beaujolais, as well as Beaujolais and Beaujolais Villages, will find it worthwhile to visit the Maison du Beaujolais at Saint Jean d'Ardières on the main N6 road. The wines can be bought in convenient, thirty-three-centilitre bottles, but if the full range is to be tasted it is better to buy three or four. To help absorb the wine, such local specialities as hot sausages and *andouillettes* are served.

Possible declassifications: Beaujolais Supérieur, Beaujolais or Bourgogne Grand Ordinaire.

Brouilly
Colour: red
Average production: 42,437 hl.
Minimum degree: 10° (with vineyard name 11°)
Area: 800 ha.

The largest in area and production of the *crus* of the Beaujolais, Brouilly is often seen on wine-lists and in many ways it is the typical wine of the Beaujolais; soft and fruity, it is best drunk quite young, up to three years old. In the words of a local writer Brouilly is 'synonymous with freshness, fruit, suppleness and charm'.

Surprisingly enough, the village of Brouilly itself does not come within the area of the *appellation*, which comprises the villages of Odénas, Saint-Lager and parts of Cercié, Charentay, Saint-Étienne-la-Varenne and Quincié. Outside the village of Odénas is the Château de la Chaize, which produces an outstanding wine, marketed in slightly dumpy bottles. The château was built at the end of the seventeenth century by the nephew of Père Lachaise, the influential confessor of Louis XIV. The cellars, which stretch for 340 feet in a single vault, reputedly the longest in Europe, can be visited on request.

The local growers' association groups together sixty-seven owners and two co-operative cellars and their tasting cellar is at Saint-Lager.

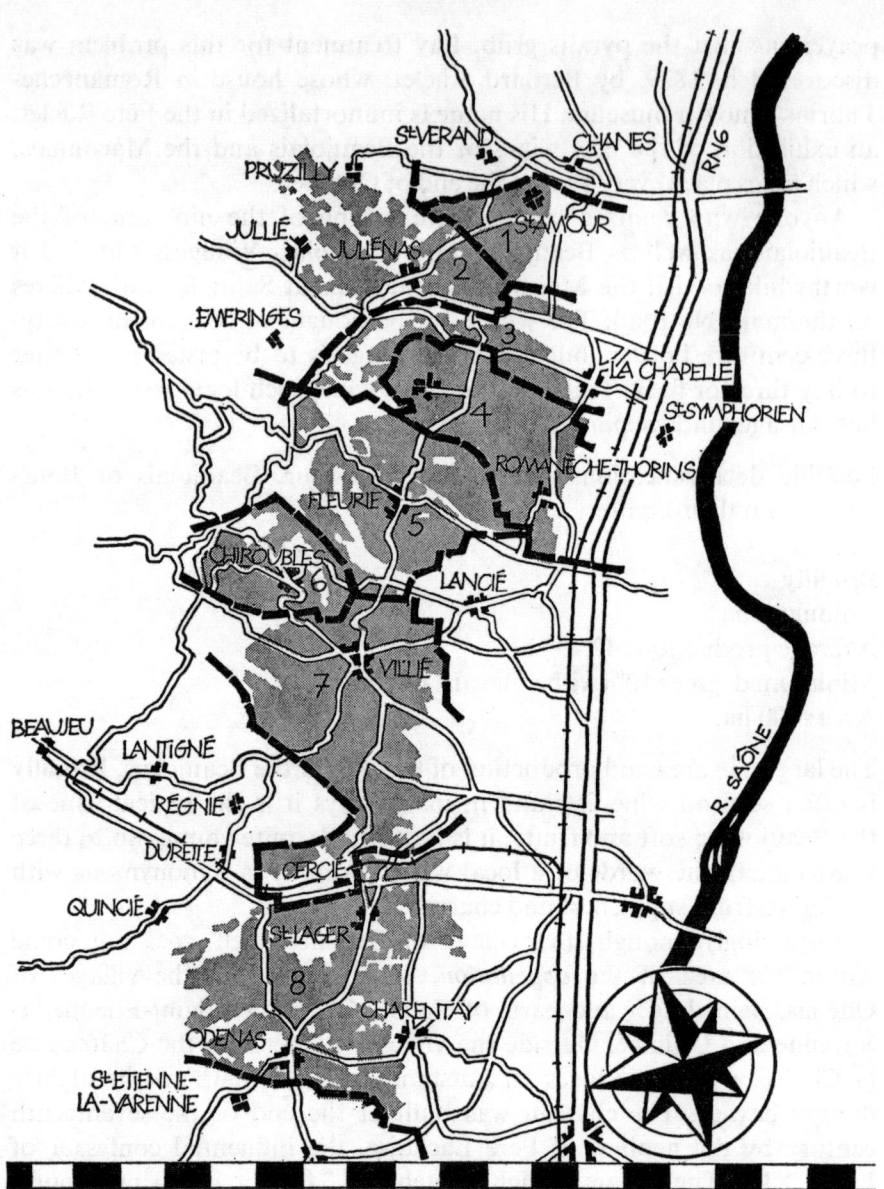

BEAUJOLAIS *GRANDS CRUS*

Possible declassifications: Bourgogne, Beaujolais Villages, Beaujolais Supérieur, Beaujolais or Bourgogne Grand Ordinaire.

Côte de Brouilly

Colour: red
Average production: 9,130 hl.
Minimum degree: 10·5° (with vineyard name 11°)
Area: 200 ha.

Almost circled by the vineyards of Brouilly, those of the Côte de Brouilly come from parts of the villages of Odénas, Saint-Lager, Cercié and Quincié. The vines climb on all sides, almost to the top of Mont Brouilly, 1,000 feet above the plain. On the summit is the rather plain Chapel of Notre-Dame-du-Raisin, built in 1857 and the scene of an annual pilgrimage on 8 September. On this occasion, the *vignerons* offer thanks for protection during the past year, by pouring many libations of fine wine, mainly down their own throats – for it is a stiff climb to the top. Halfway up the hill is a spring which has been a place of pilgrimage since pagan times and has a reputation for curing eye troubles.

The minimum degree for wines from the Côte de Brouilly is higher than that for any other of the wines of the Beaujolais. Their style is similar to those of Brouilly, but rather more pronounced. Generally they will keep for a year or two longer than their neighbours.

The wine with the best reputation in the *cru* is Château Thivin, which, until his death, belonged to Claude Geoffray, for long one of the leading promoters of the wines of the Beaujolais. His widow continues the tradition of fine wines.

Shaded areas indicate *grand cru* vineyards

1	Saint Amour	Brouilly *and Côte de Brouilly*	8
2	Juliénas	Chénas	3
3	Chénas	Chiroubles	6
4	Moulin-à-Vent	Fleurie	5
5	Fleurie	Juliénas	2
6	Chiroubles	Morgon	7
7	Morgon	Moulin-à-Vent	4
8	Brouilly *and Côte de Brouilly*	Saint Amour	1

Possible declassifications: Bourgogne, Beaujolais Villages, Beaujolais Supérieur, Beaujolais or Bourgogne Grand Ordinaire.

Morgon
Colour: red
Average production: 34,628 hl.
Minimum degree: 10° (with vineyard name 11°)
Area: 550 ha.

The village of Morgon itself is almost lost in the middle of the vineyards that bear its name; more important is Villié-Morgon, which seems to have usurped the leadership of the area. The soil of the *cru* is granite and black schist which go under the name of *roche pourrie*, or 'rotten rock'. This gives to the wine body and a flavour of wild cherry found nowhere else in the Beaujolais. The fullest wines come from the south of the *cru*, on the slopes of the Mont de Py. Just outside the limits of the appellation is the Château de Pizay, belonging to Pierre Gaidon. It has a magnificent square keep, dating from the fourteenth century and a formal garden designed by Le Nôtre, who was also responsible for laying out those at Versailles for Louis XIV. A muster of peacocks add even more colour. The vast *cuverie* is used often now for receptions and banquets. The vineyards of the *domaine*, recently purchased by the Canadian liquor firm of Seagram, lie partly in Morgon and partly in Beaujolais Villages. A little white Beaujolais is also produced. Château de Bellevue is another reputed growth.

The wines of Morgon are amongst the longest lived of the Beaujolais and are probably at their best between five and eight years old, but those of good years can last longer. Villié-Morgon has a tasting cellar and a fine restaurant in the Relais des Caveaux.

Possible declassifications: Bourgogne, Beaujolais Villages, Beaujolais Supérieur, Beaujolais or Bourgogne Grand Ordinaire.

Chiroubles
Colour: red
Average production: 11,208 hl.

Minimum degree: 10° (with vineyard name 11°)
Area: 250 ha.

The vineyards of Chiroubles, the highest-lying of the *crus*, are shaped like an arrowhead, sticking into those of Morgon. Apart from its wines, the village also has a gastronomic reputation for its turnips – an unlikely sounding combination. The local growers were the first to group together to fight the phylloxera plague in 1879. Here, too, at that time, the first grafted vines – the eventual solution – were planted by the viticulturalist Pulliat.

The fine exposure of the vineyards to the sun is emphasized by the names of such leading growths as Côte Rotie (not to be confused with the Rhône wine of the same name) and Grille-Midi. The style of the wine is somewhere between that of Morgon and Fleurie, matching body to fruit. Some experts claim that it is the Beaujolais most preferred by women, though whether it has aphrodisiac properties or not seems uncertain. Limited experiments in this direction so far carried out have given no conclusive results. The village boasts a tasting-room and a co-operative cellar.

Possible declassifications: Bourgogne, Beaujolais Villages, Beaujolais Supérieur, Beaujolais or Bourgogne Grand Ordinaire.

Fleurie
Colour: red
Average production: 27,351 hl.
Minimum degree: 10° (with vineyard name 11°)
Area: 700 ha.

Perhaps because of the evocative name, the wines of Fleurie have long been popular in Britain and the United States; and the vineyard area is important. The wines have more finesse than any other of the Beaujolais, and more fruit. They are probably best drunk about four years old. Among the single vineyards that one sees are La Chapelle des Bois and Aux Quatre Vents. The latter lies behind and above the village.

To satisfy thirsts and interests, there are two tasting cellars in the village: one at the Coopérative cellar, which is under the presidency of Marguèrite Chabert, the daughter of the founder, who combined together the gastronomic callings of *vigneron* and master-charcutier; the other is in the church square.

Possible declassifications: Bourgogne, Beaujolais Villages, Beaujolais Supérieur, Beaujolais or Bourgogne Grand Ordinaire.

Moulin-à-Vent
Colour: red
Average production: 26,230 hl.
Minimum degree: 10° (with vineyard name 11°)
Area: 700 ha.

The vineyards of Moulin-à-Vent are shared by two *départements*, Rhône, and Saône-et-Loire; and by two villages, Chénas and Romanêche-Thorins. The latter stands back from the N6 and its name shows its Roman origins. Besides wines, it has a zoo – a useful place to leave the children, when getting down to the serious matter of tasting – and a good restaurant, Les Maritonnes, where one can also stay, though its proximity to the railway-line causes problems for all but the heaviest sleepers.

Until quite recently, Romanêche-Thorins was considered a *cru* in its own right, sometimes claimed by the Mâconnais, sometimes by the Beaujolais, but the *appellation* Moulin-à-Vent was confirmed by a decree of 1936. The name for the *cru* comes from the last remaining windmill of the Beaujolais, which stands, sail-less but officially preserved, on a knoll above the hamlet of Thorins.

The wines of Moulin-à-Vent, the biggest and longest-lived of the Beaujolais, are often compared to those of the Côte d'Or. Indeed Raymond Postgate says, 'Beaujolais is best drunk young; it is a lively wine, and, except perhaps for a Moulin à Vent, does not develop the elderly and enormous grandeur of a Richebourg.' If this suggests that a Moulin-à-Vent can rival a Richebourg, he exaggerates somewhat, but it is certain that here the *gamay* produces its best wines. From the greatest vintages they can last for twenty years; some of 1929 vintage, tasted more than forty years later, still retained their class. As befits such an aristocrat the price of Moulin-à-Vent is clearly above those of other Beaujolais and reaches the levels of some lesser village wines of the Côte d'Or. (If Mr. Postgate is right in his appreciation, though, it must represent the best bargain in the world of wine!) There are several single vineyards of note and amongst those likely to be found are Le Moulin-à-Vent, Château des Jacques, Les Carquelins, Les Thorins, Château Portier and La Tour du Bief.

The local growers, realizing that many travellers have no time to drive off the N6 into the vineyards, have built a tasting house on the main road, where light meals are served. There is also a tasting cellar on the lane leading up to the windmill.

Possible declassifications: Bourgogne, Beaujolais Villages, Beaujolais Supérieur, Beaujolais or Bourgogne Grand Ordinaire.

Chénas
Colour: red
Average production: 8,291 hl.
Minimum degree: 10° (with vineyard name 11°)
Area: 185 ha.

Divided between the villages of Chénas and La Chapelle de Guinchay, the vineyards of this *cru* lie on both sides of the valley of the Mauvaise. Their name comes from the vast forest of oaks (*chênes*) that used to cover all the Beaujolais but no trace of it remains in the village. Legend has it that the first vines in the region were planted here.

The wines are similar to those of Moulin-à-Vent, but due to less favourable sun-exposure of the vineyards, they lack such full depth. Château Bonnet is perhaps the best-known vineyard of the village. There is a tasting cellar at Deschamps on the border of the vineyards of Chénas and Moulin-à-Vent.

Possible declassifications: Bourgogne, Beaujolais Villages, Beaujolais Supérieur, Beaujolais or Bourgogne Grand Ordinaire.

Juliénas
Colour: red
Average production: 20,344 hl.
Minimum degree: 10° (with vineyard name 11°)
Area: 530 ha.

The most northerly *cru* of the Rhône *département*, the *appellation* also includes some vineyards from the villages of Jullié and Pruzilly. It is doubtful whether there were vines here in the days of Julius Caesar, who gave his name to the village, but some Roman remains have been unearthed locally. The village sits on a spur overlooking the vineyards and the co-operative cellar at the Château du Bois de la Salle, where there is a tasting room. There is another in the centre of the village in a dis-established church, which in 1954 was converted into a temple to Bacchus by Victor Peyret, the owner, at that time, of the Château des Capitans. Each year a prize is awarded by the 'Association de Producteurs du Cru Juliénas' to someone particularly capable of appreciating the merits of their wines. The winner is presented, appropriately, with his own weight in the wine of the village.

The wine of Juliénas matures more quickly than that of Chénas, but it has a certain depth and life, which makes it most enjoyable at two to three years old. Perhaps the best growth is Les Capitans, but others of note are the Château de Juliénas (which belongs to the chairman of the growers' association, François Condemine), Les Mouilles, En Bessay and Les Chères. The Domaine de Beauvernais is also widely seen.

Possible declassifications: Bourgogne, Beaujolais Villages, Beaujolais Supérieur, Beaujolais or Bourgogne Grand Ordinaire.

Saint Amour
Colour: red
Average production: 8,964 hl.
Minimum degree: 10° (with vineyard name 11°)
Area: 215 ha.

The only *cru* of the Beaujolais to lie completely within the Saône-et-Loire *département*, the vineyards of Saint Amour for long belonged to the Chapter of Saint Vincent of Mâcon; and it has been uncharitably suggested that the village gets its name from the extra-mural activities of the clergy there. Like those of Moulin-à-Vent, the wines were considered, until recently, to come from the Mâconnais. The formula for producing the wine, according to a publicity leaflet is: 'In a large vat, let ferment the *gamay* from my soil. Add the laughter of a young girl, the scent of a spring garden and a good measure of the atmosphere of Montmartre. Leave them to steep for three or four days and serve cool.'

The result, according to another leaflet is 'a *rouge* with gentlemanly airs'. Neither description is likely to have the full blessing of the *appellation* authorities. In more down-to-earth terms, the wines have a lot of finesse and fruit and are best drunk young, up to two years old.

The village tasting cellar has an interesting selection of *vignerons'* implements and the white wine made locally from the *chardonnay* grape can also be sampled there. The Château de Saint Amour produces a fine wine and Les Thévenins is a reputable growth.

Possible declassifications: Bourgogne, Beaujolais Villages, Beaujolais Supérieur, Beaujolais or Bourgogne Grand Ordinaire.

To appreciate the fine wines of the area fully, you must taste them with the fine cooking of the region. This reaches its peak, either in Lyons, or in the *département* of Ain, just across the Saône from the Beaujolais, which must have more fine restaurants than any other comparably-sized district of France. Some restaurants strongly recommended are the Chapon Fin, of Paul Blanc at Thoissey, and Chez la Mère Blanc at Vonnas, where his nephew is the chef; the recent arrival amongst the highest qualified Michelin restaurants, Chez la Mère Charles of M. Chapel at Mionnay and, rather further away, though well worth the effort is the unassuming Hotel Bourgeois at Priay, where M. Berger is the proprietor-chef. In Villefranche many members of the wine trade lunch and dine at Jacques Vautrey's restaurant in the Boulevard Antonin Lassalle; it is not easy to find – in a quiet street behind the railway station – but beyond the rather small and crowded front bar there is a generous restaurant of pronounced Beaujolais character and flavour. All these restaurants have a wide range of Beaujolais wines. Particularly in the case of the Hotel Bourgeois at Priay it is advisable to reserve a table in advance.

7 THE MÂCONNAIS

The traveller leaving the Beaujolais, with its atmosphere reminiscent of more southern France, and entering the Mâconnais, finds it a transitional area. In the south the vineyards resemble those of the Beaujolais and, indeed, some of them have a choice between the *appellations*, while such former outposts of the Mâconnais as Saint Amour, Chânes and Leynes are now considered rather as part of the Beaujolais. Here the granite soil so suited to the red wines of the *gamay* gives way to the chalky clay ideal for the *chardonnay*. For this is the country of white wines: in the abundant vintage of 1973, for example, the Mâconnais produced more white wine than Chablis, the Côte d'Or, the Côte Chalonnaise combined – and Bourgogne Aligoté and Bourgogne Blanc can be added for good measure. This is a comparatively recent situation, for the area used to be well known for its red wines from the *gamay*, which now seem to be little appreciated outside Scandinavia and French bars. Attempts being made to popularize rosé wines from the area, however, are meeting with some success. Plantings are being made, too, in *pinot noir* to produce Bourgogne Rouge; but these wines lack the finesse of their cousins from the Côte d'Or. Sales of the red wines are generally falling with the growing popularity of the white.

To the north of the N80, the main road from Mâcon to Cluny, is an area of polyculture, with woods and meadows, pasturing cows and goats, and producing the well-known cheese, *chevrotton de Mâcon*, which is at its best during the summer months. The hills run from north to south and the vines are planted on the favourable slopes: though it is sometimes difficult to believe that this is a major area of production: at some points it is possible to drive for miles without seeing a single vine.

As the production of the wines of the Mâconnais is dominated by the cooperative cellars, there seems to be a much less vinous atmosphere in the villages than in the Beaujolais or the Côte d'Or. Perhaps this is also because, with the increasing production of white wines, much less is actually drunk on the spot. Thus the face of any local villager in Juliénas or Pommard will reflect his product to a greater degree than that of someone from Viré. To the Frenchman, white wine is rarely to be drunk without food, but a *petit rouge* in his neighbouring bar is something he takes for granted.

The vineyards lie roughly in the triangle formed by the towns of Tournus, Cluny and Mâcon, though two enclaves of vines away to the west have the right to the *appellation*; one lies round the village of Mancey, where there is a co-operative cellar; and the other on the right bank of the River Grosne about the village of Chapaize. There were vineyards here in Roman times, according to the poet Ausonius, who himself owned vineyards in Bordeaux and on the Moselle. The region, however, owes its reputation to the monks of Cluny, who were the first to plant extensively. Founded in 910 AD by William, Duke of Aquitaine and Count of Auvergne, the Abbey of Cluny soon became one of the most important in Christendom. The third building, begun by Saint Hugh in 1088, had as a basis for its design the church of Saint Philibert in Tournus, and when it was finally consecrated in 1131 it was matched in size only by Saint Peter's at Rome. By this time it had become the centre of the Benedictine order with as many as 10,000 monks and over 2,000 dependent houses in France, Germany, Poland, Italy, Spain and England. From the sixteenth century its importance began to decline and, though Richelieu and Mazarin each in turn became Abbot of Cluny, neither took up residence there. After the Revolution, some of the Abbey was blown up to make way for a new road and only instructions from Paris prevented it being totally destroyed. Cluny is now a quiet town with few indications of its former eminence, though the government has established there the school of *arts et métiers* and the national stud. Students of ecclesiastical architecture will find three smaller romanesque churches worth visiting, between Tournus and Cluny, at Chapaize, Uchizy and Farges; all were built in the eleventh century.

Perhaps the most famous 'worthy' of the area is Alphonse de Lamartine, the earliest of France's great romantic poets: and for his admirers the Mâconnais is of an importance similar to that of the Lake District for Wordsworth's. There is a pilgrimage route to his birthplace in Mâcon (where there is now a museum); to Milly, some eight miles to the west, where he spent his childhood and which has honoured his memory by adding his name to its own (on the Côte d'Or, they have different priorities and prefer to add the name of their most famous vineyard); to the Château of Saint-Point in the valley of the Valouze, where he lived with his English wife and where he finally died. De Lamartine's poems reflect his love for the area and provide a useful source of quotation for publicists of the local wines. (Even the growers of Santenay have rather cheekily borrowed from him in their publicity leaflet.)

The chief town of the region, Mâcon, derived its original importance from its position on the Saône, which gave it a route to the Mediterranean, the centre of the world. Nowadays it is a thriving cultural and commercial centre where, at the end of May each year, the French National Wine Fair is held. During the Fair a well known competition is staged, open to wines not only from France but from the entire world. To win a medal there is considered a great honour and recent entries have come from as far as California. The task of classifying the thousands of wines is so vast that more than a hundred judges work throughout the day in relays. For the layman, with less stamina, there are many opportunities for tasting, at a nominal charge, wines from all over France. Mâcon's twin town, Neustadt an der Weinstrasse, from the Palatinate in Germany, even has a stand to present her wines – a foreign incursion indeed to the conservative Burgundian.

Just to the west of Mâcon is the village of Charnay-les-Mâcon, which claims to be the original centre of external trade in the local wines. It is the birthplace of Claude Brosse, a local vineyard owner, who in 1660 had some difficulty in selling his wine on the local market. Undeterred, he hitched up his oxen, loaded his wagon with casks of wine and set off for Versailles. The journey took him over a month and on his arrival he met with no success in selling his wines, until one day, when he was in church, his enormous size caught the attention of Louis XIV. Summoned afterwards to the royal presence he launched into his sales-patter and made a royal convert. The king considered the wine better than the red wines of the Loire, in fashion at court at the time, and placed a shipping order with Brosse. The royal warrant carried more weight in those days than it does now, and the courtiers sought to flatter their monarch by ordering the same wine. The future of the red wines of Mâcon was assured – or at least until some years later, when the royal physician, Guy-Crescent Fagon, declared that Romanée Saint-Vivant was a useful aid in treating the king's fistula. What purpose the wine served in such a case is difficult to perceive, unless it was used as an anaesthetic during the three operations the king underwent in November and December 1686. It may be that Fagon, being a native of Nuits Saint-Georges, simply wanted to increase the reputation – and the sales – of his local wine. The memory of Claude Brosse is honoured by a carved panel in the tasting cellar at Moulin-à-Vent.

Naturally such an important wine region as the Mâconnais must have its bacchanalian order and indeed it has the Confrérie de Vignerons de Saint Vincent, an order that was resurrected in 1951. It is distinctly to Saint Vincent's advantage – the patron saint of vineyard workers, and the trade-mark of a well-known shipper in the United States – to preside over the revels, where the music is always provided by a local group of traditional musicians, Matiscona.

Mâcon
Colour: red, white or rosé. (Alternative *appellation* for white wines: Pinot Chardonnay Mâcon.)
Average production: red 14,745 hl.   white 12,749 hl.
Minimum degree: red 9°; white 10°

In all Burgundy, there is no area where the *Appellation Contrôlée* regulations present so many difficulties as in the Mâconnais, for the areas of production for red and white wines are different and the hierarchy of declassification again varies importantly between the wines. It has already been noted that here the red wines of the *gamay* generally lack distinction; certainly they lack the roundness of *gamay* from the

Beaujolais. The rosé wine now being produced is rather more successful; it has an agreeable freshness.

The white wines, on the other hand, have proved to be more profitable, particularly in the United States where the true Burgundy characteristic of the *chardonnay* grape and their reasonable price have proved important attractions. French – and other – shippers have attempted to compete with the increasingly successful Californian wines sold under a variety of names. They have offered wines of their own which are known by the name of the grape variety used. Thus one finds Cabernets, Sauvignons, Pinot Noirs, Rieslings and Pinot Chardonnays. The growers of the Mâconnais, though, have objected to this last *appellation* being used on any French wines except from their region. They base their objection on the fact that the alternative *appellation* Pinot-Chardonnay-Mâcon, granted to them by decree over thirty years ago, gives them sole rights to the usage of Pinot Chardonnay, even though it is generally accepted that it does not exist as a single grape variety. It is either the *pinot blanc* or the *chardonnay* and, whilst either variety may be used for the production of Mâcon blanc, in practice it is nearly always the *chardonnay*. The success of the Mâconnaises in propagating this doctrine has given them a useful advantage in the export markets.

Once again the co-operative cellar plays an important role; it is responsible for a third or more of the production. Another sign of the transitional nature of the area is that either the Beaujolais or the Côte d'Or hogshead is used, though occasionally one can come across a larger sized cask, the *demi-muid* of 132 gallons.

Mâcon Supérieur
Colour: red or white
Average production: see below: Mâcon (plus village name) Villages for red; Mâcon Villages or Mâcon plus village name for white.
Minimum degree: red 10°; white 11°

As with the distinction between Beaujolais Supérieur and Beaujolais, so it is with Mâcon Supérieur and Mâcon; the question is one of degree. The wine must have one extra. For the white wines a possible declassification is Bourgogne: the majority of white wine sold under this name probably comes from the Mâconnais. It is also interesting to see that the production of both red and white is about twice as much in the superior *appellation* as in the lower one. In the 1973 vintage, the proportion was as much as 12:1 in the white wines and 15:1 for the red.

Possible declassifications: red: Mâcon; white: Bourgogne, Mâcon or Bourgogne Grand Ordinaire.

Mâcon plus village name Villages (e.g. Mâcon-Lugny Villages)
Colour: red
Average production: 8,107 hl.
Minimum degree: 10°

Produced from certain of the better villages of the Mâconnais, only limited quantities of this wine are seen with this *appellation*. Certainly they are worth seeking out. They benefit from ageing and are claimed to be more 'serious' than those of the Beaujolais.

Possible declassification: Mâcon Supérieur and Mâcon.

Mâcon Villages or Mâcon plus village name
Colour: white.
Average production: 60,965 hl.
Minimum degree: 11°

Forty-three villages, mainly in the southern half of the Mâconnais, have the right to produce wines with this *appellation*. Amongst the better known are: Chardonnay (which gave its name to the grape variety), Lugny, Viré, Azé, Clessé, Igé, Verzé and la Roche Vineuse. Many of these have co-operative cellars which understandably concentrate on promoting their particular village product. Piat and Co., of Mâcon, specialize in a Mâcon Viré, and Louis Latour sell a Mâcon Lugny. One vineyard at Lugny that enjoys an outstanding reputation is the Clos du Chapitre, which belongs to the Villefranche shipper Dépagneux.

When the prices of Pouilly-Fuissé increased dramatically, these quality wines of the Mâconnais provided satisfactory alternatives and their reputation gained considerably. They are probably at their best two or three years old and provide the ideal accompaniment for shellfish or chicken in cream sauce, a speciality of the neighbouring Bresse.

There are many opportunities for tasting these wines on the spot.

Amongst other tasting-cellars are the Caveau Saint-Pierre in Lugny, the Virolis at Viré, the Réfuge at Burgy – which has a magnificent view over the vineyards and the plain of the Sâone – and the Caveau de la Roche Vineuse.

Possible declassification: Mâcon Supérieur, Bourgogne, Mâcon or Bourgogne Grand Ordinaire.

Saint-Véran
Colour: white
Average production: 13,091 hl.*
Minimum degree: 11° (with vineyard name 12°)
Area: still under negotiation

One of the most recent *appellations* of Burgundy, St-Véran only came into existence at the beginning of 1971. The wine is produced in the villages of Chanes, Chasselas (yet another grape variety), Davayé, Leynes, Prissé, Saint Amour, Saint Vérand and part of Solutré, which all lie at the extreme south of the Saône-et-Loire *département*, apart from Davayé and Prissé, which are separated from the others by the vineyards of Pouilly-Fuissé.

The *appellation* was created to offer fine wines from around the area of Pouilly-Fuissé and of a similar style. Before obtaining rights to the *appellation*, however, samples must be submitted for tasting. As the villages of Chanes, Leynes, Pruzilly, Saint-Vérand and Saint Amour are also in the Beaujolais area, the *vignerons* have a wide choice of names for their wines. At one time Saint-Véran was at a distinct premium in relation to Beaujolais Blanc so far as prices were concerned. Now, though, the gap is much narrower and as demand has increased for Beaujolais blanc at the same time as production decreased, a good Beaujolais commands as good a price as a Saint-Véran. On the face of it, the new *appellation* appears to be a failure and one must wonder whether it would be better to withdraw the possibility of alternative *appellations*.

Single vineyards that can occasionally be found are: les Chataigniers, Château Gaillard and les Plessis. At Davayé there is a well known Lycée Viticole, which is well-placed for giving its students practical experience.

THE MÂCONNAIS

Possible declassification: Mâcon Villages, Mâcon Supérieur, Bourgogne, Mâcon or Bourgogne Grand Ordinaire.

Pouilly-Fuissé
Colour: white
Average production: 25,857 hl. (with vineyard name 2,155* hl.)
Minimum degree: 11° (with vineyard name 12°)

Over the brow of the hill on the road from Leynes, an amphitheatre of vines suddenly comes into view, with the village of Fuissé at the bottom. There are no longer rolling hills to the south as in the Beaujolais nor the long ridges of the Mâconnais to the north; in Pouilly-Fuissé, crags surge out from the ground, with the rocks of Solutré and Vergisson like twin Gibraltars. The vineyards are natural suntraps in which the combination of the *chardonnay* grape and the chalky soil, produces some of the fullest wines of Burgundy. They come from the villages of Chaintré, Fuissé, Pouilly, Solutré and Vergisson which lie in a narrow strip pointing from the south-east to the north-west. Each village makes wines with a distinct characteristic; the finest are reputed to come from Pouilly itself – but those of Solutré have more body. The methods of cultivation are strictly controlled; the only permitted method of pruning being the *taille à queue du Mâconnais,* in which the producing stem is bent over and tied to the lower wire. With regard to the grape varieties, the *chardonnay* only is permitted – to the exclusion of the *pinot blanc*.

No wine can have suffered so much as Pouilly-Fuissé from the vagaries of whim and speculation. Although it is not particularly easy to pronounce, the name seems to have a singular fascination for Anglo-Saxons; and Americans and English alike seem happy to order it whenever it appears on a wine-list. Surprisingly enough, its success is comparatively recent and is largely due to a succession of small vintages in Chablis which drove customers to seek alternative white Burgundies. Pouilly-Fuissé benefited and demand for it became so great that prices rose sharply. The American market, in particular, absorbed such large quantities that there must be some serious doubt as to the authenticity of it all. The production is only limited and the prices have risen from the level of a superior Mâcon, above those of Chablis and to the level of such wines of the Côte d'Or as Meursault. Fortunately, the figure is now tending to fall and will soon perhaps find its correct level.

BURGUNDY

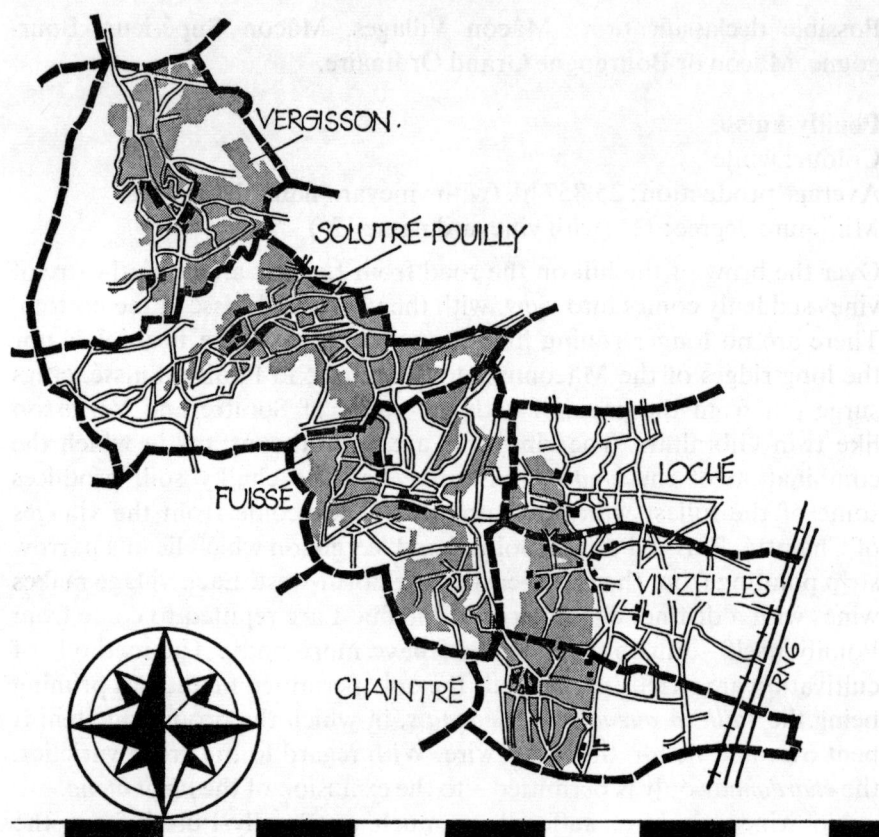

POUILLY

Shaded areas indicate *premier cru* vineyards

Appellation Pouilly-Fuissé
Vergisson
Solutré-Pouilly
Fuissé
Chaintré

How great are the wines of Pouilly-Fuissé? Only twenty years ago H. Warner Allen could write 'By no means a great wine, Pouilly-Fuissé makes an agreeable beverage, though it is too self-assertive to make such a good introductory wine as Chablis'. Morton Shand places it on the same level as such wines of the Côte Chalonnaise as Rully and Montagny. Louis Orizet says that its very name is 'enough to make an oyster yawn' – one imagines in anticipation of being eaten, rather than out of boredom.

A Pouilly-Fuissé is quite distinct from the other white wines of Burgundy; it lacks the crisp acidity of a Chablis, the nuttiness of a Meursault or the finesse of a Puligny-Montrachet, yet its dry richness has an attraction uniquely its own. Its very popularity argues that its characteristics have their own appeal. One possible disadvantage is that the vineyards are so blessed climatically that the wines can become too heavy in alcohol, with fourteen degrees or more, which is a rather tiring drink.

Several single vineyards and *domaines* have built up reputations for themselves; amongst those seen on the market are:

Vergisson: les Crays, la Maréchaude, les Charmes.
Solutré: les Crayes, les Quarts, la Mure.
Pouilly: les Bouthières, au Clos, aux Peloux, Château de Pouilly.
Fuissé: Château de Fuissé, le Clos, les Menetrières, les Perrières, en Chantenay.
Chaintre: les Quarts, les Chevrières.

The village streets are narrow and the houses colourful with flowers; at the entrance to Fuissé there is a big sign saying that 'A hundred growers bid you welcome' and by the side of the road is the diminutive château. The village of Solutré is worth a visit – gastronomically for the Relais de Solutré, one of the best restaurants in the area, and archaeologically for the small museum, which demonstrates the village's importance in pre-history. It has given its name to a world-recognized culture of the Upper Palaeolithic age, some 75,000 years ago. Indeed the oldest-known arrowheads were discovered there in the remains of a camp-site of primitive man, a man who drove thousands of wild horses to their death over the edge of the cliff. In more recent times the top of this hill became in turn the site of a druidical sacrificial ground, a Roman camp, and a castle built in the tenth century, and destroyed in the fifteenth on the orders of Philip the Good. As a further attraction the village has the tasting cellar of Pouilly-Fuissé.

Possible declassification: Mâcon Villages, Mâcon Supérieur, Bourgogne, Mâcon or Bourgogne Grand Ordinaire.

Towards Mâcon, almost on the plain, lie the villages of Loché and Vinzelles, which have right to their own *appellations*. Their production is limited and they are similar in style to the wines of Pouilly-Fuissé, though they are, in general, considerably cheaper. Between them they share a co-operative and a tasting cellar. The production of Loché is less than half that of its neighbour and it can be declassified into Pouilly-Vinzelles, though not the other way round. Single vineyards with some reputation are: aux Barres and les Mures at Loché, and les Quarts and les Verchères at Vinzelles.

Pouilly-Loché and Pouilly-Vinzelles
Colour: white
Average production: Pouilly-Loché 705 hl.; Pouilly-Vinzelles 1600 hl.
Minimum degree: 11°

Possible declassification: Pouilly-Loché: Pouilly-Vinzelles. Mâcon-Villages, Mâcon Supérieur, Bourgogne, Mâcon or Bourgogne Grand Ordinaire.

Pouilly-Vinzelles: Mâcon Villages, Mâcon Supérieur, Bourgogne, Mâcon or Bourgogne Grand Ordinaire.

8 CÔTE CHALONNAISE: RÉGION DE MERCUREY

Côte de Nuits, Côte de Beaune, Côte Chalonnaise and Côte Mâconnaise; the names roll from the tongue like the procession of royalty at a coronation. Over the past few years though, the Côte Chalonnaise has come under a different title – Région de Mercurey. This better reflects the least known of the wine-producing areas of Burgundy, for Chalon-sur-Saône has tightly linked its future to industry. Apart from a bottle factory, its connections with the wine trade are now limited, though 600 years ago wines bearing its name were much appreciated in Paris. On the other hand, over the past centuries Mercurey has had a regular body of support for its wines and neighbouring villages have even sought through the courts the right to sell their wines under its name.

The vineyards stretch in a narrow band for twenty-four kilometres from Chagny, in the north, to the village of Jully-les-Buxy in the south, with the N481 – the main road from Chagny to Cluny – as their eastern boundary. Whilst the Côte is by no means as well-defined as the Côte de Beaune to the north, it is its logical continuation. The vineyards stand well back from the road, mainly on the eastern slopes facing the plain. There is not a continuous belt of vines, but rather an archipelago of plantings, with the village of Mercurey at the centre of the largest island. It has not always been so, for, as at Chablis, the vineyard area was once very much larger. In both cases the primary cause of the decline was phylloxera, but a more particular factor in the Mercurey region was the Great War. So many of the young men were lost: for example, ninety from the village of Rully alone – about 8 per

BURGUNDY

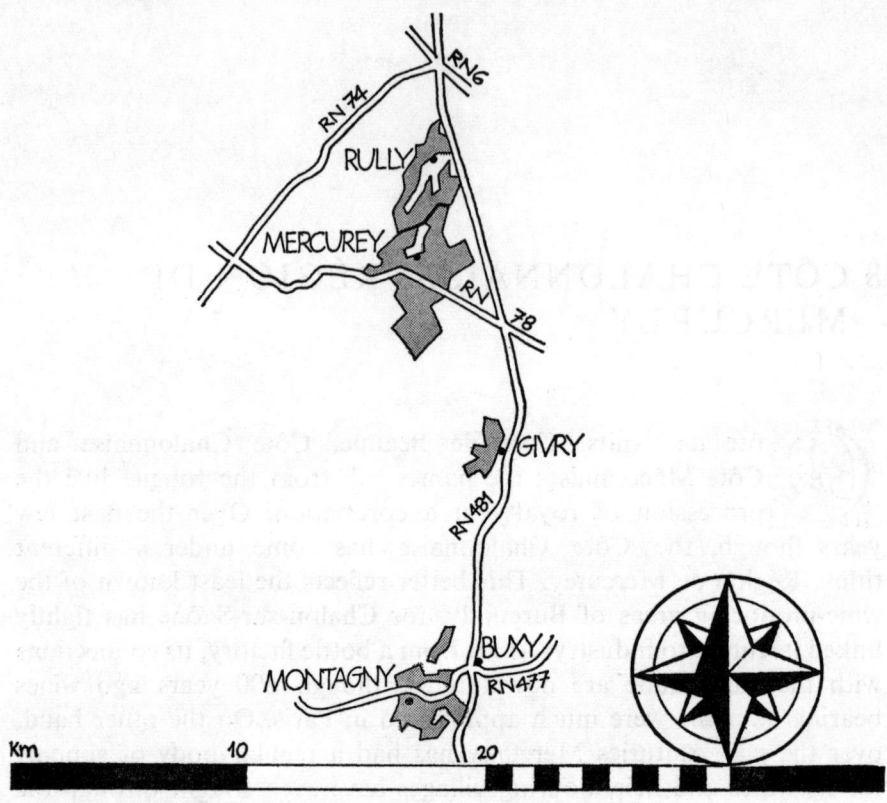

THE CÔTE CHALONNAISE

CÔTE CHALONNAISE: RÉGION DE MERCUREY

cent of its total population – died in action. With so few people to look after them, many of the vineyards went untended and reverted to scrubland. Indeed it was not until after the Second World War, and more particularly during the 'wine explosion' in the early nineteen-seventies, that replanting really began once more. As in Chablis again, the area that can be planted with full *appellation* is considerable and this has attracted capital from Paris and further afield. All through the region the hillsides are scarred where the slopes have been cleared in preparation for replanting. This access of outside finance has caused a certain amount of resentment in the area, though it is difficult to see how the recent growth in the popularity of these wines could have occurred without such an injection. Nevertheless in the Saône-et-Loire *département* the restrictions on the transfer of vineyard land are more severe than elsewhere in Burgundy and SAFER, a semi-governmental body, frequently steps in to oppose purchases of land by outsiders – or even by people of the area whom it considers to have enough vineyard holdings already – by bidding on behalf of smaller proprietors. Every transfer of vineyard land has to be referred to SAFER and it has the power to block any deal. The local Communist party, too, has stated its political view of the situation by protesting that foreign capitalists are exploiting the birthright of the local peasants by taking profits that are rightfully theirs.

P. Morton Shand says that 'Mercurey is the only real "name" of the Côte Chalonnaise – anyhow the only one that is encountered in England', but that is now by no means true. Though Mercurey is still the *appellation* of the area with the largest production, and the most firmly established reputation, the other three, Montagny, Rully and Givry are more and more frequently found. The growers are not slow to take advantage of the escalation in Côte d'Or prices, and they are in a position to offer good wine at a reasonable figure.

The sales of the wines of the Région de Mercurey have been promoted particularly by such local *négoçiants* as Antonin Rodet, Chandesais and André Delorme; certain Côte d'Or shippers with holdings in the area like J. Faiveley and Bouchard Aîné et Fils, and others who have built up a reputation for their selected wines of the area such as Louis Latour and Remoissenet Père et Fils. The French retail chain of Nicolas, too, has done much to popularize these wines.

BURGUNDY

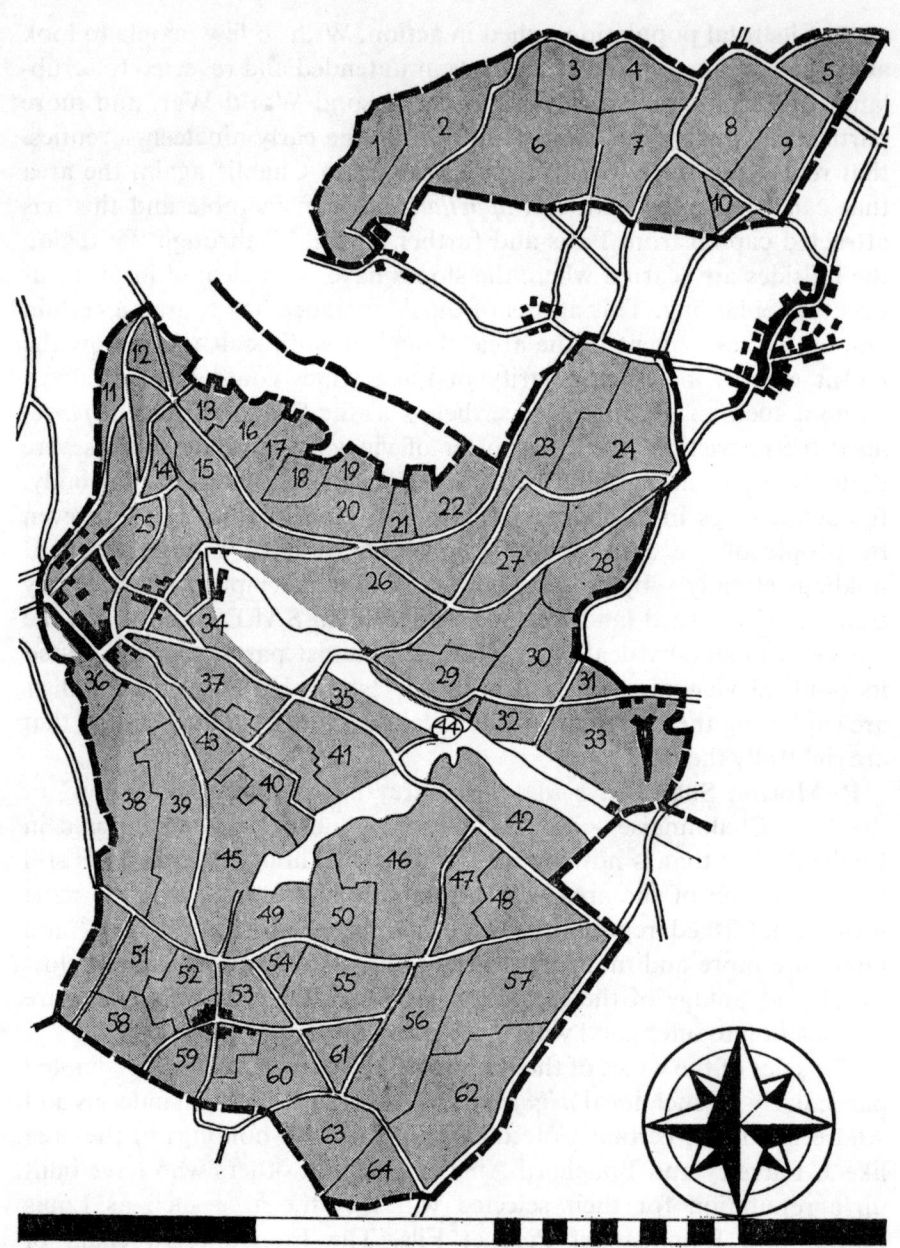

MONTAGNY

CÔTE CHALONNAISE: RÉGION DE MERCUREY

Shaded areas indicate *premier cru* vineyards

1	Clos Chaudron	les Bassets	28
2	la Grande Pièce	les Beaux Champs	39
3	les Coudrettes	les Bonnevaux	24
4	les Pidans	les Bordes	54
5	Cornevent	les Bouchots	21
6	Vignes du Puits	le Breuil	34
7	le Vieux Château	les Burnins	26
8	Vignes Longues	les Carlins	25
9	Vignes Blanches	les Champs-Toiseau	17
10	la Condemine	les Charmelottes	16
11	Sous les Roches	les Chandits	62
12	les Combes	les Chazelles	64
13	les Saint-Ytages	Clos Chaudron	1
14	les Clouzeaux	le Cloux	58
15	les Vignes Saint-Pierre	les Clouzeaux	14
16	les Charmelottes	les Coères	46
17	les Champs-Toiseau	les Coères	47
18	les Garchères	les Coères	56
19	les Vignes Couland	les Coères	57
20	Vignes sur le Clou	les Combes	12
21	les Bouchots	la Condemine	10
22	les Monts Cuchots	Cornevent	5
23	le Mont Laurent	la Corvée	33
24	les Bonnevaux	les Coudrettes	3
25	les Carlins	les Craboulettes	61
26	les Burnins	les Crets	36
27	les Monts Cuchots	Creux des Beaux Champs	45
28	les Bassets	l'Épaule	40
29	les Treuffères	les Garchères	18
30	les Vignes du Soleil	les Gouresses	53
31	la Vigne Devant	la Grand Pièce	2
32	les Thilles	les Jardins	50
33	la Corvée	les Las	55
34	le Breuil	les Males	38
35	les Marais	les Marais	35
36	les Crets	les Marocs	43
37	les Vignes Dessous	les Monts Cuchots	22
38	les Males	les Monts Cuchots	27
39	les Beaux Champs	le Mont Laurent	23
40	l'Épaule	la Mouillère	63
41	les Platières	Moulin l'Echenaud	44

continued on page 104

BURGUNDY

The Région de Mercurey is physically a continuation of the Côte d'Or and the wines are made with the same grape-varieties; the *chardonnay* and the *pinot*. In such a large proportion of recently planted vines, there has been little incentive to use the larger-cropping varieties whose wines can only be sold at much lower prices.

Whilst all the growers of the Saône-et-Loire *département* are associated for promotional purposes in the Comité Interprofessionnel des Vins de Bourgogne et de Mâcon (at Mâcon), the shippers of the Région de Mercurey turn more toward Beaune for professional grouping. Indeed there is continual complaint that, when the boundaries of the *départements* were drawn up under Napoleon, the great villages of the area were linked administratively to Saône-et-Loire – which enjoys a less profitable viticultural reputation – rather than the Côte d'Or.

42	les Varignys	les Pandars	49
43	les Marocs	les Pasquiers	60
44	Moulin l'Echenaud	les Pidans	4
45	Creux des Beaux Champs	les Platières	41
46	les Coères	les Resses	59
47	les Coères	les Saint-Mortille	51
48	la Tillonne	les Saint-Ytages	13
49	les Pandars	Sous les Roches	11
50	les Jardins	les Thilles	32
51	les Saint-Mortille	la Tillonne	48
52	les Vignes Derrière	les Treuffères	29
53	les Gouresses	les Varignys	42
54	les Bordes	le Vieux Château	7
55	les Las	Vignes Blanches	9
56	les Coères	Vignes sur le Clou	20
57	les Coères	les Vignes Couland	19
58	le Cloux	les Vignes Derrière	52
59	les Resses	les Vignes Dessous	37
60	les Pasquiers	la Vigne Devant	31
61	les Craboulettes	Vignes Longues	8
62	les Chandits	Vignes du Puits	6
63	la Mouillère	les Vignes Saint-Pierre	15
64	les Chazelles	les Vignes du Soleil	30

CÔTE CHALONNAISE: RÉGION DE MERCUREY

Montagny
Colour: white
Average production: 2,788 hl.
Minimum degree 11°; *1er cru* 11·5°
Area: 306·35 ha.

Driving to the north from the Mâconnais on the main road from Cluny, the first of the great villages of the Région de Mercurey is Montagny, whose vineyards also spread over into the villages of Buxy, Saint Vallérin and Jully-les-Buxy. Though Montagny provides the name of the wine, the village of Buxy, which stands on the main road, is probably more important. There is a tasting cellar in the historical Tour Rouge in its centre.

Not long ago, the reputed wines of the area were all red, and sold under the name of Côte de Buxy. Jullien recommended them as being soft and quick to mature, though gaining in quality with age. However, when the *appellation* Montagny was granted, the growers insisted that it should apply solely to the white wines, whereas the other three classified villages of the area have the right to produce either red or white. Another unique distinction, unparalleled in Burgundy, is that all the vineyards of the area have the right to the *appellation '1er cru'*, provided the wine has the required degree of alcohol.

From its south-easterly facing vines, Montagny produces more white wine than the other *appellations* of the Région de Mercurey: a wine that is dry and fruity; often with a considerable amount of body. This is particularly true of the wine sold under the label of Louis Latour, which fetches prices rivalling those of certain white wines of the Côte de Beaune.

A wide range of Bourgogne Passetoutgrains, Bourgogne Grand Ordinaires and red and white Bourgognes is produced in the area though they are not entitled to the *appellation* of Montagny. Much planting, particularly in the noble *cépages*, is being carried out in such lesser villages as Rosey, a couple of miles to the north of Buxy: this is typical of the rapid expansion of the area under vines.

1er cru vineyards: Montagny: Sous les Roches, les Combes, les Saint-Ytages, les Vignes-Saint-Pierre, les Charmelottes, les Champs-Toizeau (or Chantoiseau), les Garchères, les Chacolets, les Clouzeaux, les

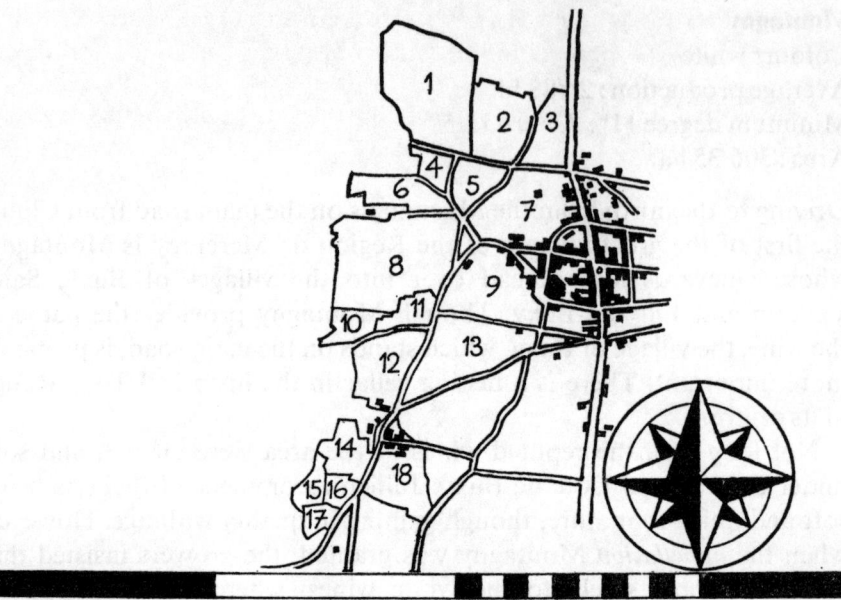

GIVRY

#	Name	Name	#
1	Cellier-au-Moines	la Baraude	14
2	Servoisine	les Bois-Chevaux	8
3	Clos Charlé	Bois Gauthier	16
4	Petit Marolle	Cellier-au-Moines	1
5	Chanevarie	Chanevarie	5
6	Clos Marolle	Clos Charlé	3
7	la Corvée	Clos Marolle	6
8	les Bois-Chevaux	Clos Saint Pierre	10
9	les Petits Pretans	Clos Saint Paul	11
10	Clos Saint Pierre	Clos Salomon	12
11	Clos Saint Paul	la Corvée	7
12	Clos Salomon	les Grands Pretans	13
13	les Grands Pretans	les Paradis	18
14	la Baraude	Petit Marolle	4
15	Plante Janlisse	les Petits Pretans	9
16	Bois Gauthier	Plante Janlisse	15
17	Vigne Rouge	Servoisine	2
18	les Paradis	Vigne Rouge	17

CÔTE CHALONNAISE: RÉGION DE MERCUREY

Carlins, le Breuil, les Champs de Coignée, les Burnins, les Monts Cuchots, les Bouchots, les Vignes-sur-le-Clou, les Vignes-Couland, les Treuffères, les Vignes-du-Soleil, les Marais, les Perrières, la Pallye, le Varignys, les Thilles, la Vigne-Devant, la Corvée, les Vignes-Dessous, les Marocs, la Thi, les Crets, les Beaux-Champs, les Males, les Pandars, les Jardins, les Saint-Mortille, le Clou, les Vignes-Derrière, le Perthuis, les Resses, les Pasquiers, les Gouresses, les Bordes, les Las.
Buxy: Clos Chaudron, la Grande-Pièce, les Pidans, le Vieux-Château, les Vignes-du-Puits, la Condemine, les Vignes-Longues, les Vignes-Blanches, Cornevent, le Mont-Laurent, les Bonnevaux, les Bassets.
Saint-Vallerin: la Mouillère, les Pasquiers, les Coéres.
Jully-les-Buxy: les Thillonnes, les Coères, les Chandits, la Mouillère, les Chazelles.

Possible declassifications: Bourgogne and Bourgogne Grand Ordinaire.

Givry
Colour: red (occasionally white)
Average production: red 2,049 hl.   white: 276 hl.
Minimum degree: red: 10·5°; white: 11°

The reputation of the wines of Givry is as strong historically as that of any wine of Burgundy. As early as the fourteenth century, they were liable to the same entry tax in Paris as those of Beaune. Henri IV, who must have supplied as many testimonials for wines available in his day as any king of France, was amongst its purchasers. (One fact that might have helped him in this choice was that when he came to taste the wines before purchasing, he could call upon the attractive Gabrielle d'Estrées, at nearby Germolles. Perhaps the wine of Givry may have been in part responsible for the two children that arrived as a result of his friendship.) When Courtepée visited Burgundy in 1776, he compared the wines of Givry to those of Volnay.

One fortunate result of such a history is that the village is exceptionally well-endowed with fine cellars, amongst which is that of Baron Thénard, the second most important proprietor of le Montrachet, and owner of the more conservative of Dijon's two daily newspapers.

Sadly, the quality of the wines of Givry fell after the First World War and their reputation suffered accordingly. Many of them were sold

BURGUNDY

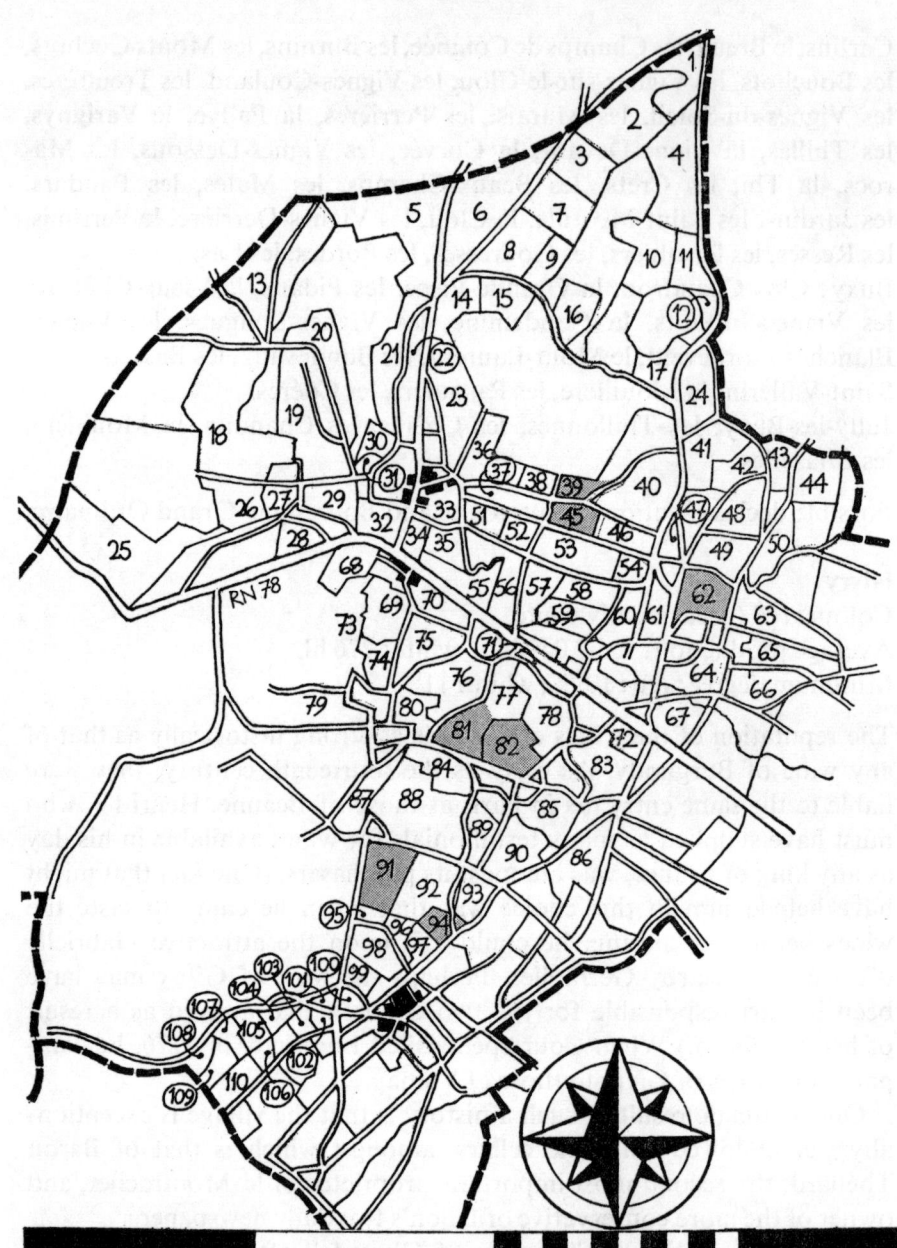

MERCUREY

CÔTE CHALONNAISE: RÉGION DE MERCUREY

Shaded areas indicate *premier cru* vineyards

1	en Villeranche	es Bauchats	3
2	en Nal	es Berlaud	10
3	es Bauchats	les Boires	101
4	en Mauvarennes	les Bosebuts	13
5	la Creuse	la Boudaillerie	98
6	les Montelants	Bourg	102
7	en Montelant	le Bourg	70
8	Creu de Montelant	le Bourg Bassot	71
9	en Pierre Milley	Boussière du Haut	16
10	es Berlaud	en Boussoy	92
11	à la Framboisière	les Byots	52
12	Vigne des Montots	les Caraby	78
13	les Bosebuts	Chamerose	31
14	les Grandes Plantes	Chamirey	85
15	les Vignes de la Brigadière	Champ Ladoy	86
16	Boussière du Haut	Champs Martin	23
17	en Montots	Champ Pillot	42
18	les Douées	Champ Rain	83
19	les Vaux	la Charmée	49
20	les Saumonts	la Chassière	97
21	les Croichots	les Chaumelottes	58
22	les Combins	les Chavance	89
23	Champs Martins	les Chenault	26
24	Clos Miglan	le Cleniseau	47
25	les Rochelles	le Clos	81
26	les Chenault	le Closeau	30
27	Pont Latin	Clos des Barraults	36
28	les Obus	le Clos l'Evêque	40
29	les Prés de l'Étang	Clos Laurent	34
30	le Closeau	Clos de la Marche	56
31	Chamerose	Clos Miglan	24
32	Mipont Château	Clos Portoul	54
33	en Tonnerre	les Combins	22
34	Clos Laurent	la Corvée	63
35	Vignes Blanches	les Coudroies	75
36	Clos des Barraults	le Cray	100
37	les Nuages	le Crét	50
38	les Crets	les Crets	38
39	les Petits Voyens	Creu de Montelant	8
40	le Clos l'Evêque	la Creuse	5
41	les Marcoeurs	les Croichots	21

continued on page 110

42	Champ Pillot	a la Croix Jacquelot	67
43	les Murgers	la Croix Rousse	68
44	les Retraits	le Douees	18
45	les Grands Voyens	les Eriglats	105
46	Jamproye Grand Clos Portoul	Etroyes	64
47	le Cleniseau	les Fourneaux	94
48	la Perrière	à la Framboisière	11
49	la Charmée	les Grandes Plantes	14
50	le Crét	les Grands Voyens	45
51	Vasées	le Grellode	106
52	les Byots	les Hâtes	104
53	les Vignes des Chazeauz	Jamproye Grand Clos Portoul	46
54	Clos Portoul	les Lamberot	84
55	Vignes du Chapitre	la Mainerie	107
56	Clos de la Marche	le Marcilly	62
57	Vignes d'Orge	les Marcoeurs	41
58	les Chaumelottes	au Mauvarennes	4
59	les Prés du Château	Mipont Château	32
60	les Pronges	Montaigu	87
61	les Morées	les Montaigus	91
62	le Marcilly	en Montelant	7
63	la Corvée	les Montelants	6
64	Etroyes	en Montots	17
65	les Noiterons	les Morées	61
66	les Varennes	la Mourandine	108
67	à la Croix Jacquelot	les Murgers	43
68	la Croix Rousse	en Nal	2
69	la Pillotte	les Noiterons	65
70	le Bourg	les Nuages	37
71	Bourg Bassot	les Obus	28
72	les Plantes	le Paradis	99
73	en Sazenay	la Perrière	48
74	les Pendaches	les Pendaches	74
75	les Coudroies	les Petits Voyens	39
76	Vigne de Malliauge	la Pidancerie	110
77	en Theurot	en Pierre Milley	9
78	les Caraby	la Pillotte	69
79	le Puits Brintet	les Plantes	72
80	Touches	Pont Latin	27
81	le Clos	les Prés du Château	59
82	du Roi	les Prés de l'Étang	29
83	Champ Rain	les Pronges	60

continued on page 111

under the name of their neighbour, Mercurey, and the abuse became so general that in 1923 the growers sought to have the position legalized. The court dismissed this application (as well as a similar one from the growers of Rully) on the grounds that the vineyard areas did not even adjoin and that the wines of Givry had their own separate traditions and reputation.

As with the majority in the Côte Chalonnaise, the vineyards of Givry generally face south-east and they produce wine rather lighter and less round than those of Mercurey. Whilst no vineyards have the classification of *1er cru*, some have built up a solid reputation for themselves, including the curiously biblical trio of Clos Saint-Pierre, Clos Saint-Paul and Clos Salomon. Le Cellier aux Moines is another known Givry wine.

Possible declassifications: Bourgogne and Bourgogne Grand Ordinaire.

84	les Lamberot	le Puits Brintet	79
85	Chamirey	la Ratte	103
86	Champ Ladoy	au Retrait	109
87	Montaigu	les Retraits	44
88	les Vellées	les Rochelles	25
89	les Chavance	du Roi	82
90	le Sant Muchiau	en Ruelle	93
91	les Montaigus	le Sant Muchiau	90
92	en Boussoy	les Saumonts	20
93	en Ruelle	en Sazenay	73
94	les Fourneaux	à la Serve	95
95	à la Serve	en Theurot	77
96	la Verrière	en Tonnerre	33
97	la Chassière	Touches	80
98	la Boudaillerie	les Varennes	66
99	le Paradis	Vasées	51
100	le Cray	les Vaux	19
101	les Boires	les Vellées	88
102	Bourg	la Verrière	96
103	la Ratte	Vignes Blanches	35
104	les Hâtes	les Vignes de la Brigadière	15
105	les Eriglats	Vignes du Chapitre	55
106	le Grellode	les Vignes du Chazeaux	53
107	la Mainerie	Vigne de Malliauge	76
108	la Mourandine	Vigne des Montots	12
109	au Retrait	Vigne d'Orge	57
110	la Pidancerie	en Villeranche	1

BURGUNDY

Mercurey
Colour: red (occasionally white)
Average production: red 13,967 hl.   white 817 hl.
Minimum degree: red 10·5°; *1er cru* 11°; white 11°; *1er cru* 11·5°

Mercurey is not only the most important village in the area that bears its name, but the aristocrat of the region, producing the finest red wines of Burgundy outside the Côte d'Or. The *appellation* is shared also with the adjoining villages of Saint-Martin-sous-Montaigu and Bourgneuf-Val d'Or and a jumble of hamlets which seem to cluster round every cross-roads. As well as its high reputation as an *appellation*, it is important for its production – greater than that of any village of the Côte d'Or, and two-thirds of the total of the four village *appellations* of the Région de Mercurey.

Mercurey takes its name from the Roman god to whom a temple above the village was dedicated. Fortunately the area has suffered less damage than most of its neighbours over the years and has managed to maintain a sound viticultural background. As a result, some shippers have established their principal cellars in the village and others from the Côte d'Or have built up substantial vineyard holdings. This outward-looking policy has led to the wines often being considered with those of the Côte d'Or, and their prices usually equal, or better, those of such Côte de Beaune villages as Savigny and Monthélie. Mercurey thus has a more solid commercial base than most of the rest of the region.

A majority of the vineyards of the village of Mercurey face the south, whilst those of Bourgneuf and Saint-Martin face more south-east. The red wines have outstanding class with a rich colour and full body. Their weight recalls the more distant Côte de Nuits, rather than the Côte de Beaune, and they benefit clearly from ageing. It is interesting to observe that the maximum permitted quantity is the same as that for the villages of the Côte d'Or, and not the larger amount allowed in Rully, Givry and Montagny.

While only five Mercurey vineyards have the right to the *appellation 1er cru*, there are a host of well-known names there: Château de Chamirey (of the leading local shipper Antonin Rodet), Château d'Etroyes-Juillet (Marcel Bureaux), Château d'Etroyes (Protheau), Clos des Myglands of the Nuits shipper J. Faiveley, who probably has the largest holding in the area, Clos Barrault and Clos la Marche of the Beaune shippers, Bouchard Aîné et Fils.

Only about 6 per cent of the wine produced in the village is white, and it generally lacks the distinction of the red.

1er cru vineyards: Mercurey: Clos Voyen (or les Voyens).
Bourgneuf-Val d'Or: Clos du Roi.
Saint-Martin-sous-Montaigu: Clos des Montaigus, Clos des Fourneaux, Clos-Marcilly.

Possible declassification: Bourgogne and Bourgogne Grand Ordinaire.

Rully

Colour: white and red
Average production: white 1,333 hl. red 619 hl.
Minimum degree: red 10·5°, *1er cru* 11°; white 11°, *1er cru* 11·5°

The first view of Rully, for the traveller approaching the village from Mercurey by the track that leads over the shoulder of Mont Morin, is of the noble château, which dates back to the thirteenth and fifteenth centuries. The vineyards of Rully, the last of the village growths of the Région de Mercurey, fall away in front of it.

The history of Rully runs back far beyond that of the château, for traces of Stone Age man have been found in the nearby Grottes d'Agneux. Roman remains have also been discovered and the village probably owes its name to Rubilium, a landlord of Gallo-Roman times. The original Rully stood on the crest of the hill, but it was moved to its present, lower, site, around a spring, after an outbreak of plague in the fourteenth century.

The wines of Rully have enjoyed mixed fortunes over the centuries. In the time of Louis XIV the white wines were recognized as being 'really excellent, with a very delicate perfume'. The red wines then came back into fashion, but in 1822 the manufacture of sparkling wine was begun in the village and this has since played an important role in the local economy, often to the detriment of the fine still wines of the area.

Phylloxera and two world wars had a disastrous effect on the local wine industry and a majority of the vineyards relapsed into scrubland. In the past few years, though, an enterprising policy of replanting has

BURGUNDY

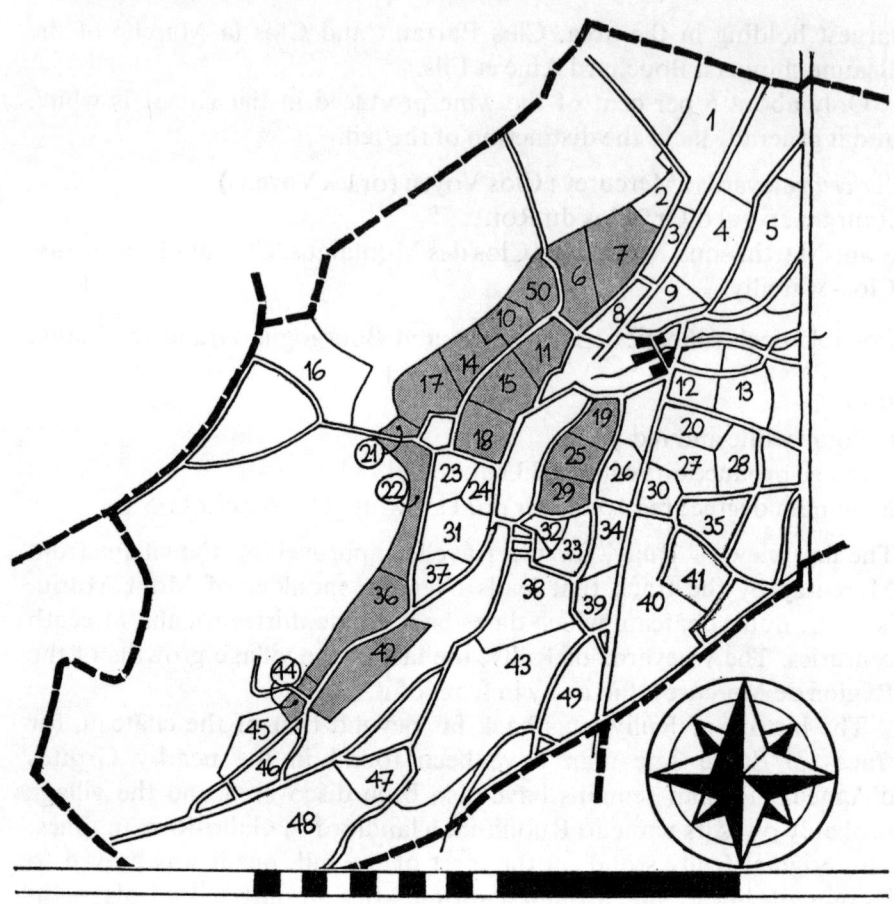

RULLY

Shaded areas indicate *premier cru* vineyards

1	Chaponnières	en l'Ane	9
2	Brange	Bas des Chênes	46
3	la Gaudine	Bas de Vauvry	42
4	en Praye	la Bergerie	38
5	en Gelée	Billerenne	28
6	la Fosse	Brange	2
7	Marrissou	la Bressande	29
8	Meix Guillaume	la Buisserolle	12
9	en l'Ane	Champ-Clou	25
10	Raclot	Chapitre	11

CÔTE CHALONNAISE : RÉGION DE MERCUREY

11	Chapitre	Chaponnières	1
12	la Baisserolle	la Chaume	43
13	Florange	en Chêne	45
14	Cloux	Clos à Dion	24
15	Préau	Cloux	14
16	Varot	la Craie	37
17	Pillot	les Crais	27
18	Moulesne	Florange	13
19	la Renarde	la Fosse	6
20	Vesignot	la Gaudine	3
21	Meix Caillet	en Gelée	5
22	Mont Palais	Grésigny	36
23	Jaquemette	es Guesne	33
24	Clos à Dion	Jacquemette	23
25	Champ-Clou	la Longeaille	31
26	Pommier	Maizière	35
27	les Crais	Margotey	44
28	Billerenne	Marrissou	7
29	la Bressaude	Meix Cadot	32
30	Pellerey	Meix Caillet	21
31	la Longeaille	Meix Guillaume	8
32	Meix Cadot	Montmorin	47
33	es Guesnes	Mont Palais	22
34	Sangeot	Moulesne	18
35	Maizière	Pellerey	30
36	Grésigny	la Perche	40
37	la Craie	Pillot	17
38	la Bergerie	Plante Moraine	41
39	Poirosot	Poirosot	39
40	la Perche	Pommier	26
41	Plante Moraine	en Praye	4
42	Bas de Vauvry	Préau	15
43	la Chaume	Raboursay	50
44	Margotey	Raclot	10
45	en Chêne	la Renarde	19
46	Bas des Chênes	Sangeot	34
47	Montmorin	les Tilles	48
48	les Tilles	Varot	16
49	Villerange	Vesignot	20
50	Raboursay	Villerange	49

been carried out by such young growers as Jean-François Delorme, who have reclaimed vast acreages of land and planted the *pinot noir* and the *chardonnay*. To illustrate the increasing importance of the village its average annual production in 1959 was quoted as being 518 hectolitres; in 1972 it had risen to 1,612 hectolitres. In 1973, admittedly an exceptional year, at least for quantity, the total production was 4,331 hectolitres. Twenty years ago, the production of white wine in Rully was almost three times as important as that of the red, but over the last two vintages they have been almost equal.

To one side of the château is the newly constructed *cuverie* of the Domaine de la Renarde, whose wines are distributed by local shipper André Delorme. Here they vinify wines from their holdings in Givry and Mercurey as well as from those vineyards in Rully itself. Every year a proportion of the wine is vinified in new oak casks to increase its keeping properties. Above the vat-room and the cask and bottle cellars, are dormitories to lodge the pickers at vintage time, and at one side the kitchens and dining-room for their team, which might number as many as seventy people.

Other established growers from Rully include the Domaine de la Folie, whose vineyards overlook the town of Chagny; and Armand Monassier, whose restaurant at Paris – Chez les Anges – is well known to lovers of the fine food, and wine, of Burgundy.

1er cru vineyards: Margotey, Grésigny, Vauvry, Mont Palais, Meix-Caillet, les Pierres, la Bressande, Champ-Clou, la Renarde, Pillot, Cloux, Raclot, Raboursay, Ecloseaux, Marissou, la Fosse, Chapitre, Préau, Moulesne.

Possible declassification: Bourgogne and Bourgogne Grand Ordinaire.

Although Rully is the last of the village *appellations* of the Région de Mercurey, two adjoining villages produce wines of some character. Bouzeron makes fine *aligoté* wines, many of which are used in Rully for making Bourgogne Mousseux. At Chassey-le-Camp, once the site of a Roman *castrum*, amongst other wines, they produce a rosé under the unlikely name of La Vierge Romaine, apparently in honour of a girl in ancient times, who defended her honour by pouring vast quantities of the local wine into her aggressor.

CÔTE CHALONNAISE RÉGION DE MERCUREY

At the northern end of the Région de Mercurey stands the town of Chagny, whose main importance is as a railway junction. It has, however, a tasting cellar and, more important, the best restaurant in the neighbourhood – and for many miles around – in 'Lameloise' which is run by the family of that name.

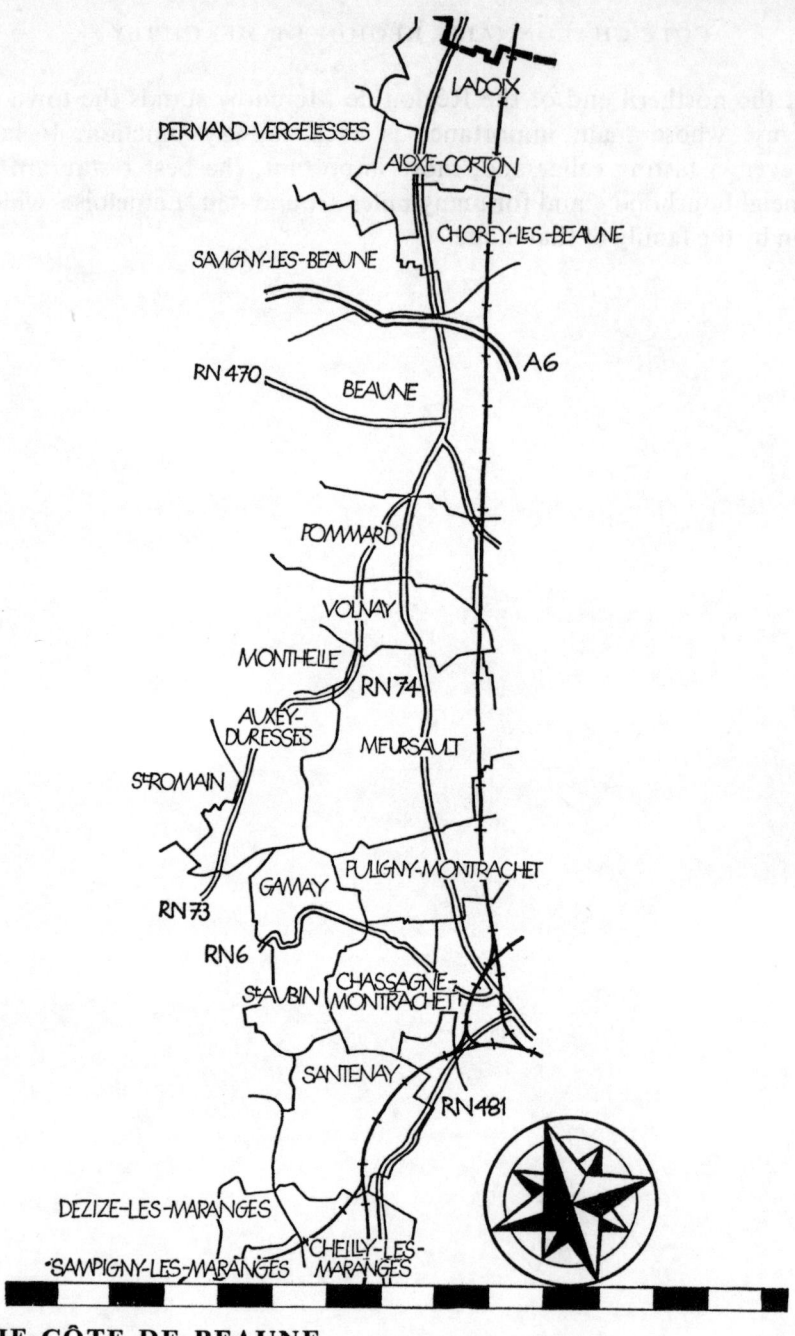

THE CÔTE DE BEAUNE

9 CÔTE DE BEAUNE

Beaune is the most satisfying of all French wine capitals. Bordeaux is a greater city but it spreads its attentions in many directions; Avignon is at the end of the Rhône vineyards; Colmar has rivals; while Reims and Épernay divide an empire. Beaune is a completely rounded wine town: the vines flow up to – and sometimes breach – its boundaries on three sides (occasionally Beaune snaps back, eating up a piece of vineyard land for building or a road); while in the cellar-city below and the vast cavities in the medieval walls, a host of shippers hold an ocean of the wines of Burgundy.

Beaune has some other interests but essentially it is a wine town. It stands at the heart of its dominion, the country mercantile centre for the peasant production of wine.

Busy; architecturally an engaging *mélange*; warm with humanity and history and cooking, eating and drinking, it is a place of tasting, buying and selling wines – fine, middling and ordinary – in large and small quantities, and in a pattern established over a dozen centuries.

Fittingly, its own vineyard range – the narrow, thirty-kilometre-long brow called the Côte de Beaune – produces a variety of fine wines. The greater part of it is red – some of it outstanding – while the smaller quantity of white includes some which are, beyond dispute, the finest dry white wines in the world. While some of those mighty names need their years to mature, others, from less famous vineyards, are made specifically to drink early; there are some mildly priced happy surprises to be found among them.

In all on the Côte de Beaune twenty villages give their names to a wine and, apart from the four most famous – Aloxe-Corton, Beaune, Pommard and Volnay – they have the right to sell their wine under the *appellation:*

Côte de Beaune Villages
Colour: red
Average production: 11,886 hl.
Minimum degree: 10·5°

Villages having right to the *appellation*: Dézize-les-Maranges, Cheilly-les-Maranges, Chassagne-Montrachet, Puligny-Montrachet, Meursault, Meursault-Blagny, Saint Aubin, Saint Romain, Auxey-Duresses, Santenay, Monthélie, Chorey-les-Beaune, Savigny, Pernand-Vergelesses, Ladoix-Serrigny.

As an alternative to the *appellation* of the commune itself, each of the sixteen may sell its red wine under the village name, followed by the term 'Côte de Beaune', printed in letters of the same size, though in certain cases this applies only to certain vineyard areas within the village itself. Until the late nineteen-thirties, it was quite common for these villages to sell their wine as Côte de Beaune (as still seems to happen with some British wine-merchants). The Beaune growers took exception to this and now, in the agreed compromise, the description can only be used after the village name, thus showing clearly that the wine does not come from Beaune itself. If the wine is blended with others of the same village or others of the sixteen villages, it is then called Côte de Beaune Villages. As this blending is carried out almost exclusively by the *négociants*, rather than the growers, it is difficult to say how much wine is sold under this *appellation* in a given year. Equally it is an interesting *appellation* for the *négociants* for, no matter how important *domaine*-bottling becomes, the blend must always remain the virtual monopoly of the shipper.

There are three other notable advantages of the *appellation* Côte de Beaune Villages. Firstly, it gives the growers of such lesser-known villages as Sampigny-les-Maranges the opportunity of selling their wines under an *appellation* that is generally known to the public. Secondly, the shippers and growers enjoy the benefit of blending the often coarse, earthy wines of, say, Chorey-les-Beaune, with the full, round ones of, say, Monthélie, to produce a well-balanced final product. Finally, for the shipper, there is the advantage that by blending wines of several sources together, he can produce a large quantity of constant quality under one name. Thus, for marketing purposes, it is easier to promote Côte de Beaune Villages than sixteen different village wines.

It is important to note that Côte de Beaune Villages is always a red wine, and that it should in no way be confused with Côte de Beaune, a sub-appellation of Beaune itself (dealt with on pages 163-4).

Possible declassifications: Bourgogne and Bourgogne Grand Ordinaire.

Dezize-les-Maranges
Cheilly-les-Maranges
Sampigny-les-Maranges
Colour: red and white
Average production: 247 hl.*
Minimum degree: red 10·5°, *1er cru* 11°; white 11°, *1er cru* 11·5°
Area: 230·56 ha.

It seems a pity to deal with three village *appellations* under one heading, but these are really the Cinderella villages of the Côte de Beaune. In some ways they are almost adopted children, for they are not part of the Côte d'Or *département* at all, but of Saône-et-Loire. In vain their mayors have asked for their villages to be transferred across the boundary-line and even to have the right to sell their wines as Santenay, which latter move was stoutly resisted by the growers of that village. Sad to say, the wines are very rarely seen under their village name; they are more generally sold as Côte de Beaune Villages, when red, or Bourgogne, when white.

These vineyards are a natural continuation of those of the Côte de Beaune, though here the slope has turned and faces due south, rather than to the east as elsewhere; as a result they benefit less from the morning sun. Dezize crouches on the hillside above Sampigny and, a mile or so away in the valley of the Dheune, lies Cheilly.

1er cru vineyards: Dezize: les Maranges (part).
  Cheilly: les Maranges (part), les Plantes de Maranges (part), la
    Boutière (part).

BURGUNDY

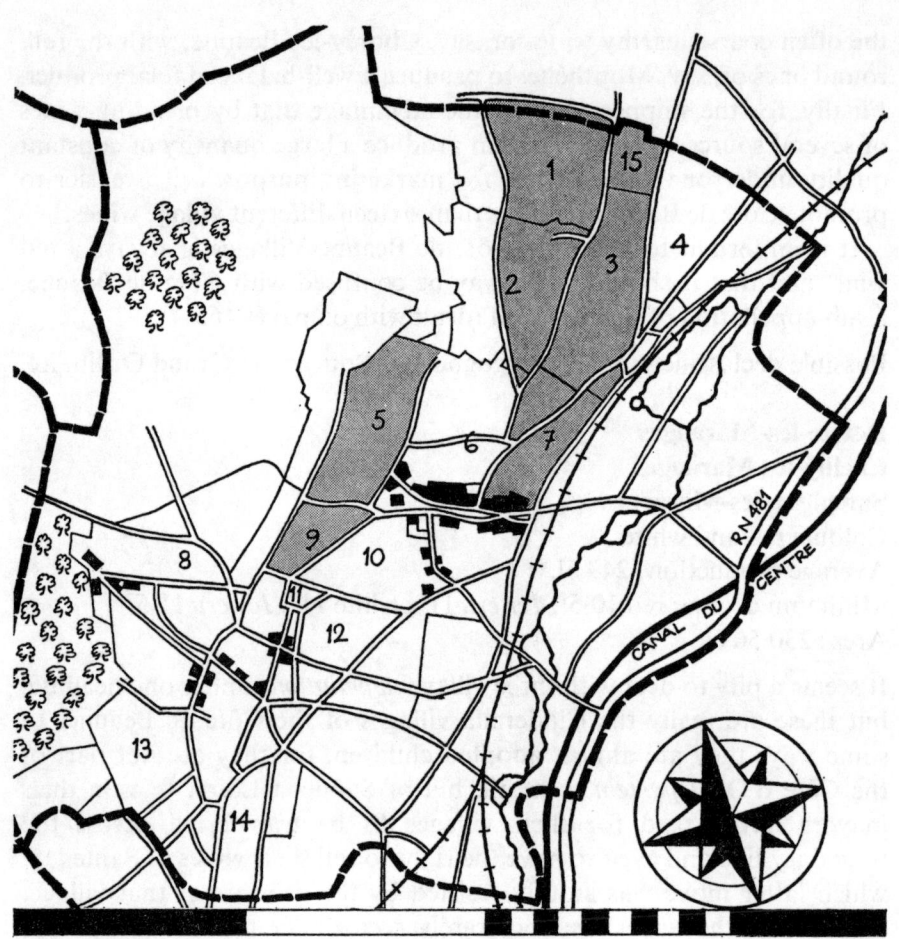

SANTENAY

Shaded areas indicate *premier cru* vineyards

1	la Comme	Beauregard	2
2	Beauregard	Beaurepaire	5
3	les Gravières	les Charmes Dessus	14
4	les Prarons Dessus	le Clos Genet	10
5	Beaurepaire	Clos des Tavannes	15
6	les Hâtes	la Comme	1
7	Passe Temps	les Cornières	12
8	Saint-Jean	Derrière la Crée	11
9	la Maladière	le Grand Clos Rousseau	13

Sampigny: les Maranges (part), le Clos des Rois (part).
Possible declassifications: Côte de Beaune Villages (red only), Bourgogne and Bourgogne Grand Ordinaire.

Santenay
Colour: red and a little white
Average production: red 7,809 hl.   white 138 hl.
Minimum degree: red 10·5°, *1er cru* 11°; white 11°, *1er cru* 11.5°
Area: 380·50 ha.

Santenay is scarcely the most attractive village of the Côte d'Or; it is dominated architecturally by a home for retired railwaymen. It can boast, however, a long and proud history, with a rubble of dolmens on the hill behind it and, in the village itself, a castle which dates back to the fourteenth century and is faced by – reputedly – the two oldest plane trees in France. In the twin village of Santenay-le-Haut the church of Saint Jean has a statue of Saint Martin dating back to the seventh century. Santenay is not just plain and ordinary Santenay; its full title is Santenay-les-Bains, whose two springs were first noted for their healing properties over 300 years ago. The springs have their devotees who come to be cured of gout and rheumatism, but, more important for many, they entitle the village to have a casino where baccarat and roulette, blackjack and *boule* prove attractions for many whose interests are not solely vinous.

In the main square an imposing building, formerly the property of Bristol wine-shippers John Harvey and Sons Limited, houses one of the more dynamic of the local shippers, Pierre Maufoux. Perhaps the most important *domaine* in the village is that of Fleurot-Larose, who are fortunate enough to own three-quarters of an acre of le Montrachet besides their holdings in Santenay itself.

10	le Clos Genet	les Gravières	3
11	Derrière la Crée	les Hâtes	6
12	les Cornières	la Maladière	9
13	le Grand Clos Rousseau	Passe Temps	7
14	les Charmes Dessus	les Prarons Dessus	4
15	Clos des Tavannes	Saint-Jean	8

Due to variations of soil between vineyards, the wines of Santenay fall into two distinct styles. Some are light and delicate, typical of lesser wines of the Côte; while others are heavy and full-coloured, more reminiscent of the Côte de Nuits. Above the vineyards, overlooking the valley, is a simple memorial to three members of the London wine-trade killed in the 1974 Paris air disaster.

1er cru vineyards: though the number of official names is limited, there are smaller plots within them which may be sold under different names; a list of which follows. Generally speaking the vineyards of les Gravières (with Clos des Tavannes) and la Comme have the best reputations.

La Comme (part).
Beauregard (part): Dessus Gravières, Murées des Forges, Commes Dessus, les Colottes, Beaurégard, Clos des Mouches.
Les Gravières (part): Clos des Tavannes, les Gravières, les Grillardes, les Ambours.
Passe Temps: Derrière l'Enclos, Passetemps, Grillarde, les Ambours, les Épiceries.
Beaurepaire: les Ruchottes, la Folie, la Foultière, sur le Château, Beaurepaire, la Maladière.
La Maladière: la Maladière, sur le Château, les Grand Murs.
Clos Rousseau: Grand Clos Rousseau, en Abdon, Petit Clos Rousseau, les Rouères, Clos de Vezon.
Les Saunières: la Gratte, les Fourneaux.

Possible declassifications: Côte de Beaune Villages (red only), Bourgogne and Bourgogne Grand Ordinaire.

Saint Aubin
Colour: red and white
Average production: red 1,241 hl.   white 782 hl.
Minimum degree: red 10·5°, *1er cru* 11°; white 11°, *1er cru* 11·5°
Area: 119·70 ha.

The village of Saint Aubin lies withdrawn slightly from the Côte, beside the N6 as it climbs up a valley to the foothills of the Morvan. Sharing the *appellation* is the hamlet of Gamay, which gave its name to the grape that caused so much trouble in Burgundy in the past. The name of the village comes from Aubin, a bishop of Angers under the medieval Frankish kings Childeric and Childebert, who dedicated an oratory to him on the site of the village. The main street is hemmed in on both sides by growers' houses as it climbs steeply up the hillside.

The production of red wine is rather more than that of white and a large proportion of it is sold as Côte de Beaune Villages. One local shipper and grower, Raoul Clerget, specializes in selling both red and white wines under the village name.

1er cru vineyards: Sur Gamay (Sous Roche Dumay), la Chatenière, les Murgers des Dents de Chien, en Remilly (les Cortons), Champlot (en Montceau), les Combes (les Combes au Sud, Pintangeret, le Charmois), sur le Sentier du Clou (le Travers de Marinot, Vignes Moingeon, en Rancrée, Marinot, Echaille), les Frionnes (les Perrières, les Champs).

Possible declassification: Côte de Beaune Villages (red only), Bourgogne and Bourgogne Grand Ordinaire.

Chassagne-Montrachet
Colour: red and white
Average production: red 4,849 hl. white 3,010 hl.
Minimum degree: red 10·5°, *1er cru* 11°; white 11°, *1er cru* 11·5°
Area: 365·38 ha.

With Chassagne we come to the first of the great wine-villages of the Côte d'Or, for within its limits lies one *grand cru* vineyard; Criots-Bâtard-Montrachet, while it shares two others – le Montrachet and Bâtard-Montrachet – with its neighbour, Puligny. Although these three vineyards produce only white wines, the reputation of Chassagne has always been based on its red which, although they may be less well-known, account for over 60 per cent of the production. Because white Chassagne fetches a higher price than red at the moment, the *chardonnay* is now being planted in many vineyards traditionally reserved for the *pinot noir*.

Like many other villages of Burgundy, Chassagne has had a stormy history and suffered much in consequence of the political inclinations of the lord of the manor. Its origins are unknown, but it is first mentioned, under the names of Cassaneas and Cassania, in ninth century

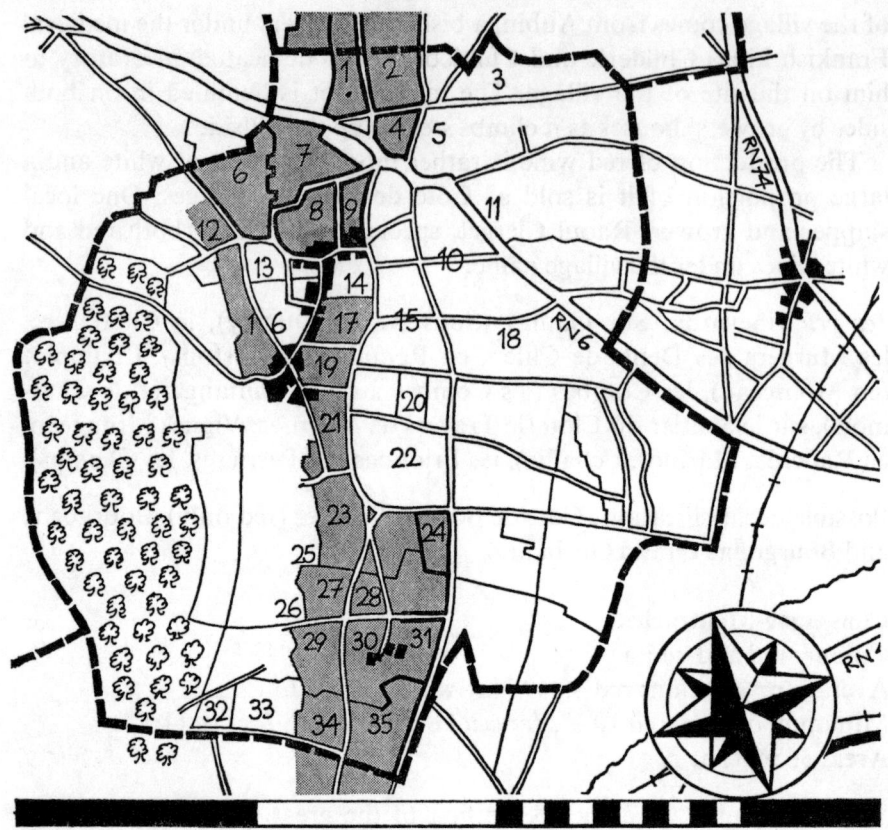

CHASSAGNE-MONTRACHET

Shaded areas indicate *premier cru* vineyards. The names of *grand cru* vineyards are shown in bold type in the legends.

1	les Montrachet	Abbaye de Morgeot	30
2	**Bâtard Montrachet**	**Bâtard Montrachet**	2
3	les Houillères	les Baudines	32
4	**les Criots-Bâtard-Montrachet**	la Boudriotte	23
5	Fontaine Sot	les Brussonnes	35
6	les Vergers	la Canière	20
7	les Chévenottes	les Champs-Gains	21
8	les Macherelles	la Chapelle	31
9	Meix Goudard	les Chaumes	24
10	Voillemot Dessous	les Chaumées	12

documents in the archives of the Abbey of Saint Seine; this would suggest that it gained its name as a diminutive of the Latin *casa*, a house. At the end of the fifteenth century the lord of the village, Jean de Chalons, Prince of Orange, supported Marie of Burgundy against Louis XI of France. At that time the village stood round his castle at the top of the hill, where the king's army under Charles d'Amboise, Lord of Chaumont besieged him. Although the prince held out for some time, he had to flee when Swiss reinforcements joined de Chaumont. The captured village was completely destroyed, apart from two houses and the Château de Chassagne-le-Bas, whose lord appears to have been rather more wise in his choice of side to support. It took

11	Plante Longe	les Chévenottes	7
12	les Chaumées	Clos Devant	15
13	les Rebichets	Clos Pitois	34
14	les Places	Clos Saint Jean	16
15	Clos Devant	les Concis des Champs	18
16	Clos Saint Jean	les Cretz	17
17	les Cretz	**les Criots-Bâtard-Montrachet**	4
18	les Concis des Champs	les Embazées	33
19	la Maltroie	Fontaine Sot	5
20	la Canière	Grands Clos	29
21	les Champs-Gains	Grandes Ruchottes en Caillerets	25
22	les Masures	les Houillères	3
23	la Boudriotte	les Macherelles	8
24	les Chaumes	la Maltroie	19
25	Grandes Ruchottes en Caillerets	les Masures	22
26	la Romanée	Meix Goudard	9
27	les Petits Clos	**les Montrachet**	1
28	Vigne Blanche	les Petits Clos	27
29	Grands Clos	les Places	14
30	Abbaye de Morgeot	Plante Longe	11
31	la Chapelle	les Rebichets	13
32	les Baudines	la Romanée	26
33	les Embazées	les Vergers	6
34	Clos Pitois	Vigne Blanche	28
35	les Brussonnes	Voillemot Dessous	10

some time for Chassagne to recover and it was probably fifty years or more before the building of a new village began on its present site.

The history of the vineyards is tied to the Church for, after Chassagne was sacked, the fields were allowed to go fallow until the Abbot of Maizières appreciated the viticultural potential of the land. He sent a team of monks to replant the vineyards and the undertaking flourished to such an extent that a priory was built on the spot to lodge the brothers working in the vines.

The extent of the Chassagne vineyards is greater now than a century ago, as can be gauged from sales-bills of that period which refer to the land to the east of the road to Santenay as being under pasture. Known at the time as Chassagne, the village followed the example of many others of the Côte d'Or and attached the name of its most famous vineyard to its own, promoting itself to the status of Chassagne-Montrachet. Similarly, Nuits became Nuits Saint-Georges, Gevrey, Gevrey-Chambertin and Vosne, Vosne-Romanée. (Others to follow the fashion – reading from north to south – were Morey-Saint-Denis, Chambolle-Musigny, Flagey-Echézaux, Aloxe-Corton, Pernand-Vergelesses, Auxey-Duresses and Puligny-Montrachet.)

The soil pattern of Chassagne is quite complicated, which suggests a stormy pre-history too. Basically the sub-soil is rich in chalk and marl, though there is a ridge of limestone, which imparts remarkable body to some of the red wines.

Of the vineyards, Clos Saint Jean, which lies on the hillside behind the village, Morgeot, Abbaye de Morgeot and la Boudriotte are particularly renowned for producing the finest red wines, with la Maltroie close behind. Apart from the *grands crus*, the finest white wines come from Cailleret and les Ruchottes; though an Abbaye de Morgeot of the Duc de Magenta recently tasted was exceptional even for a great white Burgundy. Another first growth worth mentioning is la Romanée, if only to point out that the only connection that it has with the *grand cru* of the same name at Vosne is its Roman origin.

Among the better-known growers are the Beaune shippers, de Marcilly (whose Clos Saint Jean is often seen in Britain), the Duc de Magenta, Ramonet Prudhon and Picard-Stockel, the owners of Château de la Maltroye.

How highly do the wines of Chassagne-Montrachet rate in the hierarchy of the wines of Burgundy? The local growers like to believe that, by virtue of their exceptional white, and good red wines, they are the best all-rounders in Burgundy – though the *vignerons* of Aloxe-Corton, with *grand cru* wines in both red and white, might dispute this – and they like to sum up their feelings by quoting 'Chassagne-Montrachet: the warm amber of its great white wines; the vermilion velvet of its excellent red wines; the living essentials of the slopes of purple and gold.' Whilst the prices of some of the white wines have passed the value of the product, there is no doubt that the red wines represent excellent value for money, though some of the lesser wines have to be declassified into Côte de Beaune Villages for lack of customers.

1er cru vineyards: For red wines: Clos Saint Jean (part), Morgeot (part), Abbaye de Morgeot (part), La Maltroie (part), Les Chévenottes, les Champs-Gain (part), Grandes Ruchottes, la Romanée, les Brussonnes (part), les Vergers, les Macherelles, en Cailleret (part).

For white wines: Morgeot (part), Abbaye de Morgeot (part), la Boudriotte, la Maltroie, Clos Saint Jean, les Chévenottes, Les Champs-Gain, Grandes Ruchottes, la Romanée, les Brussonnes, les Vergers, les Macherelles, Chassagne (or Cailleret).

Possible declassification: Côte de Beaune Villages (red only), Bourgogne and Bourgogne Grand Ordinaire.

Driving out of Chassagne the N6, once the main road from Paris to the Côte d'Azur, is now, after the construction of the motorway, much more tranquil. On the other side of it begins the succession of *grand crus*.

Le Montrachet
Colour: white
Average production: 205 hl.
Minimum degree: 12°
Area: 7·49 ha. (4 ha. in Puligny, 3·49 ha. in Chassagne)

Whatever one's feelings may be about the wines of Burgundy, it is generally agreed that the greatest dry white wine in the world comes from the small, unprepossessing plot of land lying astride the boundary between Chassagne and Puligny. (One exception to this generalization is Hilaire Belloc, who wrote to Bridget Herbert, 'As for the white Burgundies, they are for those that like them. I never did. Not even Chablis and Hock. I neither know nor like. Those who do cannot seek it out too carefully and will sell their souls for it.') Alexandre Dumas, on the other hand, suggests that it should be drunk in a duly reverent position, on one's knees with one's head bared. Tasting techniques have changed over the last century, but the wine still commands a similar respect, and demand far outstrips the limited supply.

Some say that the wine from the commune of Puligny, where the vines have a more south-easterly exposure, is superior to that of Chassagne, where they face more to the south, but this is a matter for the most expert and wealthy of tasters. The more ordinary drinker counts himself fortunate to taste a bottle from any of the small number of growers. It is a wine in which are combined all the finest qualities of a white Burgundy – an intense nose and a flavour of almonds, honey and ripe grapes; immense richness, yet no trace of sweetness. It has been compared to a Bach fugue, and called 'deific', 'stainless', and 'the liqueur of paradise'. A suntrap set on a streak of limestone is the rare combination which produces this 'noble and loyal lord, blood brother of the famous Bordeaux Château Yquem.'

Professor Saintsbury claimed that the second glass was always a slight disappointment after the first, indeed that the wine 'sickened' after opening. No other writer seems to have suffered from the same problem and it is interesting to note that the Professor's stock of Montrachet seems to have been of no specific vintage, which casts some doubt on its authenticity.

Even though the extent of the vineyard is small, it is shared by thirteen different owners, the wines of some of them are scarcely ever seen in general commerce. The most important is the Marquis de Laguiche, whose wine is distributed by the Beaune shipper Joseph Drouhin, followed by Baron Thénard, already mentioned as being an important owner in Givry, and Bouchard Père et Fils, of Beaune. Among the lesser proprietors are the Domaine de la Romanée-Conti (but, as they generally insist on the purchase of twenty-three bottles of their other wines – selected by them – as a pre-condition of being allowed a bottle of their Montrachet, it becomes an expensive purchase); the Fleurot-

Larose *domaine* of Santenay, and Roland Thévenin, the poet, mayor and shipper of Saint Romain.

Possible declassification: Puligny- or Chassagne-Montrachet *1er cru*, Puligny- or Chassagne-Montrachet, Bourgogne and Bourgogne Grand Ordinaire.

Above the portion of Montrachet within Puligny-Montrachet, is the *grand cru* vineyard of:

Chevalier Montrachet
Colour: white
Average production: 154 hl.
Minimum degree: 12°
Area: 7·15 ha.

Slightly smaller in size than le Montrachet, le Chevalier enjoys a reputation only fractionally less than that of its better known neighbour. The soil is distinctly more stony and although the wine has the same characteristics as le Montrachet, they are in less concentrated form. While the area is only smaller by about a twelfth, the production is generally less by about a quarter. The principal owner is the shipper Bouchard Père et Fils.

Possible declassification: Puligny-Montrachet *1er cru*, Puligny-Montrachet, Bourgogne and Bourgogne Grand Ordinaire.

Bâtard Montrachet
Colour: white
Average production: 349 hl.
Minimum degree: 12°
Area: 11·83 ha.

The largest of the *grand crus* of the southern end of the Côte de Beaune, Bâtard Montrachet lies just below the road leading from Chassagne to Puligny and is split almost equally between the villages. Here the slope begins to ease out towards the plain, and the wine, though still great, lacks some of the finesse of its neighbours on the other side of the road. Due to its size, its wines are more frequently met with, and should sell for little more than a half that of le Montrachet. Two Puligny growers to produce wines of note here are the Domaine Leflaive and Étienne Sauzet.

Possible declassifications: as for le Montrachet.

At each end of it – on the same level – lie the *grand cru* vineyards of Criots-Bâtard-Montrachet in Chassagne and Bienvenues-Bâtard-Montrachet in Puligny.

Criots-Bâtard-Montrachet
Colour: white
Average production: 41 hl.
Minimum degree: 12°
Area: 1·60 ha.

With an average total production of under 450 cases, much of which is consumed by the growers themselves, Criots is perhaps the rarest of all the white wines of Burgundy. In style it closely resembles Bâtard-Montrachet. Among the growers is the Domaine Delagrange-Bachelet.

Possible declassification: Chassagne-Montrachet *1er cru*, Chassagne-Montrachet, Bourgogne and Bourgogne Grand Ordinaire.

Bienvenues-Bâtard-Montrachet
Colour: white
Average production: 108 hl.
Minimum degree: 12°
Area: 2·30 ha.

Lying in the angle of the road which turns between the villages, is the last of the family of Montrachet *grands crus*, Bienvenues-Bâtard. The derivation of their names is lost, but there is an apocryphal story from the age of the crusades, when *droit de seigneur* (or *droit de cuissage*, as it is more graphically called in Burgundy) was a recognized part of everyday life, and bastards were apparently welcome.

The wine is produced in higher quantities per acre than its neighbours and it is possible that its quality suffers as a result. Once again, the Domaine Leflaive is a significant owner.

Possible declassifications: Puligny-Montrachet *1er cru*, Puligny-Montrachet, Bourgogne and Bourgogne Grand Ordinaire.

Puligny-Montrachet
Colour: white and red
Average production: white 4,779 hl.   red 291 hl.
Minimum degree: white 11°, *1er cru* 11·5°; red 10·5°, *1er cru* 11°.
Area: 233·91 ha.

For some reason Puligny does not seem a typical Burgundian village, for the streets are broader than elsewhere and, as a result, allow the sun to come through more easily. Though its reputation rests firmly on its *grands crus*, it has a succession of *premier cru* vineyards that do it honour. Outstanding amongst these is Caillerets (part of which was formerly known as les Demoiselles) which lies on the same level of the slope as le Montrachet and just next to it. Its name reflects the pebbly nature of the soil. This vineyard and its neighbours, les Folatières, les Pucelles and Clavoillons, produce wines similar in style to the *grands crus*. Those from the vineyards at the northern end of the village resemble rather more those of Meursault. Of these vineyards perhaps les Combettes is best known, with Champ Canet close behind.

Up on the hillside, withdrawn behind a belt of trees and a quarry, lies the sleepy hamlet of Blagny, which lies half in Puligny and half in Meursault. On the Puligny side are the three *premier cru* vineyards of Sous-le-Puits, Hameau de Blagny and les Chalumeaux. The other white wines from the Puligny side can be sold as Puligny-Montrachet-Blagny.

The reputation of Puligny, like that of many other villages now known for their white wines, was founded on red: a century ago they were recognized as the equals of those of Beaune. Perhaps more than any other Côte d'Or village, Puligny suffered from the abortive 'wine explosion' of a year or two ago. A considerable proportion of the growers signed contracts with the shippers for the exclusive sale of their wine at a price of that of the free market. As this was contracting in size, because of the limited amounts still available, prices rose steeply which, in its turn, led to speculation. Thus a large proportion of the 1972 crop was sold even before it had finished fermenting in the vats.

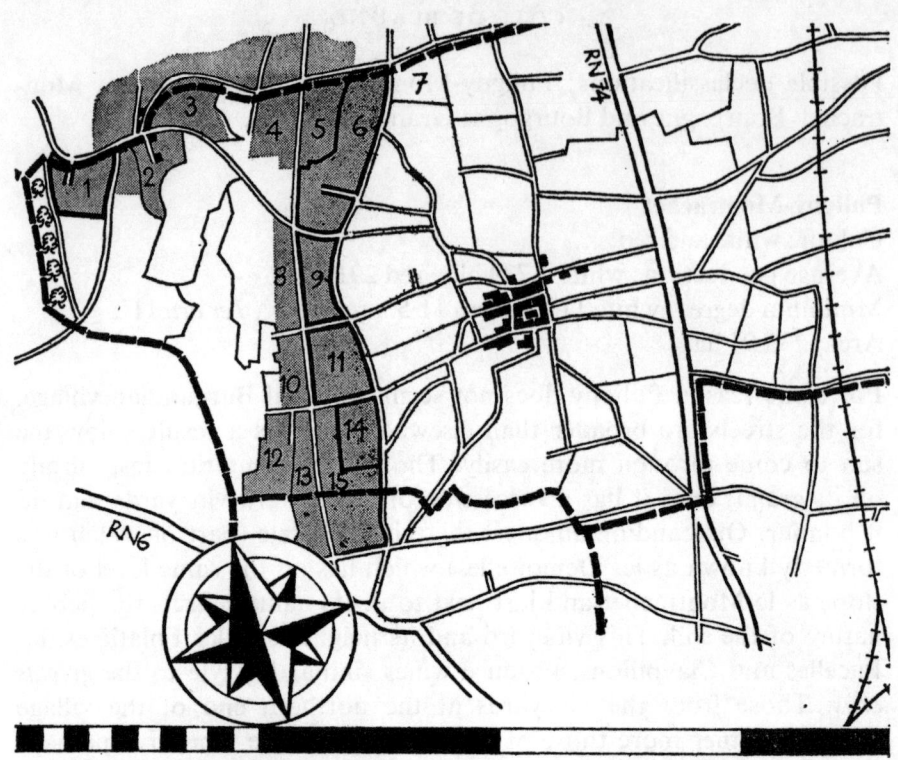

PULIGNY-MONTRACHET

Shaded areas indicate *premier cru* vineyards. The names of *grand cru* vineyards are shown in bold type in the legends

1	sous le Puits	Bâtard-Montrachet	15
2	Hameau de Blagny	**les Bienvenues-Bâtard-**	
3	les Chalumeaux	**Montrachet**	14
4	Champ Canet	le Cailleret	10
5	les Combettes	les Chalumeaux	3
6	les Referts	Champ Canet	4
7	les Charmes	les Charmes	7
8	les Folatières	**Chevalier Montrachet**	12
9	Clavoillons	Clavoillons	9
10	le Cailleret	les Combettes	5
11	les Pucelles	les Folatières	8
12	**Chevalier Montrachet**	Hameau de Blagny	2
13	**les Montrachet**	**les Montrachet**	13
14	**les Bienvenues-Bâtard-Montrachet**	les Pucelles	11
		sous le Puits	1
15	Bâtard-Montrachet	les Referts	6

It is calculated that, even now, 80 per cent of the crop of any given vintage is committed by forward contracts.

The village supports a couple of *négociants* and, among the growers regularly producing good wines, are Étienne Sauzet and the Domaine Leflaive. The Château of Puligny is the headquarters of the *domaine* of Roland Thévenin.

1er cru vineyards: le Cailleret, les Combettes, les Pucelles, les Folatières (part), Clavoillons, Champ Canet, les Chalumeaux, les Referts, Sous-le-Puits, la Garenne, Hameau de Blagny.

Possible declassification: Côte de Beaune Villages (red only), Bourgogne and Bourgogne Grand Ordinaire.

Blagny
Colour: red
Average production: 166 hl.
Minimum degree: 10·5°
Area: 14·87 ha.

One of the lesser *appellations* of Burgundy, this applies only to red wines produced in the village, from either the Puligny or the Meursault side. These, the highest vineyards on the main *côte*, produce a fine, sturdy wine which is too rarely seen. In front of the village, several acres have recently been cleared of scrub and are being planted in vines.

Possible declassification: Côte de Beaune Villages, Bourgogne and Bourgogne Grand Ordinaire.

Meursault
Colour: white and red
Average production: white 11,142 hl.   red 550 hl.
Maximum production to the acre: 293 gallons
Minimum degree: white 11°, *1er cru* 11·5°; red 10·5°, *1er cru* 11°
Area: 418·80 ha.

The village of Meursault stretches and straggles for over a mile, in a series of squares and narrow streets where every other house seems to bear the sign of a grower. The church spire dominates it all, rising

BURGUNDY

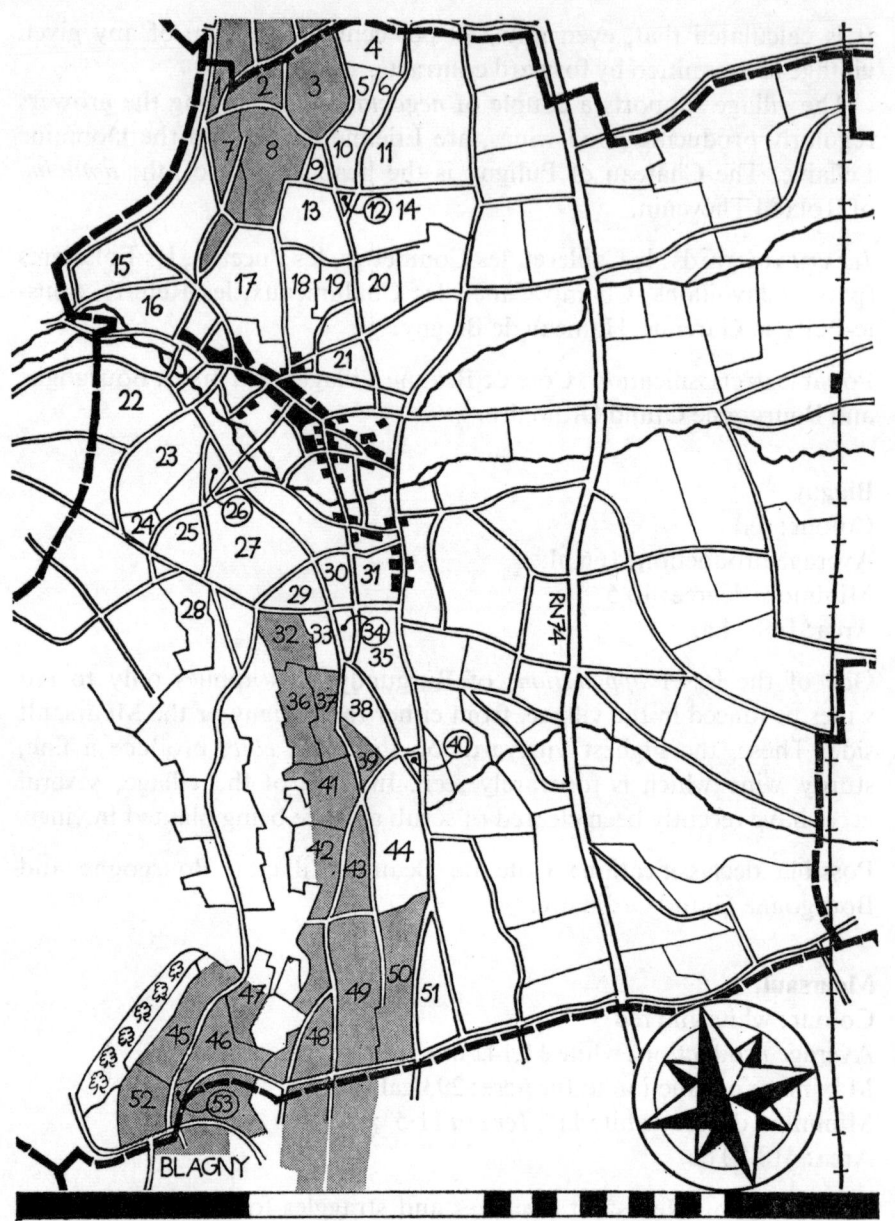

MEURSAULT

CÔTE DE BEAUNE

Shaded areas indicate *premier cru* vineyards

1	les Caillerets	en la Barre	21
2	les Santenots Blancs	la Barre Dessus	18
3	les Santenots du Milieu	sous Blagny	53
4	les Santenots Dessous	les Bouchères	36
5	en Marcausse	Buisson Certaut	40
6	les Vignes Blanches	les Caillerets	1
7	les Cras	les Casse-Têtes	29
8	les Pêtures	les Charmes Dessus	49
9	les Pêtures Vignes	les Charmes Dessous	50
10	les Criots	les Chevalières	23
11	les Durots	Clos des Mouches	12
12	Clos des Mouches	Clos de Mazeray	30
13	les Corbins	les Corbins	13
14	les Dressoles	les Cras	7
15	le Murger de Monthélie	les Criots	10
16	les Forges	le Cromin	17
17	le Cromin	les Crotots	38
18	la Barre Dessus	le Dos d'Âne	47
19	les Perchots	sous le Dos d'Âne	46
20	les Malpoiriers	les Dressoles	14
21	en la Barre	les Durots	11
22	les Meix Chavaux	les Forges	16
23	les Chevalières	les Genevrières Dessus	42
24	les Rougeots	les Genevrières Dessous	43
25	le Tesson	les Gouttes d'Or	32
26	les Petits Charrons	les Grands Charrons	27
27	les Grands Charrons	les Gruyaches	51
28	les Casse-Têtes	la Jennelotte	52
29	en Luraule	le Limosin	44
30	Clos de Mazeray	en Luraule	29
31	au Meix Gagnes	les Malpoiriers	20
32	les Gouttes d'Or	en Marcausse	5
33	les Terres Blanches	les Meix Chavaux	22
34	les Pelles Dessus	au Meix Gagnes	31
35	les Pelles Dessous	le Murger de Monthélie	15
36	les Bouchères	les Pelles Dessus	34
37	le Poruzot	les Pelles Dessous	35
38	les Crotots	les Perchots	19
39	le Poruzot Dessous	les Perrières Dessous	48
40	Buisson Certaut	la Pièce sous la Bois	45
41	le Poruzot Dessus	les Petits Charrons	26

continued on page 138

clear above the roofs for 190 feet. The Romans probably founded the village, for they had two camps in the area, protecting the road to Autun. It is likely, too, that the name has Latin roots, though it is doubtful whether the interpretation of *'muris saltus'*, or 'mouse jump' suggested by Alexis Lichine is correct.

The original *château* was built in 1337, but was demolished in 1633 on the orders of Cardinal Richelieu, after the owner, the Duke of Montmorency, had been executed. The little that remains has been incorporated in the present town-hall and post-office, and the mayor's office used to be the guardroom. There is, however, a present-day Château de Meursault which was recently bought by M. Boisseaux, the owner of Patriarche Père et Fils, from the Comte de Moucheron, who was also mayor of the village until his recent death. (Fittingly enough, the mayor's deputy, Jean Prieur, also comes from a well-known wine family.)

Half a mile or so east of the town on the main road, is the Hôpital de Meursault, which was founded as a lazar-house in 1180 by Hugues of Burgundy. When leprosy died out the building was converted into a general hospital, which also fell into disuse, and it is now used as farm out-houses.

The village's gastronomic speciality is a *terrine chaude*, or hot pâté, which is featured by one or two of the local restaurants. Perhaps better known, though, to gourmets is one of Burgundy's most prestigious banquets, La Paulée de Meursault, which takes place at midday on the day after the sale at the Hospices de Beaune. The Paulée is the traditional

42	les Genevrières Dessus	les Pêtures	8
43	les Genevrières Dessous	les Pêtures Vignes	9
44	le Limosin	le Poruzot	37
45	la Pièce sous la Bois	le Poruzot Dessus	41
46	sous le Dos d'Âne	le Poruzot Dessous	39
47	le Dos d'Âne	les Rougeots	24
48	les Perrières Dessous	les Santenots Blancs	2
49	les Charmes Dessus	les Santenots Dessous	4
50	les Charmes Dessous	les Santenots du Milieu	3
51	les Gruyaches	les Terres Blanches	33
52	la Jennelotte	le Tesson	25
53	sous Blagny	les Vignes Blanches	6

meal when the owner celebrates the end of the vintage with his workers; a vinous harvest-home supper. In 1923, the then mayor of the village, Comte Lafon, had the idea of organizing a special *paulée* for Meursault and invited thirty-five of his friends. From this small beginning sprang the famous annual function for the 300-odd guests, who are as many as can be accommodated in the largest hall in the village. The distinctive feature of this banquet is that no wines are offered, since each of the growers brings three or four of the best bottles from his cellar. This felicitous formula has led to its being described as 'the biggest bottle party in the world'. In conjunction with the lunch a prize of one hundred bottles of Meursault is presented to someone who has written an outstanding literary work on some aspect of Burgundian life.

The vineyards of Meursault stretch for two-and-a-half miles, and fall into three distinct parts. To the north of the village, bordering on Volnay, are vines producing red wines which are generally sold under the *appellation* Volnay Santenots. From the south come the succession of great white wines which have made the reputation of Meursault: les Genevrières, les Charmes, les Perrières and, only slightly behind in reputation, les Gouttes d'Or and Poruzot. Above them are the Meursault vineyards of Blagny, of which the best-known are la Pièce sous le Bois and Sous le Dos d'Âne. These last wines can be sold under the *appellation* Meursault-Blagny.

The wines of Meursault tend to be rounder than those of Puligny and Chassagne and they have an agreeably rich fullness, that makes them, for many, the most attractive white Burgundies. Their nuttiness is full of autumnal tints and they bring to mind, more than any other, vintage time and 'mellow fruitfulness'.

Two Meursault shippers have important holdings: de Moucheron sell great, full-bodied wines under the name of the Château de Meursault; and Ropiteau Frères, recently taken over jointly by Chantovent, a group with large wine interests in the Rhône Valley and the South of France, and Bordeaux shippers Dourthe Frères. Also in the village are the two important *domaines* of Poupon and Prieur, whose wines were distributed by Calvet. The Hospices de Beaune also have substantial holdings in Meursault.

1er cru vineyards: aux Perrières, les Perrières Dessus, les Perrières

BURGUNDY

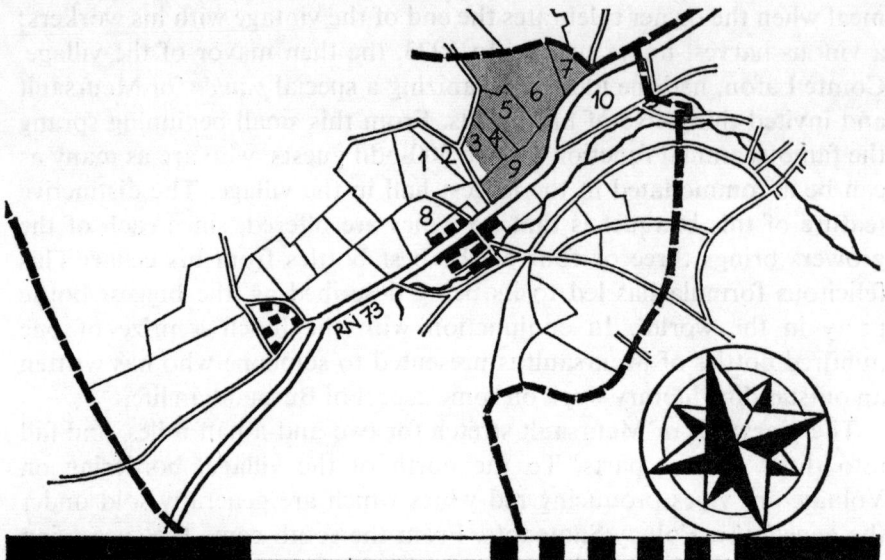

AUXEY-DURESSES

Shaded areas indicate *premier cru* vineyards

1	Climat du Val	Bas des Duresses	7
2	Clos du Val	les Bretterins	3
3	les Bretterins	la Chapelle	4
4	la Chapelle	Climat du Val	1
5	Reugne	Clos du Val	2
6	les Duresses	Derrière le Four	8
7	Bas des Duresses	les Duresses	6
8	Derrière le Four	les Ecusseaux	10
9	les Grands Champs	les Grands Champs	9
10	les Ecusseaux	Reugne	5

Dessous, les Charmes Dessus, les Charmes Dessous (part), le Poruzot Dessus, le Poruzot (part), les Bouchères, les Santenots Blancs.
Les Santenots du Milieu, les Caillerets, les Pêtures, les Cras, les Gouttes d'Or.
At Blagny: la Jennelotte, la Pièce sous le Bois, Sous le Dos d'Âne (part).

Possible declassification: Côte de Beaune Villages (red only), Bourgogne and Bourgogne Grand Ordinaire.

Auxey-Duresses
Colour: red and white
Average production: red 2,058 hl.   white 918 hl.
Minimum degree: white 11°, *1er cru* 11·5°; red 10·5°, *1er cru* 11·5°
Area: 149·98 ha.

West of Meursault, on the road to Autun, lies the village of Auxey-Duresses, whose origins date back to prehistoric times. On Mont-Mélian, overlooking the village to the south, are traces of a Stone-Age camp with two walls and a ditch. This was later occupied by the Romans and it is probable that the first vines in Burgundy were planted on these slopes.

Until 1924 Auxey was known as Auxey-le-Grand to distinguish it from its close neighbour Auxey-le-Petit, but then it added the name of its best vineyard, in imitation of its more exalted brothers on the Côte d'Or. About two-thirds of its production is of red wines and these used often to be sold under the names of Volnay and Pommard. Regrettably, though, it generally lacks the smoothness of those wines and much is declassified into Côte de Beaune Villages. The whites are round and full and resemble the lesser wines of Meursault. Roland Thévenin has an impressive property on the approach to the village; the Clos du Moulin des Moines, but perhaps its best-known label is the Cuvée Boillot of the Hospices de Beaune, produced from vines in the Duresses vineyard. The shipper, Leroy, who is a co-distributor of the wines of the Domaine de la Romanée-Conti, has cellars in Auxey, and the village restaurant, la Cremaillère, has an extensive list of local wines.

1er cru vineyards: les Duresses, les Bas des Duresses, Reugne dit la Chapelle, les Grands Champs, Climat du Val dit Clos du Val (part).
Les Ecusseaux (part), les Brettereins dits la Chapelle, les Bretterins.

Possible declassification: Côte de Beaune Villages (red only), Bourgogne and Bourgogne Grand Ordinaire.

Saint Romain
Colour: white and red
Average production: white 809 hl.   red 1,894 hl.
Minimum degree: white 11°; red 10·5°
Area: 140 ha.

More a village of the *arrière-côte* than of the main *côte* itself, Saint Romain nevertheless benefits from a full *appellation* in its own right, though it was granted this status as recently as 1967. Even after this date, though, it could not declassify its wines into Côte de Beaune Villages and it has received this right only in the past few years. In fact, only a small proportion of the wines produced within the boundaries of Saint Romain has the right to the *appellation*, and many of the vineyards to the west have the right only to the *appellation* Bourgogne.

Because the vines lie high up, the *chardonnay* is more generally planted than the *pinot*; and about twice as much white wine is produced as red. A good Saint Romain white is excellent, though rare. Local shipper Roland Thévenin is a grower to look for.

Saint Romain is one of the most attractive villages of the region; half of it is perched on a crag overlooking the rest, which is squeezed into the valley below. Its value as a stronghold was recognized so long ago that remains of Stone-Age man have been found in caves in the cliffs, together with bones of the bears and lions who were his predators and prey. Indeed, the village presents so much historical interest that for several summers past, a team from Dijon University has been conducting systematic digs and carrying out a full survey of the village to present a full picture of its development and decline over the centuries. Like much of the region, Saint Romain has suffered from the attractions of towns, and its population is barely a third of that of half a century ago.

In the higher part of the village, with a commanding view down the valley to Meursault, are the remains of a castle which used to belong to the Dukes of Burgundy, where they used to store a large proportion of their stocks of wine. They also founded there a priory, which for a time was under the control of the English Benedictine order. In the lower village is one of the few remaining cooperages in Burgundy and the stacks of maturing timber stand out in contrast against the hillside.

Possible declassification: Côte de Beaune Villages (red only), Bourgogne and Bourgogne Grand Ordinaire.

Monthélie

Colour: red (and a little white)
Average production: red 2,100 hl.   white 50 hl.
Minimum degree: red 10·5, *1er cru* 11°; white 11°, *1er cru* 11·5°
Area: 93·36 ha.

Monthélie is set on a spur, overlooking Meursault on one side and, on the other, Auxey-Duresses; its best vineyards border on those of Volnay. It relies solely on wine for its existence, for there is no spring and the soil is suitable for nothing but the vine. Indeed, the soil is so poor that, according to a local saying, even a hen would starve to death at harvest-time.

The viticultural reputation of Monthélie, like that of Auxey-Duresses, has suffered from the proximity of Pommard and Volnay and, in the past, growers did not hesitate to profit from superior *appellations* when naming their wines. Monthélie *crus* have, however, great character in their own right, and the best match those of Volnay in all but price. Realizing this, such shippers as Ropiteau and Chanson have been making efforts to popularize them, and new plantings in the valley beyond are evidence of expanding interest.

The best reputed vineyard is Champs Fulliot, which lies next to Volnay Clos des Chênes; and Ropiteau Frères are amongst the owners. On the opposite side of the village, the Hospices produce the Cuvée Lebelin from the Duresses *climat*. Another important local grower is the Suremain family, owners of the Château de Monthélie, built in 1743. The growers' association have a cellar on the main road where their wines may be tasted.

1er cru vineyards: Sur Lavelle, les Vignes Rondes, le Meix Bataille, les Riottes, la Taupine, le Clos Gauthey, le Château Gaillard, les Champs Fulliot.
Les Cas-Rougeot, les Duresses (part).

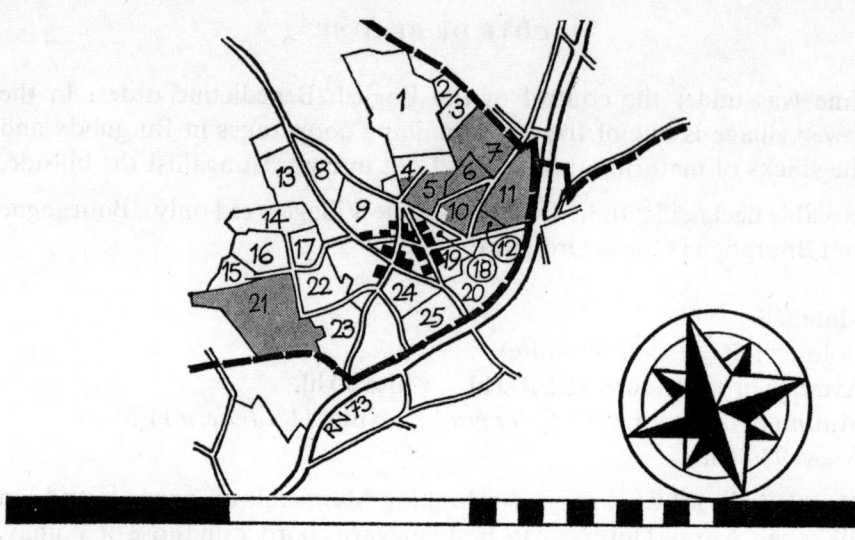

MONTHÉLIE

Shaded areas indicate *premier cru* vineyards

1	les Hauts Brins	sous le Cellier	9
2	en Pierrefitte	les Champs Fulliot	11
3	le Clou des Chênes	Château Gaillard	18
4	les Riottes	le Clos Gauthey	10
5	le Meix Bataille	le Clou des Chênes	3
6	les Vignes Rondes	les Clous	16
7	sur Lavelle	les Crays	25
8	les Longennes	les Duresses	21
9	sous le Cellier	aux Fourneaux	17
10	le Clos Gauthey	la Goulotte	15
11	les Champs Fulliot	les Hauts Brins	1
12	la Taupine	les Jouères	23
13	en Remagnin	les Longennes	8
14	les Riveaux	le Meix Bataille	5
15	la Goulotte	le Meix Garnier	19
16	les Clous	le Meix Mipont	24
17	aux Fourneaux	en Pierrefitte	2
18	Château Gaillard	en Remagnin	13
19	le Meix Garnier	les Riottes	4
20	les Toisières	les Riveaux	14
21	les Duresses	les Sous-Courts	22
22	les Sous-Courts	la Taupine	12
23	les Jouères	les Toisières	20
24	le Meix Mipont	sur Lavelle	7
25	les Crays	les Vignes Rondes	6

Possible declassification: Côte de Beaune Villages (red only), Bourgogne and Bourgogne Grand Ordinaire.

Volnay
Colour: red
Average production: 7,207 hl.
Minimum degree: 10·5°, *1er cru* 11°
Area: 214·64 ha.

Volnay is the most southerly of the four great red wine villages of the Côte de Beaune. It shares, with Pommard, Beaune and Aloxe-Corton, the distinction of not being able to declassify its wines into Côte de Beaune Villages. Hunched on the hillside above the main road, it might say with Alexander Selkirk,

> 'I am monarch of all I survey,
> My right there is none to dispute.'

Its vineyards fall away at its feet in a carpet of green, whose value is gold – as promised by the name of one of its sites, Clos de la Pousse d'Or. The reputation of Volnay is one of the most soundly established in Burgundy, though the name is probably derived from Belen, the god of springs, worshipped by the Gauls. The early Christian missionaries sent to convert them may well have preached from St Paul's text, 'Drink no longer water, but take a little wine for thy stomach's sake'. Volnay and Beaune wines were drunk at the Coronation of Philippe de Valois at Reims in 1328 and Jan Sobieski served Volnay at his coronation in Warsaw in 1673. One may assume, too, that he fortified himself with it before setting out to do battle with the Turks. When Louis XI took possession of the Duchy of Burgundy, he indemnified himself for his trouble by carrying off the entire 1477 vintage of Volnay to his castle in the Loire Valley. He may have singled out the village, since it provided the Dukes of Burgundy with a special body of cross-bowmen for the defence of the Duchy. Each May Day, they held a shooting competition: the winner had the right to be called 'King' and was excused from certain taxes for a year. Perhaps he found greater advantage in being exempted from having soldiers billeted upon him. These rights were confirmed in 1595 by the then Lord of Volnay, Henri IV. Indirectly, Henri's grandson, Louis XIV, was largely respon-

BURGUNDY

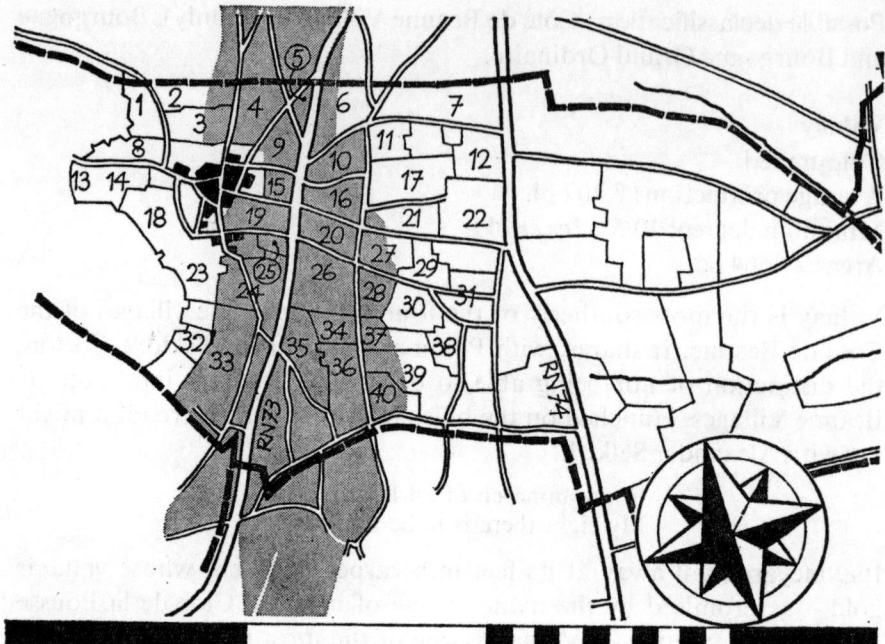

VOLNAY

Shaded areas indicate *premier cru* vineyards

1	sur Roches	les Angles	9
2	Chantin	les Aussys	37
3	Pierres Dessus	la Barre	15
4	Frémiots	Beauregard	23
5	Pointe d'Angles	les Blanches	32
6	Brouillards	la Bouchère	14
7	les Grands Poisots	Brouillards	6
8	en Vaut	en Caillerets	34
9	les Angles	Caillerets Dessus	35
10	les Mitans	Carelle Dessous	27
11	les Serpents	Carelle sous la Chapelle	20
12	les Petits Poisots	la Cave	18
13	Peux Bois	en Champans	26
14	la Bouchère	Chantin	2
15	la Barre	en Chevret	36
16	en l'Ormeau	Clos des Chênes	33
17	les Grands Champs	les Eschards	30
18	la Cave	les Famines	22

sible for spreading the reputation of the village's wines. By revoking the Edict of Nantes, he drove the solid, wealthy middle-class Protestants – including the strong community based on Volnay – out of France. Though exiled to Germany and Switzerland (and to a lesser extent England), these Burgundians retained their love for the wines of their homeland and they set up the first solid export business based neither upon the church nor the nobility.

As with most of the wines of the Côte de Beaune at that time, the wines of Volnay were not the full-bodied red wines we know today, but rather a deep pink in colour. A large proportion of white grapes were planted and the red grapes were pressed through layers of straw to prevent the colouring matter from the skins coming into contact with the must. The wine was shipped in cask and was almost always drunk in the first year of its life. It was not until the end of the eighteenth century that the *chardonnay* ceased to be the most important vine in Volnay and not unnaturally the change came in for criticism from such

19	Pousse d'Or	Frémiots	4
20	Carelle sous la Chapelle	la Gigotte	21
21	la Gigotte	les Grands Champs	17
22	les Famines	les Grands Poisots	7
23	Beauregard	les Jouères	38
24	Taille Pieds	les Lurets	39
25	en Verseuil	les Mitans	10
26	en Champans	en l'Ormeau	16
27	Carelle Dessous	les Petits Gamets	31
28	en Ronceret	les Petits Poisots	12
29	les Pluchots	Peux Bois	13
30	les Eschards	Pierres Dessus	3
31	les Petits Gamets	les Pluchots	29
32	les Blanches	Pointe d'Angles	5
33	Clos des Chênes	Pousse d'Or	19
34	en Caillerets	Robardelle	40
35	Caillerets Dessus	sur Roches	1
36	en Chevret	en Ronceret	28
37	les Aussys	les Serpents	11
38	les Jouères	Taille Pieds	24
39	les Lurets	en Vaut	8
40	Robardelle	en Verseuil	25

reactionaries as Rézerolle de Montjeu, who accepted it with bad grace, commenting that he supposed it was necessary 'because the purchaser prefers colour and keeping qualities to finesse'.

Volnay produces some of the most attractive wines of Burgundy; their delicacy is unrivalled in the Côte de Beaune. They have less colour and body than their neighbours of Pommard, but are remarkable, according to Camille Rodier, for their 'elegance, their smooth taste, their perfect balance and their extremely fine nose'. They rival in every way the Côte de Nuits wines of Chambolle-Musigny; rival them, that is, in every way but price. Some critics have said that they develop too quickly and do not have enough staying power, but a wine from a good vineyard, in a good year, should last for thirty years or more, which is enough to satisfy most consumers.

The leading vineyard is les Caillerets, which drops below the main-road. The local saying is,

> 'qui n'a pas des vignes en Cailleray,
> ne sait ce que vaut le Volnay.'

'He who has no wines in Caillerets has no idea of the worth of a Volnay.' One suggestion of the origin of the name, is that it was originally 'Caille du Roy', and it is true that the French kings had an important holding there at the beginning of the sixteenth century. Amongst present-day owners are the Marquis d'Angerville, whose *domaine* is based in the village, and Bouchard Père et Fils. The other three outstanding vineyards are Caillerets Dessus, en Champans and en Chevret; whilst Clos des Chênes, la Pousse d'Or, les Angles and Fremiet (this last adjoining the vines of Pommard) are also frequently seen. Mention should also be made of the red wine vineyards of Meursault; Santenots, Pétures and les Cras, which are sold under the *appellation* of Volnay. Amongst other local growers are the Hospices de Beaune (*cuvées* Blondeau, Gauvain, Jéhan de Massol and General Muteau), Delagrange, Domaine de la Pousse d'Or and Henri Boillot.

1er cru vineyards: En Caillerets, Caillerets Dessus, en Champans, en Chevret, Frémiots, Pousse d'Or, la Barre (or Clos de la Barre), le Clos des Chênes (part), les Angles, Pointe des Angles, les Mitans, en l'Ormeau, Taille Pieds, en Verseuil, Carelle sous la Chapelle, Ronceret, Carelle Dessous (part), Robardelle (part), les Lurets (part), les Aussys (part), les Brouillards (part), le Clos des Ducs, les Pitures Dessus, Chantin (part), les Santenots (red wines only), les Pêtures (red wines only), Village de Volnay (part).

Possible declassification: Bourgogne and Bourgogne Grand Ordinaire.

Pommard
Colour: red
Average production: 10,867 hl.
Minimum degree: 10·5°, *1er cru* 11°
Area: 339·53 ha.

Pommard has been described as the 'Grand Seigneur' of Burgundy and it is certain that its reputation is as widespread as that of any of the villages of the Côte d'Or. It may be that its name is more adaptable to the Anglo-Saxon tongue; and, certainly, nobody need fear mispronouncing it. Unfortunately, this can lead to problems, as André Simon says, talking of the wines of Beaune and Pommard: 'The fact that these two names are easily pronounced and remembered has led to much abuse. Untold quantities of red wine of doubtful origin and no uncertain nastiness have been sold under the names of Pommard and Beaune, without the names being supported on the bottle's label, by the name of any individual vineyard or that of a respectable vintner or shipper.' As a result of demand far outstripping supply, particularly to satisfy the American market – which seemed able to absorb the annual production many times over – prices for the wines of Pommard rose steeply. This in turn led to further abuse and only recently an American importer was accused of relabelling wine from Gevrey-Chambertin as Pommard, an operation that could only be profitable in a period of unbalanced prices.

Pommard is an attractive village, standing on both sides of the River Dheune, which winds down from Meloisey between meadows and allotments before it disappears under the streets of Pommard itself. The most impressive building is the Château de la Commaraine, which dates from 1180, though the attached vineyards were mentioned in records as long ago as 900 AD. The Dukes of Burgundy and the Counts of Vienne were among the owners of the *château*; and it is now the home of the well-known family of shippers, Jaboulet-Vercherre. The

BURGUNDY

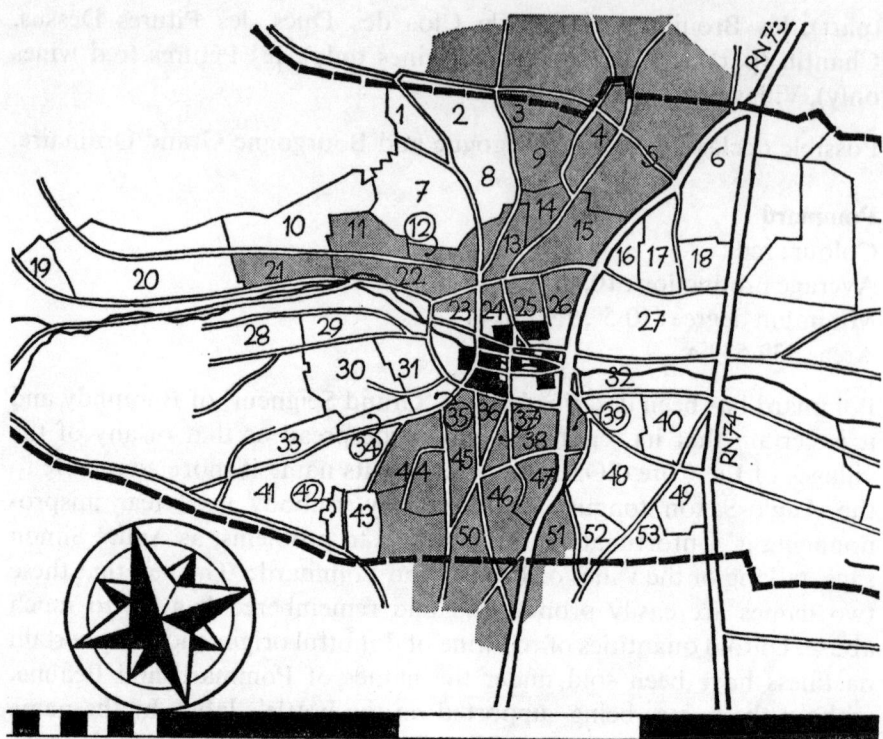

POMMARD

Shaded areas indicate *premier cru* vineyards

1	en Brescul	les Argillières	14
2	le Bas des Saucilles	les Arvelets	22
3	les Saucilles	le Bas des Saucilles	2
4	les Boucherottes	les Bertins	47
5	les Petits Épenots	les Boeufs	20
6	les Perrières	les Boucherottes	4
7	les Petits Noizons	en Brescul	1
8	les Noizons	en Challaud	32
9	les Pézerolles	la Chanière	21
10	les Vignots	les Chanlins Hauts	43
11	la Platière	les Chaponnières	36
12	les Charmots	les Charmots	12
13	les Charmots	les Charmots	13
14	les Argillières	en Chiveau	28
15	les Grands Épenots	Clos Blanc	26

CÔTE DE BEAUNE

Château de Pommard is more modern, and resembles one of the great Bordeaux châteaux of the Médoc: it belongs to M. Laplanche, a Paris surgeon. It, too, has a large vineyard but the vines, lying in the plain,

16	la Croix Blanche	Clos de la Commaraine	24
17	les Tavannes	Clos Micot	39
18	les Lavières	Clos de Verger	23
19	Plante au Chèvres	les Combes Dessus	51
20	les Boeufs	les Combes Dessous	52
21	la Chanière	la Combotte	34
22	les Arvelets	les Cras	48
23	Clos de Verger	la Croix Blanche	16
24	Clos de la Commaraine	les Croix Noires	37
25	la Refène	la Croix Planet	49
26	Clos Blanc	les Fremiers	46
27	Village de Pommard	les Grands Épenots	15
28	en Chiveau	les Jarollières	50
29	en Mareau	les Lambots	42
30	la Vache	les Lavières	18
31	Trois Follots	en Mareau	29
32	en Challaud	en Maigelot	35
33	les Vauxmuriens Bas	les Noizons	8
34	la Combotte	les Perrières	6
35	en Maigelot	les Petits Épenots	5
36	les Chaponnières	les Petits Noizons	7
37	les Croix Noires	les Pézerolles	9
38	les Poutures	Plante au Chèvres	19
39	Clos Micot	la Platière	11
40	Rue au Porc	le Poisot	53
41	les Vauxmuriens Hauts	les Poutures	38
42	les Lambots	la Refène	25
43	les Chanlins Hauts	Rue au Porc	40
44	les Rugiens Hauts	les Rugiens Bas	45
45	les Rugiens Bas	les Rugiens Hauts	44
46	les Fremiers	les Saucilles	3
47	les Bertins	les Tavannes	17
48	les Cras	Trois Follots	31
49	la Croix Planet	la Vache	30
50	les Jarollières	les Vauxmuriens Bas	33
51	les Combes Dessus	les Vauxmuriens Hauts	41
52	les Combes Dessous	les Vignots	10
53	le Poisot	Village de Pommard	27

do not produce wines rivalling those of Commaraine. It should not be thought that the economy of Pommard is tied solely to wine, for the village also supports a fire-extinguisher factory.

The vineyards of Pommard fall into two distinct groups – on either side of the village. To the south a hill rises up steeply with the best vineyards facing due east; the best-known are les Rugiens Hauts and les Rugiens Bas (if anything the latter produces better wines than the former). The name comes from the reddish nature of the soil, which has traces of iron in it, imparting a rich, full body to the wine. On the other side of the village the vineyards face more to the south and the slope is less severe. Of this group the vineyard with the highest reputation is les Épenots (or sometimes Épeneaux) which almost adjoins the vineyards of Beaune. It produces a wine with more delicacy and finesse than those of Rugiens. Other wines commonly seen from the south of the village are la Platière, les Arvelets and Clos de la Commaraine.

During the middle ages many powerful nobles and monastic and lay orders owned vineyards in Pommard. These included Dukes of Burgundy, the Abbots of Citeaux, the Order of Malta and Nicolas Rolin, the founder of the Hôtel-Dieu in Beaune. Such patronage assured widespread prestige and Henri IV and Louis XV were among the royal admirers of these wines. More surprising is that the poet Ronsard could find time amongst his eulogies of Genèvre, Helène, Astrée, Marie, Cassandre, Sinopé and a number of other sixteenth-century beauties, to sing their praises.

The Hospices de Beaune is an important owner, producing two *cuvées* from its own vines in the village, and other owners include Comte Armand and Jaboulet-Vercherre. This last company has cellars in the village, as do other shippers Louis Latour and Cruse.

1er cru vineyards: to the north of the village: les Petits Épenots (part), Clos de la Commaraine, les Épenots, Clos Blanc, les Arvelets, les Charmots, les Argillières, les Pézerolles, les Boucherottes, les Saucilles, la Refène, Clos de Verger, la Platière (part), la Chanière (part).

To the south of the village: les Rugiens Bas, les Rugiens Haut (part), les Croix Noires, les Chaponnières, les Fremiers, les Bertins, les Jarollières, les Poutures, le Clos Micot, Derrière Saint Jean, les Chanlins Bas (part), les Combes Dessus (part).

Possible declassification: Bourgogne and Bourgogne Grand Ordinaire.

Beaune
Colour: red and white
Average production: red 9,845 hl. white 476 hl.
Minimum degree: red 10·5°, *1er cru* 11°; white 11°, *1er cru* 11·5°
Area: 538·21 ha.

Undisputed capital of the wines of Burgundy and one of the leading tourist towns of France, Beaune has its feet firmly planted in the past, but its eyes look forward to the future. It is on the motorway from Paris to Lyon, Marseilles and Italy and soon other motorways under construction will skirt it on the way to Mulhouse, eastern France, Champagne and the Channel ports. Hence the mayor of Beaune has described it as 'the navel of Europe'. Plans are under way for the construction there of a *port terrestre*, which one can only imagine as a rallying point for international juggernauts. Beaune also suffers from the endemic French disease of eruptions of hideous blocks of flats on every side. Happily, though, the old town centre retains all its charm and provides an admirable backdrop for the succession of celebrations and festivals that take place there throughout the year. Of these, the most attractive are the Fêtes de la Vigne, held each September, when groups of traditional dancers and musicians from all over the world parade through the streets and afterwards perform in the open-air theatre; and the Hospices de Beaune sale, which takes place each year on the third Sunday in November.

Tightly linked with the nobility and the Church, Beaune's historic importance starts in 40 BC, when the Romans established a camp there, but it was not until the fourteenth century that its wines really became known. Amongst the vineyard owners at that time were the Cistercians, the Carthusians and the knights of Malta. Over the next 300 years, at least eleven religious orders established houses in the town and several others had cellars stocked from their holdings in the area.

The majority of the leading shippers of the wines of Burgundy are

BURGUNDY

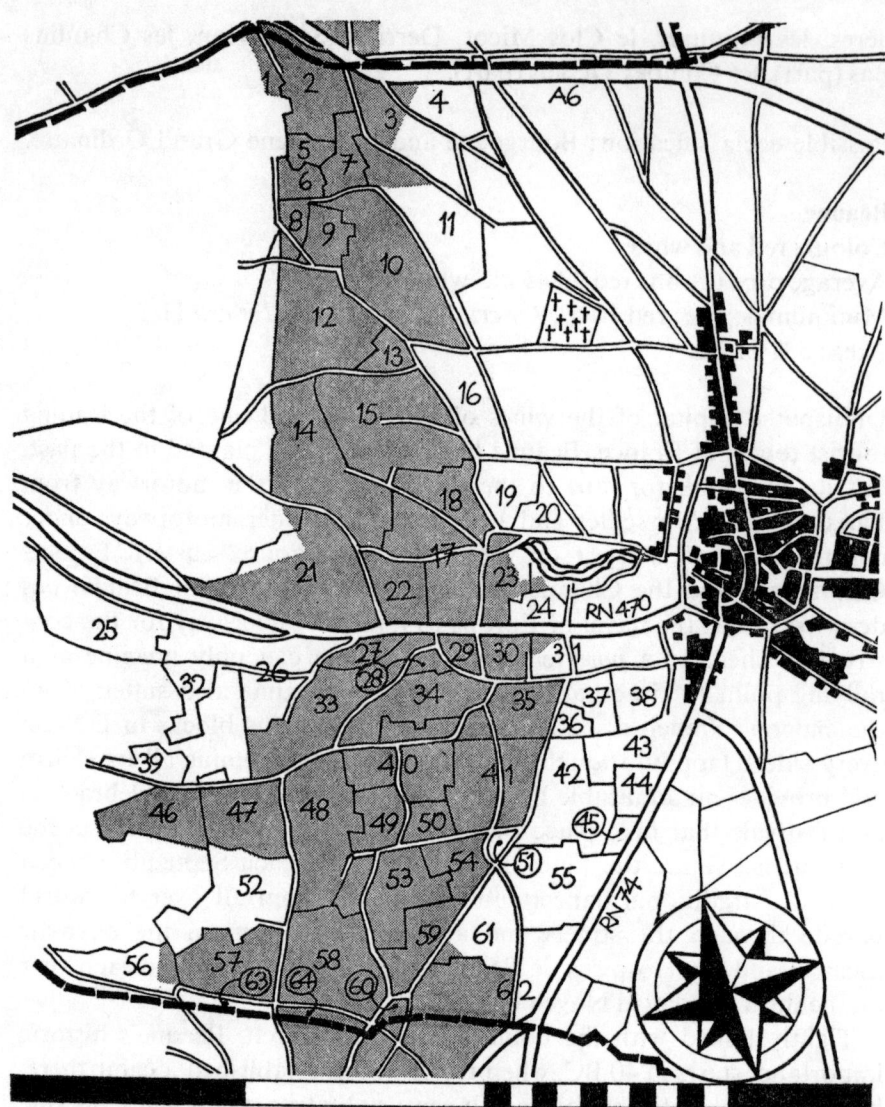

BEAUNE

Shaded areas indicate *premier cru* vineyards

1	Dessus des Marconnets	les Aigrots	47
2	les Marconnets	les Aigrots	48
3	Clos du Roi	les Avaux	34

CÔTE DE BEAUNE

4	Blanchefleurs	le Bas des Saucilles	63
5	en Orme	le Bas des Teurons	18
6	les Perrières	les Beaux Fougets	61
7	en Genet	Belissand	35
8	à l'Écu	Blanchefleurs	4
9	les Fèves	la Blanchisserie	19
10	les Cent Vignes	les Bonnes Feuves	55
11	les Chilènes	les Boucharottes	60
12	les Bressandes	les Boucherottes	59
13	les Toussaints	les Bressandes	12
14	sur les Grèves	les Cent Vignes	10
15	les Grèves	Champs Pimont	33
16	les Mariages	les Chardonnereux	43
17	les Teurons	Chaume Gaufriot	25
18	le Bas des Teurons	les Chilènes	11
19	la Blanchisserie	les Chouacheux	54
20	le Foulot	le Clos des Mouches	58
21	aux Couchéries	Clos de la Mousse	29
22	aux Cras	Clos du Roi	3
23	les Theurons	aux Couchéries	21
24	la Creusotte	aux Cras	22
25	Chaume Gaufriot	la Creusotte	24
26	Montée Rouge	Dessus des Marconnets	1
27	la Mignotte	à l'Écu	8
28	les Seurey	les Epenottes	62
29	Clos de la Mousse	les Fèves	9
30	les Reversées	le Foulot	20
31	les Sceaux	en Genet	7
32	au Renard	les Grèves	15
33	Champs Pimont	sur les Grèves	14
34	les Avaux	les Levées	45
35	Belissand	Longbois	39
36	les Paules	Lulunne	56
37	les Verrottes	les Marconnets	2
38	les Verrottes	les Mariages	16
39	Longbois	la Mignotte	27
40	les Sizies	Montagne Saint-Désiré	52
41	les Tuvillains	Montée Rouge	26
42	les Prevoles	les Montrevenots	57
43	les Chardonnereux	en Orme	5
44	les Pirottes	les Paules	36
45	les Levées	les Perrières	6

continued on page 156

now established in Beaune where they can make use of a network of cellars and towers dating back to the Middle Ages. Even these resources, however, have proved insufficient for many and rapidly expanding businesses which have had to build premises outside the traditional limits of the town walls. To the north of the town an estate for light industry has recently sprung up and at least four local wine companies have built press-houses, bottling-halls or storage cellars there. On the other side of the town Joseph Drouhin has built a large modern complex, with in front of it a tank standing in the memory of the liberation of the town during the Second World War.

The vineyards of the town of Beaune are the most extensive of the Côte d'Or and take a kidney shape on the slopes to the west of the town. The southern bulge stretches from the boundary with Pommard on the sides of Mont Saint Désiré, to the N470 which leads up to the quaintly named village of Bouze-les-Beaune and over the *arrierè-côte* to the valley of the Ouche. The northern bulge is on the steeper slopes of the Montagne de Beaune, cut off at the north by the motorway to Paris.

Though Beaune still has the largest vineyard area of the Côte, an important proportion of its vines has been lost in relatively recent years.

46	Siserpe	Pertruisots	49
47	les Aigrots	les Pirottes	44
48	les Aigrots	les Pointes de Tuvillains	51
49	Pertruisots	les Prevoles	42
50	Tiélandry	au Renard	32
51	les Pointes de Tuvillains	les Reversées	30
52	Montagne Saint-Désiré	les Saucilles	64
53	les Vignes Franches	les Sceaux	31
54	les Chouacheux	les Seurey	28
55	les Bonnes Feuves	Siserpe	46
56	Lulunne	les Sizies	40
57	les Montrevenots	les Teurons	17
58	le Clos des Mouches	les Theurons	23
59	les Boucherottes	Tiélandry	50
60	les Boucharottes	les Toussaints	13
61	les Beaux Fougets	les Tuvillains	41
62	les Epenottes	les Verrottes	37
63	le Bas des Saucilles	les Verrottes	38
64	les Saucilles	les Vignes Franches	53

CÔTE DE BEAUNE

In the nineteen-thirties, the building of an airstrip cost two vineyards, les Chilènes and la Champagne de Savigny. A new airstrip is at present being built on the plain east of the town; and, while most of the earlier airport land will be used for the building of flats, some is scheduled to be replanted in vines. The construction of the N6 motorway, too, took a slice off the *premier cru* vineyards of Beaune: les Marconnets, in particular, suffered.

The large extent of vines means that Beaune produces varying styles of wines. The greatest rival the finest of the Côte de Nuits. Maurice Marion, in his *Illustration et Défense du Vin de Beaune*, compares les Marconnets with le Chambertin, les Fèves with Richebourg (we have already seen that they used to sell at the same price a hundred years ago) and the Clos des Mouches with Chambolle-Musigny. One interesting fact not generally appreciated, is that the growers of Beaune have long concentrated on producing quality wines, rather than large quantities. Thus the Pommard vineyards, although they are only two-thirds the area of those of Beaune, regularly produce more wine. So do those of Gevrey-Chambertin, four-fifths the area of those of Beaune. This is not a recent phenomenon, as is shown by M. Marion's figures for the villages of the Côte de Beaune for the vintages of 1933, 1934 and 1935. In each case Beaune had the lowest production per acre of vines.

In all thirty-four vineyards have the right to the *appellation* Beaune *premier cru*: and each authority seems to have differing ideas as to which are outstanding: there is even no agreement on which are *têtes de cuvée*, an old classification which has largely fallen into disuse. The only vineyard on which everyone seems to agree is Fèves, which is described, with Grèves, by the American writer, Harold Grossman, as being the outstanding example of Côte de Beaune wine, noted 'for its fine, rich softness and elegance'. The majority of this vineyard belongs to the shippers Chanson Père et Fils who sell it under the name of Beaune Clos des Fèves. (In many cases, a particular owner will add *'clos'* before the vineyard name to distinguish a certain portion of the vineyard. Thus one can find Clos des Corton Faiveley, Pommard Clos des Épeneaux of the Comte Lafon, Beaune Clos des Avaux of the Hospices de Beaune, and many others. Such an *appellation* is only accepted by the authorities when it has a sound historical basis, and may not be adopted at the whim of any and every grower.) Second in reputation is the largest vineyard in Beaune Grèves, which extends over eighty acres. The growers here are numerous, but the best-known plot, Vigne de l'Enfant Jésus, is the monopoly of Bouchard Père et Fils. The vineyard immediately to its north, les Bressandes, is also highly regarded for wines with 'the perfect union of body and bouquet'. Les Marconnets is at the northern extremity of Beaune, with only the motorway separating it from the *climat* of the same name in Savigny. It has been known for over 700 years and its name is probably derived from that of the Germanic tribe, the Mercomani, who settled the area in the third century. In the southern half of the vineyards lies, amongst others, the small (eight-acre) Clos de la Mousse, which is the sole property of Bouchard Père et Fils. In 1220 Edmé de Saudon presented it to the church of Notre Dame in Beaune. A hundred and fifty years ago, it belonged to the writer Dr Morelot, who described it as having its own 'special charm and delicacy'. Further south still is the Clos des Mouches, where a fine red wine is produced, as well as an interesting white, which is the speciality of Joseph Drouhin.

Although the area of *premier cru* vineyards in Beaune is considerable, a large proportion lies in the hands of three growers: Bouchard Père et Fils, Chanson Père et Fils and the Hospices de Beaune, who each have holdings in ten or more different plots. As in some cases the holding is quite small, both Bouchard and Chanson produce 'branded' wines blended from certain of their vineyards in Beaune *1er Cru*. Bouchard's is called Beaune du Château, Chanson's Beaune Bastion, both names derived from the old cellars of the respective houses. Most shippers have some holdings in the vineyards of Beaune and the Clos des Ursules of Louis Jadot is well reputed. Other growers of note are Louis Latour, Remoissenet Père et Fils, Bouchard Ainé, Darviot, Pierre Ponnelle, Champy Père et Fils, Albert Morot and Patriarche Père et Fils.

The Hospices de Beaune
The Hospices de Beaune consists of two charitable institutions in the centre of the town, the Hôtel-Dieu and the Hospice de la Charité, which have in the past been largely financed by legacies and donations, particularly of top quality vineyards in the Côte de Beaune.

The Hôtel-Dieu was founded in 1443 by Nicolas Rolin, chancellor of Philippe le Hardi, Duke of Burgundy, and his wife Guigone de

Salins. The building was designed by the Flemish architect Jacques Wiscrere, who took as his model the hospital at Valençiennes. It was inaugurated in 1451 and has ever since been run by the same order of lay nuns, who even retained control after the French Revolution, although they were forced to give up wearing habits, and despite their numbers being depleted by arrests. The most impressive features are a cobbled courtyard, with wrought-iron well, surrounded by wooden arcades and galleries; and, immediately on the left inside the gateway, on entering, the ward – the Salle des Pôvres – with its enormous carved and gilded beams, the walls lined with beds each with a view of the altar of the chapel at the far end (in 1501 there were thirty-two beds each holding two patients) and the picture of the Last Judgement by Roger van der Weyden.

The Hospice de la Charité was founded by Antoine Rousseau and his wife Barbe Deslandes in the seventeenth century. It is now used as an old people's home. Within the welfare state, these two institutions are no longer financed solely by the proceeds from the sale of their wines. They owe their modern amenities, however, to this income and even a proportion of the cost of Beaune's new hospital came from this source. These two institutions are now under the control of the town of Beaune with the mayor as the nominal chairman of the board of directors, though the position of vice-chairman is of great importance, and traditionally goes to a member of one of the leading wine families of the town.

The vineyard estates of the Hospices spread over 131 acres of *grands* and *premiers crus* of the Côte de Beaune, ranging from Meursault to Corton. The more recent donations include holdings in Beaune from Maurice Drouhin and, in 1974, part of the Corton vineyard planted in white vines, given by Paul Chanson. The importance of these holdings is likely to increase over the coming years.

Until 1851 the Hospices wines were sold by private tender, but in that year Joseph Pétasse, a Beaune accountant, sought permission to go out and look for customers. Two years later he was able to arrange the first auction and this has since been held traditionally on the third Sunday in November, the second of the 'Trois Glorieuses'. The quantities of wine on sale naturally vary considerably with the vintage and in exceptionally bad years, such as 1968, no sale is held.

Until 1899, the names of the different wines on offer were those of the vineyard worker responsible for their production, but since then they have been named after the principal benefactors of the Hospices. (This does not necessarily mean that the benefactor gave the vineyard that produced the actual *cuvée* of wine named after him. Indeed, many of the principal legacies the Hospices have received have not been of vineyard land at all.) As the Hospices sale is the first general appearance of the wines of the new vintage, it used to be considered that the prices fetched influenced the general prices for all the wines of that vintage. Recently, however, the atmosphere has become more artificial, particularly as many of the parcels were knocked down to foreign buyers prepared to pay heavily for charity – and publicity. Thus, in the decade from 1960 to 1970, the average price for a wine from the Hospices was approximately the same as a wine from Clos de Vougeot. From 1971 to 1973, however, the premium for Hospices wine became as much as 40 per cent. The feeling now is that the Hospices Sale is an event apart from general commerce and that it should no longer be used as a weathercock of price trends in the trade.

Average prices in francs per hogshead of Hospices Cuvées during the past six years

Cuvée	1970	1971	1972	1973	1974	1975
White wines						
CORTON CHARLEMAGNE FRANÇOIS DE SALINS	10,200	20,000	35,100	30,000	30,000	50,000
MEURSAULT CHARMES de BAHEZRE DE LANLAY	4,000	5,300	8,800	7,900	4,750	6,290
MEURSAULT LOPPIN	3,200	5,000	7,500	6,800	5,100	6,500
MEURSAULT GENEVRIÈRES BAUDOT	2,600	5,800	8,230	7,600	5,150	7,880
MEURSAULT GENEVRIÈRES PHILIPPE LE BON	3,500	7,000	9,000	8,200	8,000	6,300
MEURSAULT (Poruzot) HUMBLOT	2,400	7,600	8,200	8,500	7,000	6,000
MEURSAULT (Poruzot) GOUREAU	3,400	6,700	7,500	7,100	11,100	6,400
MEURSAULT CHARMES ALBERT GRIVAULT	3,500	7,500	10,000	8,600	10,000	7,730
Red wines						
CORTON CHARLOTTE DUMAY	5,925	13,900	14,900	9,975	8,365	9,550
CORTON DOCTEUR PESTE	3,225	11,865	11,240	11,875	6,950	10,600
PERNAND (Basses-Vergelesses) RAMEAU-LAMAROSSE	3,050	6,200	7,000	8,100	5,300	5,000
SAVIGNY (Marconnets) ARTHUR GIRARD	3,230	7,065	7,760	8,150	5,150	6,650

CÔTE DE BEAUNE

Cuvée	1970	1971	1972	1973	1974	1975
SAVIGNY (Vergelesses, Gravains) FORNERET	3,600	6,300	7,665	6,825	5,295	4,690
SAVIGNY (Vergelesses, Gravains) FOUQUERAND	2,665	7,250	8,775	6,975	6,070	6,050
BEAUNE (Grèves, Aigrots) HUGUES ET LOUIS BETAULT	3,350	7,975	10,265	6,700	5,425	6,100
BEAUNE (Avaux, Boucherottes, Champimonts, Grèves) MAURICE DROUHIN	2,565	5,830	8,800	9,120	5,235	6,250
BEAUNE (Bressandes, Mignotte) DAMES HOSPITALIÈRES	6,925	11,900	10,400	11,500	8,200	7,630
BEAUNE (Centvignes, Grèves) NICOLAS ROLIN	4,900	10,950	10,440	11,225	9,600	7,950
BEAUNE (Bressandes, Mignotte) BRUNET	2,950	8,000	8,900	9,360	6,495	5,830
BEAUNE CLOS DES AVAUX	4,230	9,600	10,080	10,840	6,835	6,870
BEAUNE (Bressandes, Champimonts) GUIGONE DE SALINS	4,500	11,230	12,425	10,200	7,695	6,700
BEAUNE (Centvignes, Montremenots) ROUSSEAU-DESLANDES	3,065	8,000	9,300	7,820	6,635	6,700
POMMARD (Épenots, Rugiens) DAMES DE LA CHARITÉ	4,800	10,000	12,400	14,360	8,790	8,050
POMMARD (Épenots, Noizons) BILLARDET	3,525	9,000	12,175	8,025	7,260	10,050
VOLNAY (Champans, Taille-Pieds) BLONDEAU	3,375	8,400	9,630	6,750	5,665	7,200
VOLNAY (Village, Carelle) GENERAL MUTEAU	3,230	9,550	10,330	10,150	8,500	6,240
VOLNAY SANTENOTS GAUVAIN	3,465	7,565	8,200	9,530	6,325	6,550
VOLNAY SANTENOTS JEHAN DE MASSOL	3,800	7,100	9,030	9,230	6,295	5,250
MONTHÉLIE (Duresses) LEBELIN	2,500	6,500	7,750	7,200	4,600	4,300
AUXEY-DURESSES (Duresses) BOILLOT	2,200	7,000	8,000	6,000	5,800	4,600
Total number of hogsheads in sale	679	341	755	871	490½	267

These figures are particularly interesting because they cover the period of the wine 'boom', when speculation in fine wine was at its peak, and also the subsequent dramatic fall-away in demand. The variations in prices, particularly between 1970 and 1971, are quite striking and the relations in price between the different *cuvées* illogically erratic. Thus it is only at such a sale that one finds an Auxey-Duresses and a Pernand-Vergelesses costing more than a Beaune or a Volnay. These variations depend on a number of imponderables, such as the order in which the wines are auctioned, which changes from year to year and depends on a draw. For example the buyer of the first lot is traditionally Patriarche Père et Fils and this will fetch a good price as others are prepared to push up the bidding, knowing that they risk little. Another factor of some importance is the effect of Burgundian hospitality before the event!

How good are the wines from the Hospices? Like any others, their quality varies considerably from year to year, and even from wine to wine. They are well-vinified, but this in itself is not a reason for paying a substantial premium, for other growers take care with their wines. Another factor to be considered is that the *élévage* of the wine is the responsibility of the purchaser. He must take delivery of it – in barrel – not later than the January following the sale. What he does with it then is his responsibility and it is quite possible for two different bottles from the same *cuvée* of the same year to vary considerably. A bottle of Hospices wine will always be expensive, but some allowance should always be made for charity.

The Hospices also produce a white wine from Beaune, which is not put on sale, but is reserved for banquets, guests and – perhaps – the staff. Mention should also be made of the *marc* of the Hospices, which is auctioned in the year following its distillation. It always commands a high price and two traditional purchasers are the local liqueur houses, Vedrenne of Nuits Saint-Georges, and Labet of Beaune.

After the sale is over, the day is completed by a banquet in the bastion of the Hospices – indeed the event has become so popular that an overflow meal has been held in a spare ward of the Hôtel-Dieu. The Hospices sale provides the excuse for this great weekend, but there is no doubt that the attraction for many is the series of banquets: on Saturday evening at Clos de Vougeot, Sunday evening at Beaune and Monday lunchtime at Meursault.

The visitor to Beaune should see the admirably laid-out wine-museum, in the former palace of the Dukes of Burgundy. The many cellars in the town are worth visiting; among others those of Calvet, Patriarche and Drouhin offer hospitality all the year round. Most growers and shippers are pleased to welcome visitors, but not all have regular facilities for tourists, so it is wise, as well as courteous, to contact them in advance.

As the natural complement to wine, the food of Burgundy is seriously considered in Beaune, where there are many fine restaurants. The Hôtel de la Poste of M. Chevillot attracts gourmets from all over the world. Outside the town is Au Petit Truc, at Vignolles, where Edith Remoissenet holds court in her minute kitchen, which serves also as a bar. For value for money it must be difficult to beat Chez Nono on the Montagne de Beaune, where in summer it is most agreeable to sit out and look down over the vineyards to Beaune.

Until recently it was not easy to buy a bottle of fine Burgundy in Beaune but within the space of a year three retail shops opened in the centre of the town and now the choice is wide. The most impressive is Denis Perret, a name which groups together five of the leading shippers and growers; Joseph Drouhin, Bouchard Père et Fils, Louis Latour, Louis Jadot and Chanson Père et Fils. In all, a range of 250 different Burgundies is offered, as well as a small selection of fine wines and spirits from elsewhere. The Vinothèque, the only independent shop, offers a variety of wines from a range of shippers. The Patriarche group have a retail shop opposite the Hôtel-Dieu and the Barenzai, the latest comer, in Petit Place Carnot, offers growers' wines.

1er cru vineyards: les Marconnets, les Fèves, les Bressandes, les Grèves, les Teurons, le Clos des Mouches, Champs Pimont (or Champimonts) Clos du Roi (part), aux Couchéries (part), en l'Orme, en Genêt, les Perrières, a l'Écu, les Cent Vignes, les Toussaints, Sur les Grèves, aux Cras (or Crais), le Clos de la Mousse, les Chouacheux, les Boucherottes, les Vignes Franches, les Aigrots, Pertuisots, le Tiélandry (or Clos Landry), les Sizies, les Avaux, les Reversées, le Bas de Teurons, les Seurey, la Mignotte, Montée Rouge (part), les Montrevenots (part), les Blanchefleurs (part), les Epenottes (part). (It should be mentioned that les Teurons and les Theurons are separate vineyards and not just alternative spellings of the same name.)

Possible declassification: Côte de Beaune, Bourgogne and Bourgogne Grand Ordinaire.

Côte de Beaune
Colour: red and white
Average production: red: no recent declarations   white 118 hl.
Minimum degree: red 10·5°; white 11°
Area: the vineyards of Beaune, plus 8·94 ha.

If there are any redundant *appellations* in Burgundy, this must be one of them. It came into being in 1937, in an effort to prevent confusion in the mind of the customer, since there was a tendency for some of the villages of the Côte de Beaune to sell simply under that name. The growers of Beaune protested that such a name indicated that the wine came from the slopes above the town of Beaune itself. To protect them it was decided that a bottle from Santenay, for example, could be called Santenay, Santenay Côte de Beaune, or Côte de Beaune Villages; but that Côte de Beaune should apply solely to wines from Beaune itself. In practice four other small vineyards also have a right to the *appellation*: Dessus des Marconnets, Pierres Blanches and les Mondes Rondes, on the hillside above the vineyards of Beaune, and la Grande Châtelaine, on the right of the road leading to Bouze. As these vineyards are better exposed than some of those entitled to the Beaune *appellation* it seems logical to give them that status. The *appellation* is not commonly seen, though there is an interesting white wine under the name of Clos des Pierres Blanches, and the shipper Louis Max is the owner of la Grande Châtelaine.

Possible declassification: Bourgogne and Bourgogne Grand Ordinaire.

Chorey-les-Beaune
Colour: red and white
Average production: red 2,058 hl.   white 11 hl.
Minimum degree: red 10·5°; white 11°
Area: 121·57 ha.

Chorey, whose vineyards lie in the plain, makes no claim to making distinguished wines and the majority of them are blended off into Côte de Beaune Villages. Even the growers themselves do not impute greatness to their products, but describe them as best drunk young and suitable for the 'wine-lover seeking a good wine at a reasonable price, for are not its finesse on the nose and its elegance on the palate the true charms of a Burgundy?' One bonus with the wines of Chorey is that in drinking them, one is protected by the village's generous allocation of four patron saints – Luke, Hubert, Vernier and Vincent.

Among the few growers whose wines are found in bottle are Jacques Germain of the fourteenth-century Château de Chorey, Tollot-Beaut, and Voarick, who also own the Baleuzai restaurant on the main Dijon road.

Possible declassification: Côte de Beaune Villages (red only), Bourgogne and Bourgogne Grand Ordinaire.

Savigny
Colour: red and white
Average production: red 8,180 hl.   white 317 hl.
Minimum degree: red 10·5°, *1er cru* 11°; white 11°, *1er cru* 11·5°
Area: 378·47 ha.

Although the vineyard area of Savigny is third in size on the Côte de Beaune – after those of Beaune and Pommard – its wines do not enjoy quite the same reputation. In some ways this is difficult to understand for some truly outstanding bottles are produced there. In earlier times they were not wanting for admirers and the last Duke of Burgundy, having been well entertained by the Marquis de Migieu, announced that, on account of the superlative quality of his wines, his host was worthy of being raised to the ranks of the immortals. Perhaps, though, like many of the best after-dinner speeches, the phrases had been rehearsed in advance.

Though Savigny's reputation may have fallen slightly, it was for long considered to be the most advanced viticultural village in Burgundy, for there vines were first planted in rows, and the *taille à cordon* Guyot was first introduced. To maintain, and increase, the reputation of the wines of the village a Bacchic brotherhood was founded in 1960. The Cousinerie de Bourgogne has as its first tenet that basic principle of Burgundian hospitality – the first necessity is a bottle in front of you.

Savigny's vineyards lie on both sides of the River Rhoin; some of those to the south, on the boundaries of Beaune, have the peculiar north-east exposure but, surprisingly enough, some of the greatest wines of the village come from those vines. Savigny Marconnets differs considerably from its neighbour of the same name in Beaune, for its slope is at a slightly – but significantly – different angle. Perhaps the most attractive wine from this group of vineyards is Dominode, whose name indicates its former ecclesiastical ownership. It is typical of those wines of Savigny described as having 'fire and strength'. Amongst the owners

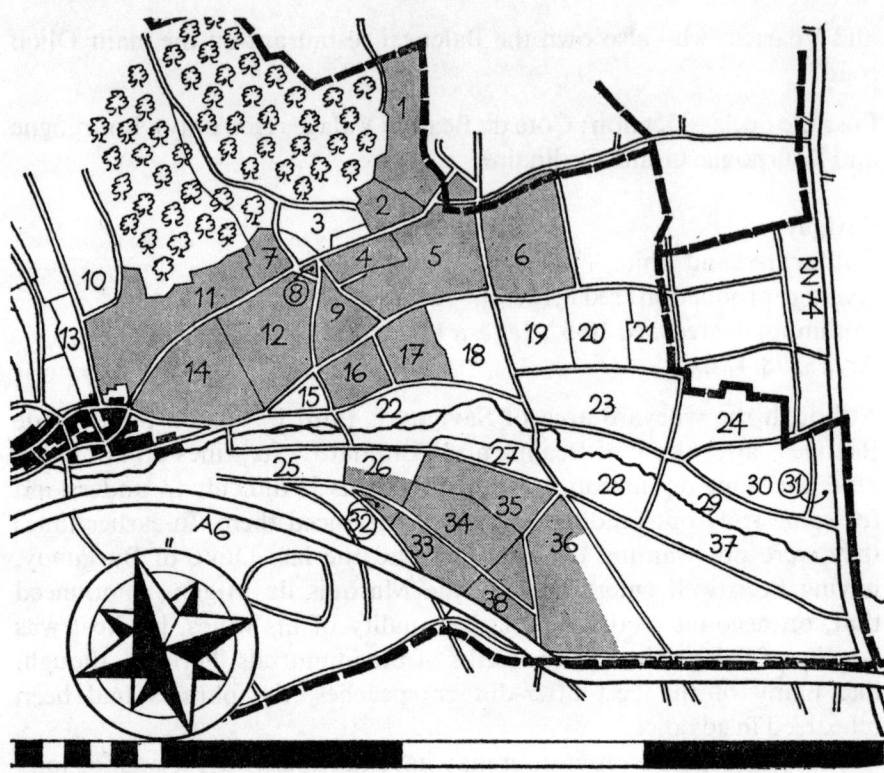

SAVIGNY-LES-BEAUNE

Shaded areas indicate *premier cru* vineyards

1	aux Vergelesses	les Bas Liards	22
2	les Talmettes	les Bourgeots	28
3	les Godeaux	aux Champs Chardons	20
4	les Charmières	aux Champs des Pruniers	21
5	les Lavières	les Charmières	4
6	aux Fourneaux	aux Clous	14
7	Ruichottes	les Conardises	18
8	Petits Godeaux	Dessus de Montchenevoy	10
9	aux Gravains	la Dominode	34
10	Dessus de Montchenevoy	aux Fourches	19
11	aux Guettes	aux Fourneaux	6
12	aux Serpentières	les Godeaux	3
13	Guelottes	aux Grands Liards	17
14	aux Clous	Grande Picotins	24

there are Chanson Père et Fils, Champy Père et Fils and Joseph Drouhin. Another vineyard in this group is Redrescul and the label of the local shippers, Doudet-Naudin, who are owners there, shows a bare-bottomed boy similar to the German Krover Nacktarsch. Of the northern group of vineyards, les Vergelesses probably produces the best wine, though the Lavières of Bouchard Père et Fils is also excellent.

Though the village of Savigny is not very large it is easy to lose one's way for the narrow streets twist and turn. The most impressive building is the *château*, originally built in 1340, but largely destroyed on the instructions of Louis XI, because its owner had supported the wrong side in the struggle between the Burgundians and the French. It was rebuilt in 1672 and has recently been purchased by an English company, who, it is said, intend to turn it into an hotel. Fortunately their subsequent liquidation has postponed development.

15	aux Pointes	aux Gravains	9
16	aux Petits Liards	Guelottes	13
17	aux Grands Liards	aux Guettes	11
18	les Conardises	aux Jarrons	33
19	aux Fourches	les Lavières	5
20	aux Champs Chardons	aux Marconnets	38
21	aux Champs des Pruniers	Moutier Amet	27
22	les Bas Liards	les Narbantons	35
23	les Pimentiers	Petits Godeaux	8
24	Grande Picotins	aux Petits Liards	16
25	les Saucourts	Petits Picotins	30
26	les Rouvrettes	les Peuillets	36
27	Moutier Amet	les Pimentiers	23
28	les Bourgeots	les Planchots de la Champagne	37
29	les Planchots du Nord	les Planchots du Nord	29
30	Petites Picotins	aux Pointes	15
31	les Ratausses	les Ratausses	31
32	en Redrescul	en Redrescul	32
33	aux Jarrons	les Rouvrettes	26
34	la Dominode	Ruichottes	7
35	les Narbantons	les Saucourts	25
36	les Peuillets	aux Serpentières	12
37	les Planchots de la Champagne	les Talmettes	2
38	aux Marconnets	aux Vergelesses	1

Savigny holds an important position in the commerce of the wines of Burgundy, for it is the base of three important shippers including the Swiss-owned company of Henri de Villamont, which purchased the extensive and remarkable cellar of old wines, known as the Dr Barolet collection. The village is also a centre of Bourgogne Mousseux production.

To eat in the village, one cannot do better than go to the Ouvrée, a restaurant belonging to the local councillor, Monsieur Petitjean, who is also an important vineyard owner. (An *ouvrée* is an old Burgundian measurement, still used locally when talking of land, particularly vineyard land. It is the equivalent of 512 square yards or approximately a tenth of an acre.)

1er cru vineyards: aux Vergelesses, aux Vergelesses dit Bataillière, les Marconnets, la Dominode, les Jarrons, Basses-Vergelesses, les Lavières, aux Gravains, les Peuillets (part), aux Guettes (part), les Talmettes, les Charmières, aux Fourneaux (part), aux Clous (part), aux Serpentières (part), les Narbantons, les Hauts Marconnets, les Hauts Jarrons, Redrescul (part), les Rouvrettes (part), aux Grands Liards (part), aux Petits Liards (part), Petits Godeaux (part).

Possible declassification: Côte de Beaune Villages (red only), Bourgogne and Bourgogne Grand Ordinaire.

Pernand-Vergelesses
Colour: red and white
Average production: red 1,751 hl.   white 257 hl.
Minimum degree: red 10·5°, *1er cru* 11°; white 11°, *1er cru* 11·5°
Area: 143·31 ha.

The village of Pernand lies back from the main run of Côte de Beaune villages at the junction of a Y; to the west its vineyards are on the slope leading up to the Bois de Noël; on the east, on the slope leading up to the Bois de Corton and – directly behind – its own hill, surmounted by a shrine in a clearing in the wood. With little passing traffic, it remains calm and tranquil, though it hardly deserves Alexis Lichine's description as 'the most primitive of all the hamlets along the Côte d'Or'.

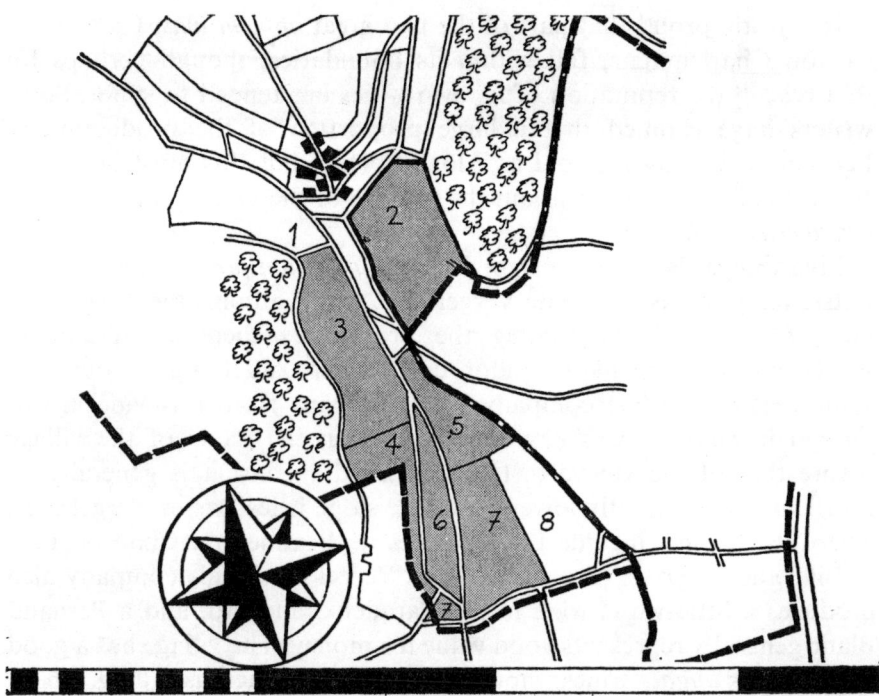

PERNAND-VERGELESSES

Shaded areas indicate *premier cru* vineyards, except those bordered with a heavy boundary line, which are *grand cru*. The names of *grand cru* vineyards are shown in bold type in the legends

1	sous le Bois de Noël et Belles Filles	les Basses Vergelesses	7
2	**en Charlemagne**	sous le Bois de Noël et Belles Filles	1
3	en Caradeux	les Boutières	8
4	Creux de la Net	en Caradeux	3
5	les Fichots	**en Charlemagne**	2
6	Îles des Hauts Vergelesses	Creux de la Net	4
7	les Basses Vergelesses	les Fichots	5
8	les Boutières	Îles des Hauts Vergelesses	6

It is justly proud that part of the two great *appellations*, Corton and Corton Charlemagne, fall within its boundaries, though perhaps for that reason the reputation of its own wines has tended to suffer. Some writers have claimed that a large proportion of the production of Pernand-Vergelesses is sold as Aloxe-Corton, but this must be due to confusion in their minds about the portion of the village entitled to the *grand cru appellations*.

Five vineyards have the right to the *appellation premier cru*, but the outstanding one is the Île de Vergelesses, which adjoins the Vergelesses vineyard of Savigny. Among the proprietors there are Dubreuil-Fontaine, the Domaine Chandon de Briailles, and Louis Latour. For some reason this last company labels its wine from this vineyard as though it were a *grand cru*, that is without the name of the village before that of the vineyard. (Notwithstanding this, it is generally an excellent wine.) Slightly lower down the slope is les Basses Vergelesses, where the owners include the Hospices de Beaune and Chanson Père et Fils; the latter sell the wine as Les Vergelesses. This company also produces a little white wine in the Caradeux vineyard, and a Pernand Blanc generally represents good value for money. The village has a good name for its *aligoté* wines, though production of them is falling. Those of Dubreuil-Fontaine enjoy a particularly high reputation.

The red wines of Pernand, though somewhat overshadowed by their neighbours from Aloxe-Corton, are rather hard at first, but make excellent *vins de garde*. A Les Vergelesses of the 1904 vintage, tasted in 1974, proved to be enjoyable, rather than simply interesting, which is often the case with wines of such an age. It would have put to shame many much younger wines from villages with a greater reputation.

The mayor of the village is M. Dubreuil who, like his colleague at Savigny is both vineyard-owner and restaurateur. His restaurant, Le Charlemagne, maintains sound standards and reasonable prices.

1er cru vineyards: Îles des Vergelesses, les Basses Vergelesses, Creux de la Net (part), les Fichots, en Caradeux (part).

Possible declassification: Côte de Beaune Villages (red only), Bourgogne and Bourgogne Grand Ordinaire.

Corton

Colour: red and white
Average production: red 2,574 hl.   white 61 hl.
Minimum degree: red 11·5°; white 12°

The *cru* of Corton is complex for it is not one single vineyard, but several; one of which – to increase the confusion – is called le Corton. All these vineyards have the right to call their wine either Corton – alone – or Corton plus the name of the *climat*. Thus Corton-Bressandes could equally be sold as Corton, or it might be blended with a Corton-Clos du Roi and still sold as Corton. In any case, any wine with Corton at the beginning of its name should be outstanding and has *grand cru* classification. In no case should it be confused with a wine whose name begins with Aloxe-Corton. For whilst Corton-Maréchaudes is a *grand cru*, Aloxe-Corton-Maréchaudes is just a *premier cru* of Aloxe-Corton. The vineyards of Corton are not only on the territory of Aloxe-Corton, they also overlap into Ladoix-Serrigny and Pernand-Vergelesses.

The reputation of the wines of Corton is almost as old as that of the wines of Burgundy and one interpretation of the name is '*curtis d'Othon*' – *domaine* of Othon (one of the less successful Roman emperors of the first century). It is more certain that Charlemagne held land in Pernand and Aloxe, and that later owners included the Abbots of Citeaux, the Dukes of Burgundy, Charlotte Dumay (who left her land to the Hospice in 1584) and the Kings of France, whose tenure 400 years ago is still remembered in Corton Clos du Roi. It may be that they were attracted by the local proverb which says that 'Give a dumb man a glass of old Corton and he will chatter like a magpie'. On the strength of this, Pierre Forgeot suggests that it is the ideal wine for diplomats, barristers and politicians.

Voltaire was a devoted admirer of Corton: indeed as he grew older he could not do without it – though he philosophically plied his guests with Beaujolais. Professor Saintsbury's last purchase of Burgundy was 'a comparatively humble Corton of 1881, bought when it was nineteen years old for sixty-eight shillings a dozen, and quite cheap at its price.'

The slowest developing wine of the Côte de Beaune, Corton, given the opportunity to mature fully, turns into an outstanding bottle: but, as Hilaire Belloc says, 'As for Corton, if it is soft, then it is good, if it is not, it is not.' The character of the wine can vary considerably, due to the large extent of the vineyards entitled to the name, and to the fact that they face in different directions and are at different levels on the slope.

There are a myriad of owners, but by far the most important is the shipping company of Louis Latour. They sell much of their production under the label Corton-Grancey, which, confusingly, is not a vineyard name at all, but comes from their property at Aloxe, the Château de Grancey. All wines which bear this label must come from their own *domaine* and, of course, from vines having the right to the *appellation* Corton. The *château*, built in 1749, faces their *cuvérie* and cellars, dug into the face of one of the finest wine-hillsides in the world.

About a twentieth part of the production of Corton is white wine, which is similar to that of Corton-Charlemagne. The Hospices de Beaune is one of the producers of white Corton. Stephen Gwynn claimed that a white Corton of the 1923 vintage which he purchased tasted more like a hock than any French wine. This sounds extraordinary, unless it was bottled by an unreliable London shipper.

Vineyards having the right to the *appellation* Corton:
In Ladoix-Serrigny: les Vergennes (part), le Rognet et Corton (part).
In Aloxe-Corton: le Corton, le Clos du Roi, les Renardes, les Bressandes, les Maréchaudes (part), en Pauland (part), les Chaumes, la Vigne au Saint, les Meix Lallemand, les Meix (part), les Combes (part), le Charlemagne (part), les Pougets (part), les Languettes (part), les Chaumes de la Voirosse, les Frêtres, les Perrières, les Grèves.
In Pernand-Vergelesses: le Charlemagne (part) (red wines only).

Possible declassification: Aloxe-Corton *1er cru*, Aloxe-Corton, Bourgogne and Bourgogne Grand Ordinaire.

Corton-Charlemagne
Colour: white
Average production: 960 hl.
Minimum degree: 12°
Area: Not finalized

The vines producing Corton-Charlemagne lie in a band above those of Corton, curling round the hillside, just below the wooded summit. Confusingly enough, Corton-Charlemagne can be produced from part of the plot called Corton, while Corton can also come from part of the plot called Charlemagne. The chalky soil produces a white Burgundy second only to Le Montrachet. With its flinty flavour and spicy nose, Corton Charlemagne can be pleasant when drunk young, but the fine vintages may not reveal their full richness for eight or ten years.

The popular story relates that Charlemagne used to take great pleasure in drinking wine from his vines in Corton, but as he grew older it tended to stain his snow-white beard. His wife became so ashamed of seeing him like this, that she nagged him continually, which got on his nerves. Finally he decided the best way to disguise the fact that he drank was to plant vines which produced white wines. History does not relate, even apocryphally, whether the stratagem was successful. If the story is true, though, Charlemagne's wife must be given credit for the persistence that prompted one of the world's great wines.

For many years a proportion of *aligoté* grapes was permitted to be planted, but this was finally forbidden in 1938 and they had to be replaced by 1948.

Again Louis Latour is the leading grower and the other fine Beaune shipping-house of Louis Jadot also has a holding.

Vineyards having the right to the *appellation* Corton Charlemagne:
In Ladoix-Serrigny: le Rognet et Corton (part).
In Aloxe-Corton: le Corton (part), le Charlemagne (part), les Pougets (part).
In Pernand Vergelesses: le Charlemagne.

Possible declassification: as for Corton.

Charlemagne

Colour: white
Average production: no recent declarations
Minimum degree: 12°

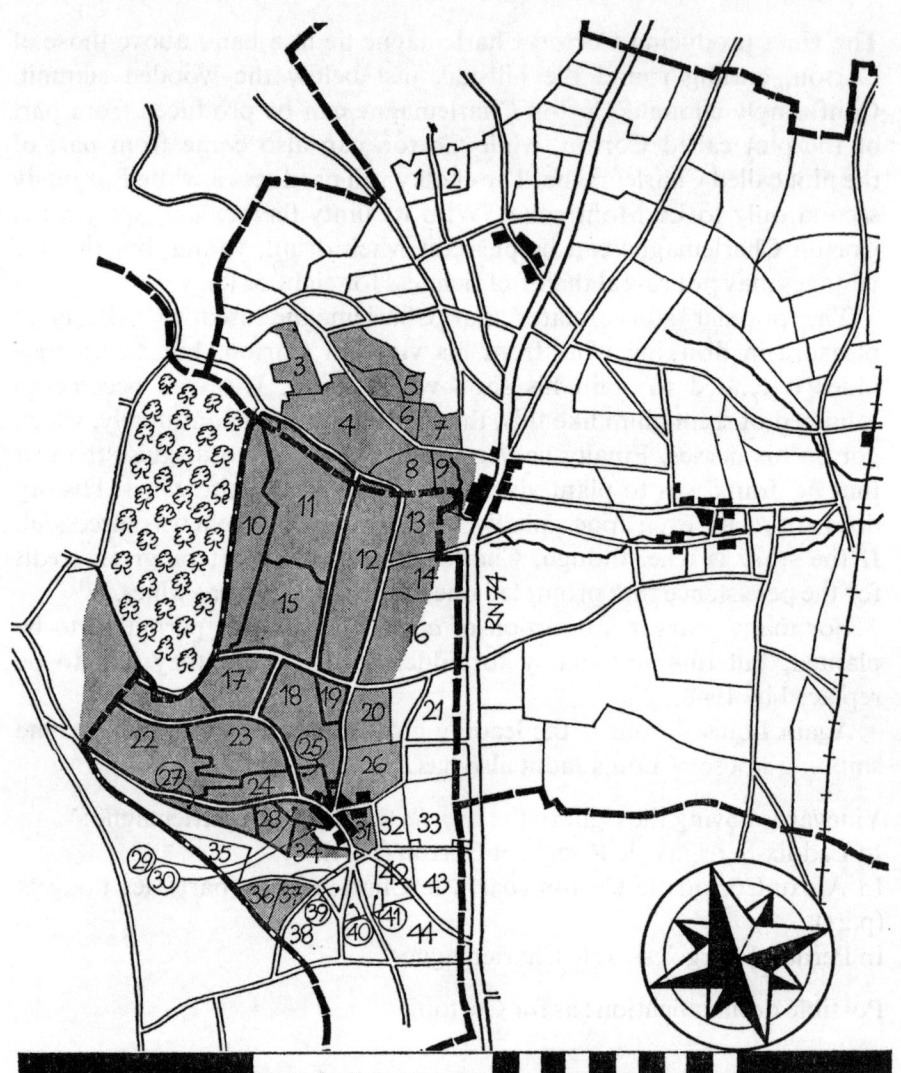

LADOIX-SERRIGNY and ALOXE-CORTON

Shaded areas indicate *premier cru* vineyards, except those bordered with a heavy boundary line, which are *grand cru*. The names of *grand cru* vineyards are shown in bold type in the legends, asterisks indicating that only a part of the vineyard is *grand cru*

	LADOIX-SERRIGNY			LADOIX-SERRIGNY	
1	les Buis			Basses Mourettes	3
2	le Clou d'Orge			les Buis	1
3	Basses Mourettes			le Clou d'Orge	2
4	**le Rognet et Corton**			la Coutière	7
5	Petites Lolières			les Grandes Lolières	6
6	les Grandes Lolières			Petites Lolières	5
7	la Coutière			**le Rognet et Corton**	4
8	**les Vergennes***			la Toppe-au-Vert	9
9	la Toppe-au-Vert			**les Vergennes***	8
	ALOXE-CORTON			**ALOXE-CORTON**	
10	**le Corton**			la Boulotte	32
11	**les Renardes**			**les Bressandes**	12
12	**les Bressandes**			les Brunettes	42
13	les Maréchaudes			les Caillettes	33
14	**en Pauland**			les Chaillots	20
15	**le Clos du Roi**			**le Charlemagne**	22
16	les Valozières			**les Chaumes**	27
17	**les Languettes**			**les Chaumes de la Voirosse**	24
18	**les Perrières**			les Citernes	38
19	**les Grèves**			**le Clos du Roi**	15
20	les Chaillots			les Combes	34
21	les Morais			**le Corton**	10
22	**le Charlemagne**			les Cras	43
23	**les Pougets**			les Cras Poussuets	44
24	**les Chaumes de la Voirosse**			les Fournières	26
25	**les Piètres**			les Genevrières	39
26	**les Fournières**			**les Grèves**	19
27	**les Chaumes**			les Guérets	36
28	**Vigne au Saint-Meix**			**les Languettes**	17
29	**les Meix Lallemand**			les Maréchaudes	13
30	**les Meix**			**les Meix**	30
31	les Meix			les Meix	31
32	la Boulotte			**les Meix Lallemand**	29
33	les Caillettes			les Morais	21
34	les Combes			**en Pauland**	14
35	la Toppe Martenet			**les Perrières**	18
36	les Guérets			**les Piètres**	25
37	les Vercots			les Planchots	41
38	les Citernes			**les Pougets**	23
39	les Genevrières			**les Renardes**	11
40	Suchot			Suchot	40
41	les Planchots			la Toppe Martenet	35
42	les Brunettes			les Valozières	16
43	les Cras			les Vercots	37
44	les Cras Poussuets			**Vigne au Saint-Meix**	28

This is an *appellation* which has fallen completely out of use and no declarations of crop under this name have been made for several years. The area of production is the same as for Corton-Charlemagne, excluding those parts of the vineyard on Ladoix-Serrigny. If this foreshadows the disappearance of other redundant *appellations* in Burgundy, it is welcome news, for the multiplicity of small *appellations* in the region can only cause confusion in the mind of the consumer.

Possible declassification: as for Corton.

Aloxe-Corton
Colour: almost exclusively red
Average production: red 4,289 hl.   white 44 hl.
Minimum degree: red 10·5°, *1er cru* 11°; white 11°, *1er* cru 11·5°

The reputation of the village wines of Aloxe-Corton has been rather overwhelmed by those of the *grand crus* of the neighbourhood, whose total output is almost as great as that of the more ordinary wines, even allowing for the fact that the better vineyards of Ladoix-Serrigny have the right to the *appellation* Aloxe-Corton *premier cru*. Nevertheless these *climats* have qualities in their own right and their perfect exposure to the south-east makes for full-bodied wines which often appear retarded in development. This led Dr Morelot to suggest that their hardness, when young, may come as a shock to the uninitiated.

Surprisingly, for a village with wines of such quality, Aloxe has almost no history and is the most modern of the villages of the Côte. In earlier days, it used to be a dependency firstly of Échevronne and then of Pernand. Among the more recent constructions in the village are the cellars and bottling-hall of the Reine-Pédauque.

1er cru vineyards: In Aloxe-Corton: les Valozières (part), les Chaillots (part), les Meix (part), les Fournières, les Maréchaudes (part), en Pauland (part), les Guérets.
In Ladoix-Serrigny: la Maréchaude, la Toppe-au-Vert, la Coutière, les Grandes Lolières, les Petites Lolières, Basses Mourettes.

Possible declassification: Bourgogne and Bourgogne Grand Ordinaire.

Ladoix-Serrigny
Colour: red and white
Average production: red 1,360 hl.   white 60 hl.
Minimum degree: red 10·5°; white 11°
Area: 135·59 ha.

Ladoix, the viticultural half of the twin villages Ladoix-Serrigny, stands astride the N74, the main road from Beaune to Dijon. The width of the main street baits an inviting trap for the unwary motorist unaware of the radar machine which so frequently lies in wait there. Serrigny is some two miles or so away to the east on the plain, near the railway line.

On the right-hand side of the road from Beaune to the village, is the chapel of Notre Dame du Chemin, begun in the eleventh-century but not finished for almost 400 years when Duc Philippe le Bon financed its completion. By the beginning of this century, it had become a private house and has been restored to its religious purpose only during the past few years.

So much of its wine has the right to the *grand* and *premier cru appellations* of Aloxe-Corton, that the amount left to be sold as Ladoix-Serrigny is unimportant. In practice, much of this is declassified into Côte de Beaune Villages.

After the village of Ladoix, there comes a physical break in the hill-line and the three picturesquely named vineyards of les Madones, la Mort and Vigne Adam – all entitled to the *appellation* Ladoix-Serrigny – mark the northern end of the Côte de Beaune.

Possible declassification: Côte de Beaune Villages (red only), Bourgogne and Bourgogne Grand Ordinaire.

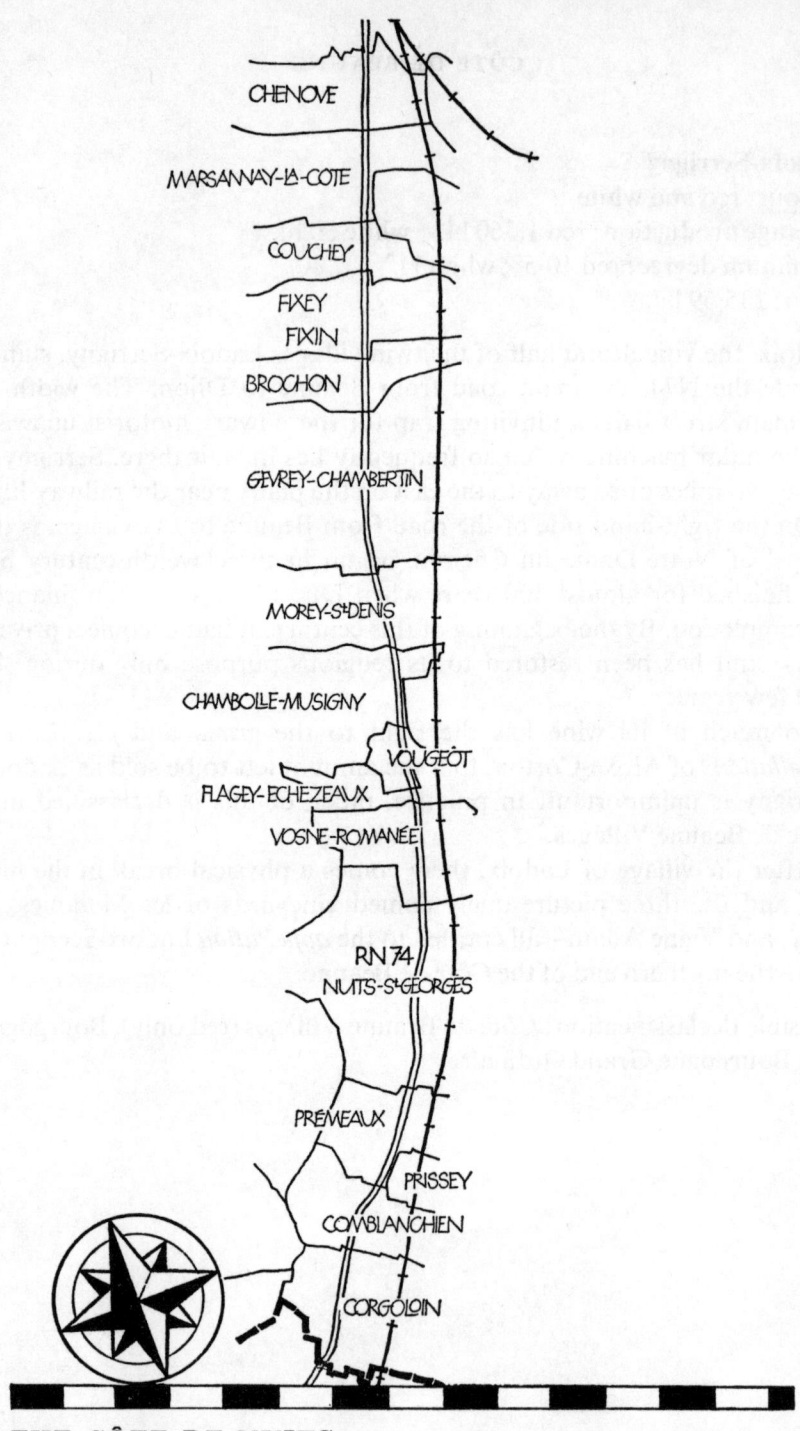

THE CÔTE DE NUITS

10 CÔTE DE NUITS

The 'regal reds' is Alexis Lichine's term for the wines of the Côte de Nuits, for this short and narrow stretch of vines produces most of the finest red wines of Burgundy, the essence of Burgundy itself. Regal may be the word, for in 1888 a local wine-lover drew up a list of the 'royal family' of Burgundy, with Chambertin as the King and Romanée-Conti as the Queen. The nearest relation from the Côte de Beaune was le Corton – no more than royal standard-bearer – and well down the list of heirs to the throne. An alternative *Almanach de Gotha*, rather less chauvinistic, accepted Le Corton and Le Montrachet as 'royal children'.

However regal the family may be, it remains close to the soil and, while the Burgundian respects his great wines, they hold no mystery for him. Some of the local restaurants seduce the tourist by serving even the most ordinary wines in a glass resembling an elephant's hip-bath; and the foreign wine-buff may bring out his thermometer and decanter; but these are not for the Burgundian. He makes his wine to be appreciated, talked about, and enjoyed, but not to be exploited. For him there can be as much to discuss in a humble *passetoutgrain* as in the most royal Chambertin.

The production of the Côte de Nuits is much smaller than that of the Côte de Beaune; the strip of vineyards is narrower, and often the slope is steeper. In many cases towards the crest of the hill the soil has become so eroded that vines are no longer planted there. Recently, though – particularly at Nuits Saint-Georges – there has been some replanting at this level after the bare rock was crushed and topped with earth from the lower reaches. Because of the poverty of the soil, the *grand cru* vineyards are often well down the slope, where a slight fold in the ground has allowed earth to gather, giving a richer base on which the vine can thrive. With only a handful of exceptions only red wine is produced, and it is here that the *pinot noir* has its greatest successes.

Côte de Nuits Villages
Colour: almost entirely red
Average production: red 5,013 hl.   white 6 hl.
Minimum degree: red 10·5°; white 11°
Villages having right to the *appellation:* Fixin, Brochon (part), Prissey, Comblanchien, Corgoloin, Marsannay-la-Côte and Couchey
Total area: 320·87 ha. (subject to final confirmation)

The outsider could well believe that the *appellations* of Burgundy were designed specifically to confuse, for it must seem logical that the legislation for Côte de Nuits Villages would parallel that of Côte de Beaune Villages. Once again the power of the winegrower took over, with the result that there is little resemblance, or even coherence. Of the villages entitled to the *appellation*, one – Fixin – has a full *appellation* in its own right (like all the villages of Côte de Beaune Villages); another – Marsannay – has its own *appellation* for its rosé wines; while for all the others, Côte de Nuits Villages is the highest *appellation*. Even more oddly, the white wines (in an area preponderantly red) can be called Côte de Nuits Villages, yet there is no such thing as a white Côte de Beaune Villages.

Of the seven villages, four – Marsannay, Couchey, Fixin and Brochon – are at the northern extremity of the Côte, whilst Prissey (which seems recently to have amalgamated with Prémeaux), Comblanchien and Corgoloin are at the southern end. The wines do not have to be blended and one occasionally comes across single vineyard names. Such a one is the Clos des Langres, the southernmost vineyard of the Côte de Nuits which, until the Revolution, belonged to the Bishops of Langres. They were the most important vineyard-owners, with the Abbey of Citeaux, on the Côte de Nuits. Fortunately the vineyards of Burgundy came within their diocese, for the bishopric of Dijon is of comparatively recent foundation. The vineyard now belongs to La Reine Pédauque.

According to Camille Rodier, this vineyard is unfortunate not to have been classified as a *premier cru*. Two main reasons may be assigned to this argument. In the middle of the last century the majority of the vineyards of Corgoloin belonged to two growers, M. Marey of Pommard and M. Duret of Nuits. They vinified their wines in their own home villages and all their produce appeared under those village names. As a result the value of the wines of Corgoloin was not appreciated. Moreover, when the classification committee sat in 1861, no representative from Corgoloin appeared at the meeting and, although the growers of the village later produced their own classification it met with no general acceptance.

Of the villages, Fixin is better known for the red wines which bear its own name; Marsannay for the best rosé wines of Burgundy; and Comblanchien and Corgoloin for the marble from their quarries, which graces, amongst other buildings, the Paris Opéra and Orly airport.

Until recently the *appellation* Côte de Nuits Villages was Vin Fin de La Côte de Nuits. Due to growers' protests, the inclusion of Marsannay and Couchey in the *appellation* has yet to be ratified.

Possible declassification: Bourgogne and Bourgogne Grand Ordinaire.

Nuits Saint-Georges
Colour: almost entirely red
Average production: red 8,172 hl. white 32 hl.
Minimum degree: red 10·5°, *1er cru* 11°; white 11°, *1er cru* 11·5°
Area: 375·74 ha.

In acreage of vineyards, Nuits is second in importance only to Gevrey on the Côte that bears its name, but its importance in the commerce of wine is demonstrated by the succession of important shippers with their cellars in the town: Faiveley and Moillard, Dufouleur and Geisweiler, Chauvenet and Lupé-Cholet are some of the names seen on labels round the world. The Scandinavian monopolies particularly come to Nuits to make their purchases. Liqueur and sparkling Burgundy producers also have an important share in the town's commerce. More surprisingly, Nuits is an important centre for the production of fruit-juices. This industry dates from the difficult times of the thirties when one enterprising wine-shipper sought to counter the slump in sales of

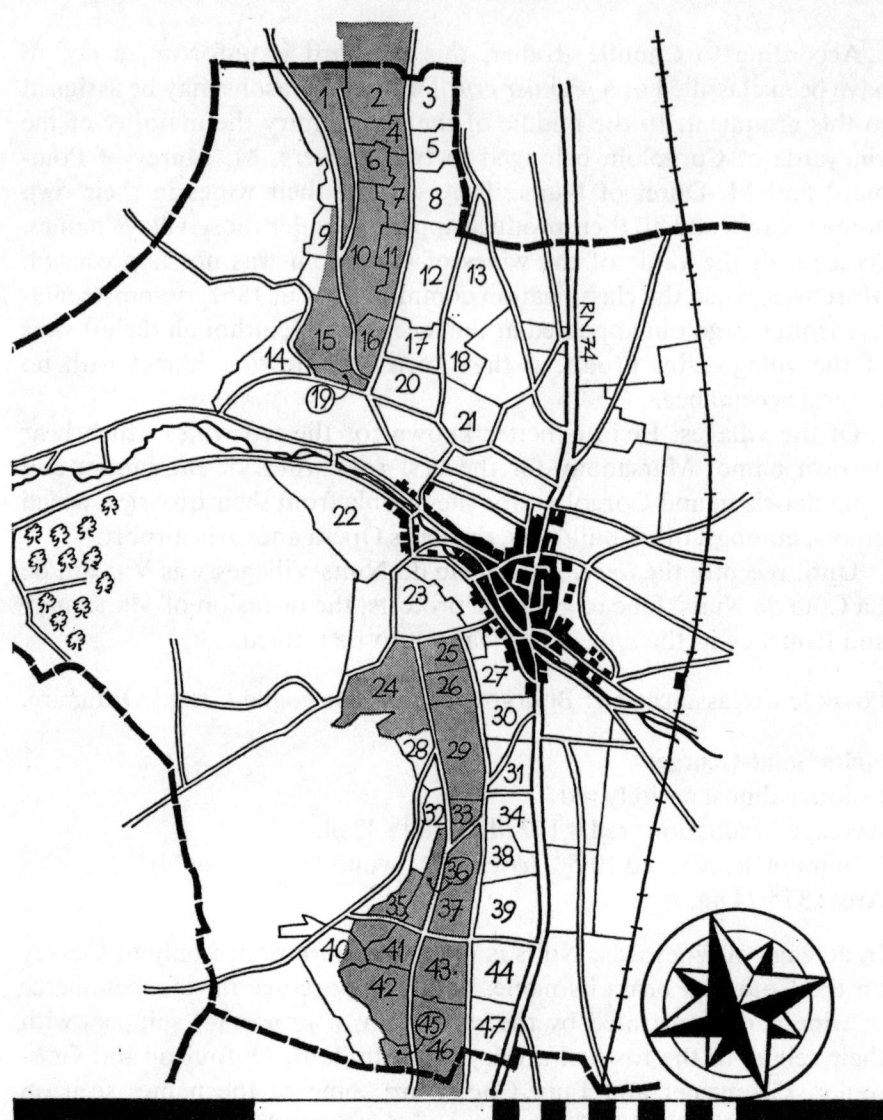

NUITS SAINT-GEORGES

Shaded areas indicate *premier cru* vineyards

1	aux Damodes	aux Allots	12
2	aux Boudots	aux Argillats	19
3	au Bas de Combe	les Argillats	14

CÔTE DE NUITS

4	aux Cras	aux Barrières	5
5	aux Barrières	au Bas de Combe	3
6	le Richemone	Belle Croix	30
7	aux Murgers	aux Boudots	2
8	aux Lavières	aux Bousselots	16
9	en la Perrière Noblet	les Brulées	38
10	aux Chaignots	les Cailles	43
11	aux Vignes Rondes	les Chaboeufs	41
12	aux Allots	aux Chaignots	10
13	aux Saint-Jacques	Chaînes Carteau	45
14	les Argillats	les Chaliots	39
15	aux Thorey	les Charmois	22
16	aux Bousselots	la Charmotte	20
17	la Petite Charmotte	au Chouillet	18
18	au Chouillet	aux Cras	4
19	aux Argillats	aux Crots	24
20	la Charmotte	aux Damodes	1
21	aux Saint-Juliens	aux Fleurières	31
22	les Charmois	les Hauts Poirets	32
23	les Plateaux	les Hauts Pruliers	28
24	aux Crots	aux Lavières	8
25	Rue de Chaux	les Longecourt	47
26	les Procès	la Maladière	34
27	Tribourg	aux Murgers	7
28	les Hauts Pruliers	la Perrière	36
29	les Pruliers	en la Perrière Noblet	9
30	Belle Croix	la Petite Charmotte	17
31	aux Fleurières	les Plateaux	23
32	les Hauts Poirets	les Poisets	44
33	Roncière	les Porrets	37
34	la Maladière	les Poulettes	35
35	les Poulettes	les Procès	26
36	la Perrière	les Pruliers	29
37	les Porrets	le Richemone	6
38	les Brulées	Roncière	33
39	les Chaliots	Rue de Chaux	25
40	les Vallerots	les Saint-Georges	46
41	les Chaboeufs	aux Saint-Jacques	13
42	les Vaucrains	aux Saint-Juliens	21
43	les Cailles	aux Thorey	15
44	les Poisets	Tribourg	27
45	Chaînes Carteau	les Vallerots	40
46	les Saint-Georges	les Vaucrains	42
47	les Longecourt	aux Vignes Rondes	11

his produce by promoting non-alcoholic grape-juice. From this humble beginning sprang one of the most important fruit-juice factories in Europe.

The original Nuits dated from Roman times and lay further down the valley of the Meuzin from the centre of the modern town. At the beginning of the middle-ages the present town was established upstream and in the fourteenth century, as a result of damage done by English armies, King Jean gave the people of Nuits permission to build a fortress. Despite this defence, the town was regularly attacked and, in 1576, it was largely destroyed after a lengthy siege by Jean-Casimir, Duke of Deux-Ponts, with an army of 25,000 men. When the Duchy of Franche-Comté was incorporated into the kingdom of France in 1678, the strategic importance of Nuits declined and the walls surrounding it were gradually dismantled over the following centuries. Nuits thus lacks much of the medieval atmosphere that Beaune, for example, still retains.

The *appellation* of Nuits has been extended to the next village to the south, Prémeaux, which houses two esteemed shippers, Charles Viénot and Jules Belin. The village has a spring, whose medical properties were recognized over 300 years ago. It now enjoys little favour and, after some years as a swimming-pool, its purchase by the Nuits liqueur family of Vedrenne may herald a renaissance. No plans have been announced yet for its development, but some must hope that the waters of Prémeaux-les-Bains may in future rival those of Évian – and its Casino perhaps tempt the oil-sheikhs from Divonne.

The vineyards of Nuits fall into three sections. Those north of the town, towards Vosne, produce the wines that show themselves earliest, and in many ways resemble their neighbours to the north. The best-known vineyards in this area are aux Murgers and aux Boudots. The vineyards to the south, on the other side of the Meuzin, produce the greatest wines: les Saint-Georges (which gave the town its name in 1892 and which Camille Rodier says needs ten to twenty years to show its full merits), les Vaucrains, and les Cailles. Prémeaux has a succession of *premiers crus* of which the most commonly seen is Clos de la Maréchale, the largest vineyard on the Côte de Nuits in the hands of a single owner. The wine is distributed by the Nuits shipper Faiveley. A little white wine with the *appellation* Nuits is produced from the vineyards of la Perrière and Clos Arlots; but the former, at least, tastes more like a wine from the Rhône valley than from Burgundy.

The vineyard of les Saint-Georges was first surrounded with a wall and planted about the year 1,000, though for several years it was known as les Vaillerots. During the eighteenth century it enjoyed a very high reputation, being considered superior to Corton and sold at a price not far short of that of Richebourg.

Among the most important growers with vineyards in Nuits Saint-Georges are the Hospice de Nuits, Faiveley, Moillard and Gouges. The Hospice de Nuits owns about twenty-five acres of *premier cru* vineyards. Like the Hospices de Beaune it sells its wines at auction. The sale is on the second Sunday before the Easter following the vintage. This does not generally attract attention but, in 1974, when the prices fell by about 40 per cent, it was headlined in all the French newspapers and achieved national publicity for the first time. There is also a cooperative cellar run by some of the smaller growers.

Though Nuits suffered at the hands of the English 600 years ago, they have recently damaged its reputation more harshly by fostering its popularity. The reason for this must lie in its name, a gesture of Anglo-Saxon daring in asking for a wine which conjures up a picture of exotic (or erotic) nights, coupled with the patriotic image of Saint George. Undoubtedly this demand led to much optimistic labelling, encouraged in some cases by local shippers. Now that *appellation contrôlée* has arrived in the United Kingdom, consumers must be surprised by the price they are asked to pay for a genuine bottle. As a result of the demand, Nuits Saint-Georges has become the most expensive village wine of Burgundy.

Premier cru vineyards: to the north of Nuits: aux Murgers, la Richemone, aux Boudots, aux Chaignots, aux Thorey (part), aux Vignes Rondes, aux Bousselots, aux Damodes (part), les Argillats (part), les Champs Perdrix (part), en la Perrière Noblet (part).
To the south of Nuits: les Saint-Georges, les Vaucrains, les Cailles, les Porrets (or Poirets), les Pruliers, les Haut Pruliers (part), les Chaboeufs, la Perrière, la Roncière, les Procès, Rue de Chaux, aux Cras, les Poulettes, aux Crots (part), les Vallerots (part), en la Chaînes-Carteau.
In Prémeaux: Clos de la Maréchale, Clos Arlots, Clos des Argillières,

BURGUNDY

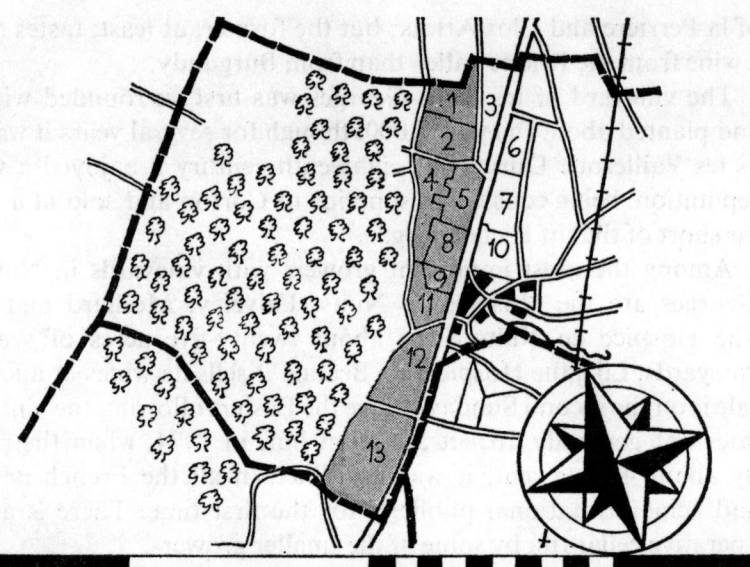

PRÉMEAUX

Shaded areas indicate *premier cru* vineyards

1	les Didiers	les Argillières	11
2	le Clos des Forêts	Charbonnières	7
3	Plantes au Baron	Clos Arlots	12
4	aux Perdrix	le Clos des Corvées	5
5	le Clos des Corvées	le Clos des Forêts	2
6	les Tapons	Clos de la Maréchale	13
7	Charbonnières	les Clos Saint-Marc	9
8	les Corvées Paget	les Corvées Paget	8
9	les Clos Saint-Marc	les Didiers	1
10	les Grandes Vignes	les Grandes Vignes	10
11	les Argillières	Plantes au Baron	3
12	Clos Arlots	aux Perdrix	4
13	Clos de la Maréchale	les Tapons	6

Clos des Grandes Vignes, Clos des Corvées, Clos des Forêts, les Didiers, aux Perdrix, les Corvées Paget, le Clos Saint-Marc.

Though Nuits may produce the most expensive village wines of Burgundy, the area does not rely on the villages for its reputation. The next village, Vosne-Romanée, has the distinction of producing the most expensive vineyard wine of Burgundy, Romanée-Conti: and, together with the neighbouring village of Flagey, six other *grand cru* wines little less esteemed – Romanée and Romanée Saint-Vivant, la Tâche and Richebourg, Grands-Echézeaux and Echézeaux. These names can be mentioned with those of the greatest wines of France and of the world.

Romanée-Conti
Colour: red
Average production: 59 hl.
Minimum degree 11·5°
Area: 1·80 ha.

It is doubtful whether any vineyard in Burgundy has changed hands so rarely as Romanée-Conti: for this is a plot of land that has been particularly cherished by its owners. Even the prosaic valuers at the time of the French Revolution dug deeply into their resources of evocative language when they described it on the bill of sale. In all, from the thirteenth century – when the vineyard belonged to the priory of Saint-Vivant – until the present day, the property has come on to the market on only nine occasions. The last time was in 1869 when it was purchased by M. Durand-Blochet, whose descendants, in the shape of the Domaine de la Romanée-Conti (the de Vilaine family and Leroy, the Meursault shippers) are the present owners. They have made sustained and determined efforts to produce outstanding wines. Indeed, it was not until after the Second World War that they first grafted their French vines on to American rootstock, for until then, by dint of using all the most expensive processes, they had been able to hold phylloxera at arm's length. As a result of the rooting up of the old vines and subsequent replanting, the first post-war vintage of the wine was the 1952.

The wine is all bottled at the *domaine*, whose unprepossessing cellars are at Vosne-Romanée. The Domaine de la Romanée-Conti are also the sole owners of La Tâche and have vines in Richebourg, Grands

Echézeaux, Echézeaux and le Montrachet. The *domaine* is also responsible for the production and marketing of the Romanée Saint-Vivant holding of the Domaine Marey-Monge.

Holding such tight control of a considerable proportion of the finest wines of Burgundy, the Domaine has been able to mount an admirable marketing operation, implicit in the fact that there are always more people eager to buy their wine than the production will supply. As a result their wines have, in the past, been a most satisfactory investment, small parcels regularly making high prices in the auction rooms. Unfortunately it is true that some of their wine, particularly of less favoured vintages, has been sold at a price above its actual worth. In consequence, certain signs of disillusionment are beginning to creep in, particularly in the United States, where about 60 per cent of the wine has been sold. It must be hoped that the quality of the wine does not fall. In any case the limited amount produced will always mean that it is a bottle for the wealthy man. As Dr Ramain wrote in 1931, 'Rare are those chosen for the honour of appreciating this outstanding wine with its deep scent of violets mixed with cherries, with its brilliant ruby colour and the most distinguished smoothness on the palate'.

Possible declassification: Vosne-Romanée *1er cru*, Vosne-Romanée, Bourgogne and Bourgogne Grand Ordinaire.

La Romanée
Colour: red
Average production: 26 hl.
Minimum degree: 11·5°
Area 0·83 ha.

The smallest *appellation contrôlée* in Burgundy (and in terms of area, in the whole of France, though the white wine vineyard of Château Grillet, in the Rhône valley, has a smaller production), la Romanée has long been the sole property of Nuits shippers Liger-Belair. Perhaps the wine lacks the finesse of Romanée-Conti, but it never seems to have matched it for prestige. It has been popular in England, though André Simon's description of the 1915 vintage as a 'most gracious wine to introduce a greater wine' was perhaps uncharitable.

Possible declassification: as for Romanée-Conti.

CÔTE DE NUITS

Romanée Saint-Vivant
Colour: red
Average production: 253 hl.
Minimum degree: 11·5°
Area: 9·54 ha.

Romanée Saint-Vivant takes it name from the monastery of Saint-Vivant, which traditionally was the viticultural enemy of the Cistercians. The monastery was founded in the Arrière Côte de Nuits at the beginning of the eleventh century. The monks were presented with part of the vineyard in 1232 and purchased the rest in 1246. As mentioned earlier, the wine achieved popularity as a result of Guy-Crescent Fagon dosing Louis XIV with it to cure him of a fistula. (Partisans of Nuits say that a wine from a vineyard of that village, belonging to the monks of Saint-Vivant, was responsible, but that may be dismissed as chauvinism.) In any case it took two operations and several hours' largely experimental surgery by the royal specialist Félix to clear up the problem.

The vineyard of Saint-Vivant lies at the foot of Richebourg and Romanée-Conti and is split between a number of owners including the Domaine Marey-Monge already mentioned. The Marey family purchased the whole vineyard for 91,000 francs at the time of the Revolution and, in a fit of republican zeal, destroyed all traces of the former monastic owners. A portion of the vineyard, called les Quatre Journaux, belongs to Beaune shipper Louis Latour, and many other shippers sell the wine under their own label.

Possible declassification: as for Romanée-Conti.

La Tâche
Colour: red
Average production: 184 hl.
Minimum degree: 11·5°
Area: 6·02 ha.

Separated from the other *grands crus* of the village by the narrow strip of the *1er cru* vineyard la Grande Rue, la Tâche lies next to another well known *1er cru*, les Malconsorts, a portion of which it has absorbed over the years. The vineyard has been the sole property of the Domaine de la Romanée-Conti since 1933. When the wine of Romanée-Conti, instead of being sold on the open market, was reserved for the personal needs of its owner the Prince de Conti, la Tâche was regularly the most expensive Burgundy, a fact mentioned when it came up for sale after the Revolution. Once again a member of the Marey family was the purchaser.

Possible declassification: as for Romanée-Conti.

Richebourg
Colour: red
Average production: 254 hl.
Minimum degree: 11·5°
Area: 7·99 ha.

For many, Richebourg is the most attractive of Burgundies, for of the *grands crus* of Vosne it is the easiest to find (the two foster-sons of Flagey-Echézeaux, Grands Echézeaux and Echézeaux, cannot really be considered full members of the family). Raymond Postgate said he always found it 'the wine in which all the standard qualities of red Burgundy are found in their highest degree'. On a rather different level, Hilaire Belloc recounts of Richebourg 1928: 'I bought a bottle of it in Salisbury at a grocer's and I am keeping it for my grandson. It was in his window. He did not know its value and I gave him eight shillings, which was only fair'. Sadly there is no report as to how this bottle from the grocer's window tasted. Maurice Healy, too, enjoyed a bottle of Richebourg, but Warner Allen found that it often had a dry finish which prevented it dying away gradually in the mouth 'like the last chord of a symphony'.

Among the owners are Beaune shippers Bichot and the Gros and Noëllat *domaines*.

Possible declassification: as for Romanée-Conti.

Grands Echézeaux
Colour: red
Average production: 307 hl.

Minimum degree: 11·5°
Area: 9·14 ha.

For some distant and forgotten reason, the village of Flagey, which lies on the plain on the 'wrong side of the railroad tracks', has an enclave of vines squeezed behind the rear boundary of Clos Vougeot. This area is largely composed of the two *grand cru* vineyards of Grands Echézeaux and les Echézeaux. While Flagey has been certain enough of its importance in the world of wine to tack Echézeaux on to its name, it has never had its own *appellation*, but has relied on that of its neighbour, Vosne.

Reputedly because it is hard for the Englishman to pronounce, Grands Echézeaux has never enjoyed a great reputation in Britain. That is a pity, for this is truly one of the great wines of Burgundy. It is full and rich and loses nothing in comparison with some of its more expensive neighbours. Among the owners are the Domaine de la Romanée-Conti and René Engel, who is respected not only as a grower but as a raconteur without equal in Burgundy. His anecdotes have enlivened many an otherwise dull banquet.

Possible declassification: as for Romanée-Conti.

Les Echézeaux
Colour: red
Average production: 819 hl.
Minimum degree: 11·5°
Area: 30·08 ha.

Les Echézeaux is not really one vineyard but eleven, lying on both sides of the lane from the village of Vosne-Romanée to Clos Vougeot. Not too long ago, only one of these, les Echézeaux-du-Dessus, was considered of *grand cru* standing, but the rights of the others to the *appellation* was confirmed by decree in 1937.

One disadvantage of the Burgundy classification system is that the same designation often applies to wines of widely varying quality and price. Les Echézeaux, together with the other *grands crus* – Clos Saint Denis and Clos de la Roche – of Morey-Saint-Denis, generally finds itself at a price level below the *premiers crus* of some other villages.

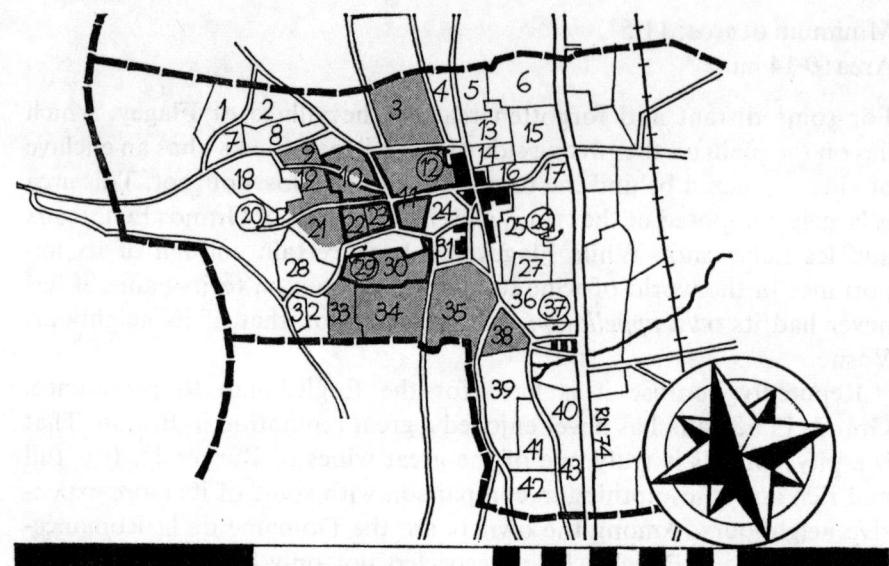

VOSNE-ROMANÉE

Shaded areas indicate *premier cru* vineyards, except those bordered with a heavy boundary line, which are *grand cru*. The names of *grand cru* vineyards are shown in bold type in the legends

1	les Hauts Beaumonts	les Barreaux	18
2	les Beaumonts	aux Bas de Combe	35
3	les Suchots	Basses Maizières	5
4	Hautes Maizières	les Beaumonts	2
5	Basses Maizières	Bossières	14
6	les Chalandins	aux Brulées	8
7	la Combe Brulée	les Chalandins	6
8	aux Brulées	Champs Condins	27
9	Verroilles ou Richebourg	Champs de Perdrix	28
10	**le Richebourg**	Clos de Réas	38
11	**Romanée Saint-Vivant**	la Colombière	25
12	la Croix Rameau	la Combe Brulée	7
13	Vigneux	aux Communes	36
14	Bossières	la Croix Blanche	43
15	aux Ormes	la Croix Rameau	12
16	aux Jachères	les Damaudes	32
17	aux Saules	Derrière le Four	24
18	les Barreaux	Derrière le Four	31
19	Gros Parantoux	au Dessus de la Rivière	40

A wine bearing this label from a good grower, or a well-reputed shipper, will have a great deal of finesse and should provide a very good bottle.

Vineyards having right to the *appellation:* en Orveaux (part), les Treux, Clos Saint-Denis, les Cruots (or Vignes Blanches), les Rouges du Bas, Champs Traversins, les Poulaillières, les Loachausses, les Quartier-de-Nuits (part), les Echézeaux du Dessus, les Rouges du Dessus.

Possible declassification: as for Romanée-Conti.

Vosne-Romanée
Colour: red
Average production: 5,590 hl.
Minimum degree: 10·5°, *1er cru* 11°
Area: 239·01 ha.

Courtepée, when he wrote 'There are no common wines in Vosne', summed up in a few words the village, for here one runs the least risk

20	les Petits Monts	au Dessus de Malconsorts	33
21	les Reignots	Genevrières	37
22	**Romanée**	la Grand Rue	29
23	**Romanée-Conti**	Gros Parantoux	19
24	Derrière le Four	les Hauts Beaumonts	1
25	la Colombière	Hautes Maizières	4
26	Pré de la Folie	aux Jachères	16
27	Champs Condins	les Jacquines	41
28	Champs de Perdix	aux Malconsorts	34
29	la Grande Rue	aux Ormes	15
30	**la Tâche**	les Petits Monts	20
31	Derrière le Four	Pré de la Folie	26
32	les Damaudes	aux Raviottes	42
33	au Dessus de Malconsorts	aux Réas	39
34	aux Malconsorts	les Reignots	21
35	au Bas de Combe	**le Richebourg**	10
36	aux Communes	**Romanée**	22
37	Genevrières	**Romanée-Conti**	23
38	Clos de Réas	**Romanée Saint-Vivant**	11
39	aux Réas	aux Saules	17
40	au Dessus de la Rivière	les Suchots	3
41	les Jacquines	**la Tâche**	30
42	aux Raviottes	Verroilles ou Richebourg	9
43	la Croix Blanche	Vigneux	13

of being disappointed. Round, soft and rich, they could only prove unattractive to the hardest-hearted drinker. While the village may be best known for its phalanx of *grand cru* vineyards, it also has some classed as *premiers crus* which have an excellent reputation in their own right and would probably, if they were placed elsewhere on the Côte, have a more exalted rank. Les Malconsorts was only cleared of scrub and planted in vines at the beginning of the seventeenth century. La Grand'Rue, the exclusive property of the Lamarche *domaine*, remains a *premier cru*, despite being squeezed between Romanée-Conti and la Tâche. Suchots and Beaumonts, too, are well considered. Part of the latter lies on the territory of Flagey-Echézeaux, but the vineyards of that village have right to the *appellation* of Vosne-Romanée.

Vosne was mentioned in documents over 1,200 years ago, but the village suffered particularly from depredations by the Austrian army at the end of the Napoleonic wars, and again by the Germans in 1870. Thus, apart from one house from the sixteenth century, little remains of the earlier village. In former times the Dukes of Burgundy had a hunting-lodge there which they let out for a rent of five francs a year, on the undertaking that, on request, the huntsman and his hounds were to be looked after free of charge for up to three days at a time.

1er cru vineyards: aux Malconsorts, les Beaumonts, les Suchots, la Grand' Rue, les Gaudichots, aux Brulées, les Chaumes, les Reignots, le Clos de Réas, les Petits Monts.

Possible declassification: Bourgogne and Bourgogne Grand Ordinaire.

Clos de Vougeot
Colour: red
Average production: 1,485 hl.
Minimum degree: 11·5°
Area: 50·22 ha.

The largest of the *grand cru* vineyards of the Côte d'Or, Clos de Vougeot, produces what was once probably the best-known wine of Burgundy, thanks to the exalted contacts of the owner, the Abbot of Citeaux, who used to offer the finest of his wines to the crowned heads of Europe and the princes of the Church. With the total production under the control of a single owner, there was every incentive to produce only the finest wines.

Now, however, the situation has changed. To possess a portion of Clos Vougeot is a matter of prestige and there are more than eighty different owners ranging from small local proprietors to the most exalted shippers of Beaune, Nuits, Dijon, and even Mâcon. Round the vineyard runs a stone wall, frequently pierced by gates surmounted by the names of many of the owners. When so many different wines are produced, it is scarcely surprising that the quality is variable, more so since the average production over the past few years has approached thirty hectolitres to the hectare, when, in the days of the monks, it was no more than thirteen.

At a time when wine fetches a high price almost irrespective of its quality, some growers have made quantity their main objective. In such circumstances, it is wisest to buy a bottle of Clos de Vougeot (or Clos Vougeot, as it is now more commonly called) bearing the name of a reputable shipper or grower. The new regulations, which will make the tasting of *appellation contrôlée* wines obligatory and the manipulation of wines more difficult, the vineyard name should again be considered sufficient guarantee of quality.

The most important proprietor is the Nuits house of Morin Père et Fils, who sell their wine in a dumpy bottle under the name of the Château de la Tour de Clos Vougeot. Other proprietors of some importance are Champy Père et Fils, Engel, Noëllat, Faiveley, Drouhin-Laroze and La Reine Pédauque.

While all Clos Vougeot may not be outstanding, its best wines rank with the finest in Burgundy, with, according to Camille Rodier, a nose that combines the flavours of liquorice and truffles, violet and wild mint: while Jullien ranks it with Chambertin and Richebourg.

The basis for the present vineyard was some vines presented to the Cistercians as early as 1110, and about fifty years later they built a press-house on some adjoining land given by Waldo Gile of Vergy. Over subsequent centuries they extended their holding by means of legacies and purchases, but it was not until 1336 that they finally constituted the vineyard as we know it today. Each parcel of vines had its own name, though these are no longer used. Originally, apart from some of the tilling, the work was done by monks detached from the

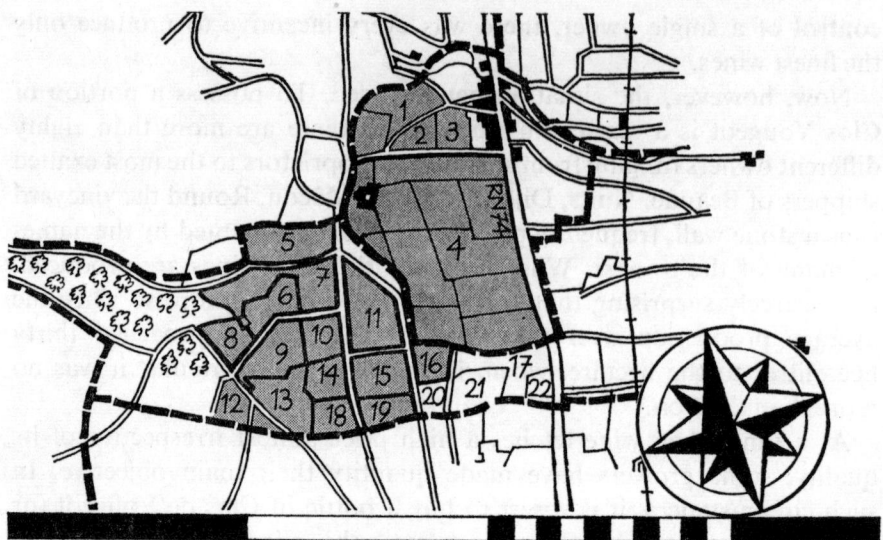

VOUGEOT and FLAGEY-ECHÉZEAUX

Shaded areas indicate *premier cru* vineyards, except those bordered with a heavy boundary line, which are *grand cru*. The names of *grand cru* vineyards are shown in bold type in the legends

VOUGEOT
1 les Petits Vougeots
2 Vigne Blanche ou Clos Blanc de Vougeot
3 les Cras
4 **Clos de Vougeot**

FLAGEY-ECHÉZEAUX
5 **en Orveaux**
6 **les Champs Traversins**
7 **les Poulaillières**
8 **les Rouges des Dessus**
9 **les Rouges du Bas**
10 **Echézeaux du Dessus**
11 **les Grands Echézeaux**
12 **les Beaumonts Hauts**
13 **les Beaumonts Bas**
14 **les Loachausses**
15 les Treux
16 **les Cartiers de Nuits**

VOUGEOT
Clos de Vougeot 4
les Cras 3
les Petits Vougeots 1
Vigne Blanche ou Clos Blanc de Vougeot 2

FLAGEY-ECHÉZEAUX
les Beaumonts Bas 13
les Beaumonts Hauts 12
les Cartiers de Nuits 16
les Champs Traversins 6
Clos Saint-Denis 19
les Cruots ou Vignes Blanches 18
Echézeaux du Dessus 10
les Grands Echézeaux 11
les Loachausses 14
Maizières Basses 21
Maizières Hautes 20
en Orveaux 5

mother house at Citeaux, but after the fourteenth century, vineyard workers from the village of Gilly were employed at the princely rate of four to six francs a year. Later still, when the system of 'half-fruits' became general, the Abbot used to buy back the half of the crop that was not monastery property, and that system lasted until the Revolution.

The senior monk in charge of production had the title of *magister cellarii* and the last to hold this title, Dom Goblet, was important enough to be able to tell Napoleon – when he passed through Dijon and expressed interest in having some Clos Vougeot – that he would have to make a detour if he wanted to taste the best wine. It is not recorded whether Napoleon availed himself of the invitation. At the time of the appropriation of monastic property in February 1790, this same Dom Goblet was held in such professional respect that he was asked to remain to maintain the vineyard until it was auctioned in the following January. After that he was presented with two silver dinner-services and enough wine to last him for the rest of his life.

At about the same time, according to Stendhal, in his *Mémoires d'un Touriste*, a certain Colonel Bisson, who was leading his regiment to join the Army of the Rhine, made his troops halt before the vineyard and present arms to the sound of bugles and beating drums. This tradition was continued by such notable generals as MacMahon, but does not seem to appeal to the present French army.

Tradition, or at least Dr Morelot, has it that the monks used to produce three separate wines from Clos Vougeot: the Cuvée des Papes from the top part of the vineyard, the Cuvée des Rois from the middle and the Cuvée des Moines from the bottom; and that only the last was sold through the normal commercial channels. Records, though, are

17	les Violettes	les Portefeuilles ou Murailles du Clos	22
18	**les Cruots ou Vignes Blanches**	les Poulaillières	7
19	**Clos Saint-Denis**	les Rouges du Bas	9
20	Maizières Hautes	les Rouges des Dessus	8
21	Maizières Basses	les Treux	15
22	les Portefeuilles ou Murailles du Clos	les Violettes	17

incomplete and there are some that claim that the wine was produced from three separate vertical – rather than horizontal – strips. Jules Ouvrard, who owned the vineyard from 1818 until 1861, did, for one vintage, make three separate wines under the horizontal principle, but apparently opinion was divided as to which was the best.

It is more certain that, until about 1820, as much as 40 per cent of the vineyard's vines produced white wines; and even as late as 1855 there remained a fifth of Clos Vougeot in *chardonnay*, though this and some *pinot gris* may have been used to add finesse to the wine. The *appellation* now is only available for red wines and white vines are no longer planted.

The press-house of Clos Vougeot, which, together with the *château*, is open to visitors, is one of the most impressive sights of the Côte. A hollow square, some hundred feet long on the outside, it holds a number of traditional open oak vats and four enormous wooden presses which apparently had the most perilous moments of their long and honourable career during the Second World War, when some German prisoners, suffering from a Burgundian winter, wanted to chop them up for firewood.

The *château*, so the story goes, was not built to the original design. The Abbot, wishing to humble a proud architect-monk, ordered one of his colleagues to make some cruel and ugly alterations to the plans. The original monk had then to sign the amended design as his own work and, reputedly, died of pique soon afterwards. The construction was begun in 1551, but was not fully completed until 1891, when it was privately occupied by Léonce Bocquet.

In 1944, the *château* and *cuvérie* were bought from M. Étienne Canazet and restored by the Confrérie des Chevaliers du Tastevin, the senior and best-known wine brotherhood, not only of Burgundy, but of France. Founded in 1934 by Camille Rodier and Georges Faiveley to promote 'the wines of Burgundy in general and the wines of Nuits in particular', it took as its model an earlier brotherhood – l'Ordre de la Boisson – which had flourished, and died, under Louis XIV. The first banquet was held in a cellar at Nuits Saint-Georges on the eve of the Hospices de Beaune sale in 1934, and this is still the most important of the twenty or so similar celebrations held every year. At each meal, 500 or more sit down in the old cask-cellar of Clos Vougeot to an evening of Burgundian gastronomy, humour and songs, the last provided by the Cadets de Bourgogne, a 'folk' group that truly appreciates the local produce. The atmosphere is a skilful blend of Molière and Rabelais which attracts visitors from all over the world. At each banquet there is a guest of honour, who might be a member of a royal family, an ambassador or a well-known writer. The banquet on the eve of the Hospices de Beaune sale is now the first of the 'Trois Glorieuses' and it makes an unforgettable occasion for the few able to be there.

The Confrérie is far from being simply a social drinking club. Since 1950 it has awarded special labels to those wines submitted to a blind tasting by a panel composed of growers, shippers, restaurateurs and consumers. The labels are granted only to outstanding examples of their *appellation* and vintage. Thus even wines produced in unfashionable years may bear the label as an excellent example of what it claims to be. The label is not awarded to every wine submitted: a considerable proportion are rejected every year. Most shippers, and some growers, have some *tastevin* wines to add prestige to their lists.

The brotherhood is also responsible for the organization of the Saint Vincent Tournante, the festival of thanksgiving held at the beginning of each year and mentioned in an earlier chapter.

The *tastevin* in the title of the brotherhood is the traditional shallow tasting cup still widely used in Burgundy by cellarmen, growers and brokers. Its dimpled sides best reflect the true colour of the wine and show up clearly the slightest haze.

Possible declassification: Vougeot *1er cru*, Vougeot, Bourgogne and Bourgogne Grand Ordinaire.

Vougeot
Colour: red and white
Average production: red 543 hl.   white 56 hl.
Minimum degree: red 10·5°, *1er cru* 11°; white 11°, *1er cru* 11·5°
Area: 12·89 ha.

Since the village vineyards of Vougeot cover only a quarter of the area of its famous Clos, their wines are not frequently found. Perhaps the most interesting is the white Clos Blanc de Clos Vougeot, exclusively owned by the Dijon company of l'Héritier Guyot, better known perhaps for their blackcurrant liqueur. The Clos Blanc, just across a lane from Clos Vougeot, used also to belong to the Cistercian monks and has always produced white wine. Its current production averages just over twenty-two hogsheads a year of a wine resembling Meursault.

Pierre Ponnelle produces wines in Vougeot, which he sells as the Domaine du Prieuré: and the *domaine* of Bertagna also has some vines there.

Possible declassification: Bourgogne and Bourgogne Grand Ordinaire. *1er cru* vineyards: le Clos Blanc, les Petits-Vougeots, les Cras (part), Clos de la Perrière.

Le Musigny
Colour: red and a little white
Average production: red 275 hl.   white 10 hl.
Minimum degree: red 11·5°; white 12°
Area: 10·65 ha.

The vineyard of le Musigny lies on a crest of the hillside behind Clos Vougeot and adjoining Grands Echézeaux. The wine, smooth and satiny, is perhaps the most elegant of all Burgundies. As a *grand cru*, it may lack the masculinity of a Chambertin or the richness of a Romanée-Conti. For many, however, it is more attractive than either and, although expensive, is almost invariably satisfying. Gaston Roupnel calls it a wine of 'silk and lace' and compares its nose to 'roses and violets under the morning dew'.

Once again the monks of Citeaux were among the proprietors, but the vineyard has always been split between several *climats* of which at present there are about ten. The honour of producing the wine with the best reputation goes to Comte Georges de Vogüé, who has family connections in the Champagne trade. A proportion of his wine is made from '*vieilles vignes*' which make an outstanding bottle. Other proprietors include the *domaines* of Clair Däu, Prieur and Joseph Drouhin.

Le Musigny is split into two almost equal halves by a track; to the south lies les Petits Musigny and to the north, Grand Musigny. Since a court decision of 1928, about an acre and a half of la Combe d'Orveau is also entitled to the *appellation* of Musigny.

Each year a minute quantity of white Musigny is produced by two growers. In an average year this amounts to no more than a total of one hundred cases.

Possible declassification: Chambolle-Musigny *1er cru* (red only), Chambolle-Musigny (red only), Bourgogne and Bourgogne Grand Ordinaire.

Bonnes-Mares
Colour: red
Average production: 440 hl.
Minimum degree: 11·5°
Area: 13·71 ha.

For some reason Bonnes-Mares has never enjoyed the reputation it deserves, for it is one of the great wines of Burgundy and sells at a price exceeded only by the highest nobility of the *crus* of the region.

The vineyard lies on the far side of the village of Chambolle from le Musigny, and a small portion overlaps into the neighbouring village of Morey-Saint-Denis. The wine, too, is a coda between the two villages, matching the rich softness of Chambolle with the fuller firmness of Morey.

There seem to be at least three different theories as to the origin of the name. Harry Yoxall suggests that it should, in fact, be Bonnes-Mères, in honour of an order of nuns who once owned the vineyard. Camille Rodier suggests that on the site was found a statue of the *Déesses-Mères*, a trinity of goddesses, worshipped as protecting deities of crops in Roman times, but whose origin probably dates back to a pagan fertility cult. Yet a third interpretation, owing nothing to religion, comes from the old Burgundian verb, *marer*, to plough; the vineyard was well-tended.

The Comte de Vogüé is again an important owner, together with the *domaines* of Roumier and Clair Däu.

Possible declassification: Chambolle-Musigny *1er cru*, Chambolle-Musigny (or Morey-Saint-Denis *1er cru* and Morey-Saint-Denis for wines produced from the portion of the vineyard in that village), Bourgogne and Bourgogne Grand Ordinaire.

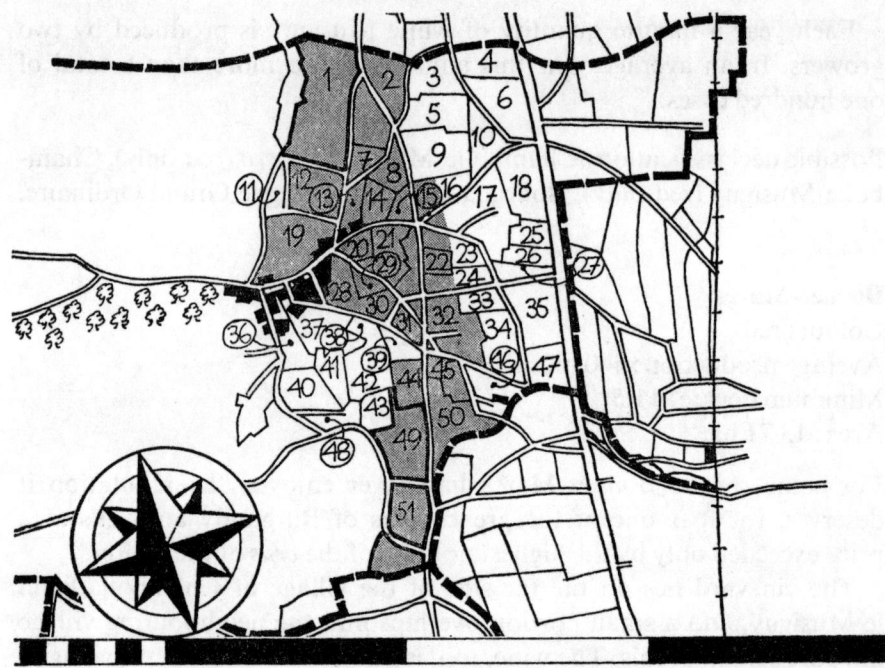

CHAMBOLLE-MUSIGNY

Shaded areas indicate *premier cru* vineyards, except those bordered with a heavy boundary line, which are *grand cru*. The names of *grand cru* vineyards are shown in bold type in the legends

1	**les Bonnes-Mares**	les Amoureuses	50
2	les Sentiers	les Argillères	43
3	les Bussières	les Athets	18
4	les Gamoires	les Babillières	35
5	les Grazey	les Barottes	30
6	les Herbues	les Bas Doix	46
7	les Lavrottes	aux Beaux Bruns	16
8	les Noirots	**les Bonnes-Mares**	1
9	les Fremières	les Borniques	44
10	les Chardannes	les Bussières	3
11	les Cras	les Carrières	20
12	les Fuées	les Chabiots	39
13	Derrière Grange	les Chardannes	10
14	les Gruenchers	les Charmes	32
15	les Groseilles	les Châtelots	21
16	aux Beaux Bruns	aux Combottes	23

CÔTE DE NUITS

Chambolle-Musigny
Colour: red
Average production: 5,003 hl.
Minimum degree: 10·5° *1er cru* 11°
Area: 172·93 ha.

17	aux Échanges	les Condemènes	34
18	les Athets	les Cras	11
19	les Cras	les Cras	19
20	les Carrieres	les Creux Baissants	40
21	les Châtelots	aux Croix	24
22	les Plantes	les Danguerins	48
23	aux Combottes	Derrière Grange	13
24	aux Croix	Derrière le Four	37
25	les Maladières	aux Échanges	17
26	les Monbies	les Echeseaux	36
27	les Mals Carrées	les Fouchères	42
28	les Fousselottes	les Fousselottes	28
29	les Grands Murs	les Fremières	9
30	les Barottes	les Fuées	12
31	les Plantes	les Gamoires	4
32	les Charmes	les Grands Murs	29
33	les Sordes	les Grazey	5
34	les Condemènes	les Groseilles	15
35	les Babillières	les Gruenchers	14
36	les Echeseaux	les Gueripes	41
37	Derrière le Four	les Herbues	6
38	les Pas de Chats	les Hauts Doix	45
39	les Chabiots	les Lavrottes	7
40	les Creux Baissants	les Maladières	25
41	les Gueripes	les Mals Carrées	27
42	les Fouchères	les Monbies	26
43	les Argillères	**les Musigny**	49
44	les Borniques	les Nacoires	47
45	les Hauts Doix	les Noirots	8
46	les Bas Doix	les Pas de Chats	38
47	les Nacoires	**les Petits Musigny**	51
48	les Danguerins	les Plantes	22
49	**les Musigny**	les Plantes	31
50	les Amoureuses	les Sentiers	2
51	**les Petits Musigny**	les Sordes	33

Chambolle-Musigny is a narrow village, drawn-out along the banks of the Grône stream, whose turbulent nature gave its name to the village in the second century when it first appeared in records under the name of '*campus ebulliens*' or 'boiling field'. Until the sixteenth century, the village was dependent on Gilly-les-Vougeot and it was only then that it was allowed to have its own church. In 1895, some richly coloured paintings of the saints, dating from the foundation period, were discovered in this church. The village also has a number of pleasing galleried houses and boasts two *châteaux*, the older of which dates back to the early eighteenth century.

Many of the villages of Burgundy are twinned with other famous wine-growing villages abroad; for example, Aloxe-Corton with Zell on the Moselle, and Gevrey-Chambertin with Nierstein on the Rhine, but Chambolle-Musigny seems to have outranged the others by selecting as its partner Sonoma, in the heart of the vineyards of northern California.

Though nineteen Chambolle-Musigny vineyards hold the *appellation premier cru*, two have an outstanding reputation – les Amoureuses and les Charmes. The price of the former exceeds that of many *grands crus* and often matches that of Bonnes-Mares. The vineyard lies on the slope, just below le Musigny, and makes a wine as attractive as its name. Warner Allen says 'there is no Burgundy which possesses a finer and more subtle bouquet than these Chambolle growths. Indeed with their deep colour and rich abundance of esters, those volatile elements which affect nose and palate so rapturously, they are regarded by certain connoisseurs as unrivalled among the wines of the Côte d'Or for charm, as well as for fascination of bouquet'.

1er cru vineyards: les Amoureuses, les Charmes, les Cras (part), les Borniques, les Baudes, les Plantes, les Hauts Doix, les Châtelots, les Gruenchers, les Groseilles, les Fuées, les Lavrottes, Derrière Grange, les Noirots, les Sentiers, les Fousselottes, aux Beaux Bruns, les Combottes, aux Combottes.

Possible declassification: Bourgogne and Bourgogne Grand Ordinaire.

Clos Saint-Denis
Colour: red
Average production: 166 hl.
Minimum degree: 11·5°
Area: 6·56 ha.

Though Clos Saint-Denis achieved the status of *grand cru* in 1936 and its name was tacked on to Morey by the village in 1927, not long ago it was considered of less than *tête de cuvée* quality; and even now it is one of the most reasonably priced wines of its rank.

Its name comes from the church of Saint-Denis, originally established at Vergy in the Hautes-Côtes, but later transferred to Nuits, and landlord for some time of an important viticultural *domaine*.

The vineyard lies to the north of the village and the *appellation* applies not only to the vineyard of Clos Saint-Denis itself, but also to the adjoining Maison Brulée, Calouère and part of les Chaffots. The wine tends to be rather lighter than that of the neighbouring *grand cru* of Clos de la Roche.

Possible declassification: Morey-Saint-Denis *1er cru*, Morey-Saint-Denis, Bourgogne and Bourgogne Grand Ordinaire.

Clos de Tart
Colour: red
Average production: 181 hl.
Minimum degree: 11·5°
Area: 7·22 ha.

Clos de Tart has long had a good reputation on the British market, and is distinctive in that for many years the whole vineyard has been in the hands of a single owner. Originally called Climat de la Forge, it was the property of the Prior of Brochon. He sold it in 1145 to the Cistercian Bernardine order of nuns of Notre Dame of Tart l'Abbaye, which lies, on the banks of the River Ouche before it joins the Saône. They increased the size of the vineyard over the years by purchases and legacies, and surrounded it with a wall. It remained their property until the Revolution, when it was bought by a certain Charles Dumagner of Nuits for 68,200 francs. In due course it passed to the Marey family and was finally bought during the slump in 1932, for what at the time seemed a large sum, by the Mommessin family of the Grange Saint Pierre, outside Mâcon. It has remained their sole property ever since. An impressive press-house and two stories of cellars are attached to the vineyard.

Warner Allen considered the 1904 vintage of this vineyard, tasted in 1930, to be one of the greatest wines ever produced, but they seem now to be vinified for quicker consumption, though they have a finesse more typical of a Chambolle than a Morey.

Possible declassification: as for Clos Saint-Denis.

Clos de la Roche
Colour: red
Average production: 374 hl.
Minimum degree: 11·5°
Area: 15·34 ha.

The largest in area and producing the fullest-bodied wine of the *grand cru* vineyards of Morey, Clos de la Roche is frequently seen and generally at a reasonable price. Like that of Saint-Denis, the *appellation* has spread to include, apart from Clos de la Roche itself, les Mauchamps, les Froichots, les Fremières, les Chabiots and part of les Monts Luisants.

Possible declassification: as for Clos Saint-Denis.

Morey-Saint-Denis
Colour: red and a little white
Average production: red 2,107 hl.   white 36 hl.
Minimum degree: red 10·5°; white 11°
Area: 103·66 ha.

Like such villages as Auxey-Duresses and Monthélie of the Côte de Beaune, Morey has suffered from the proximity of better-known villages and from the unwillingness of the shippers of the eighteenth and nineteenth centuries to offer their customers a broad selection of wines. As

It is the weekend of the Hospice wine sale and the *Trois Glorieuses*; the great occasion of the year in Beaune. Visitors come from all over the world; some from near at hand, like this folk group from Romenay in the Plain of Bresse, who make the point that food – especially the *coq au vin de bourgogne*, made with a cockerel from Bresse – is as much part of the Burgundian scene as wine.

The square-shaped, vertical wooden press traditional in the Beaujolais. This is one of the few examples still in use; most have been replaced by the automated, horizontal rotary press. The worker in the foreground is not treading grapes, but conducting his ablutions.

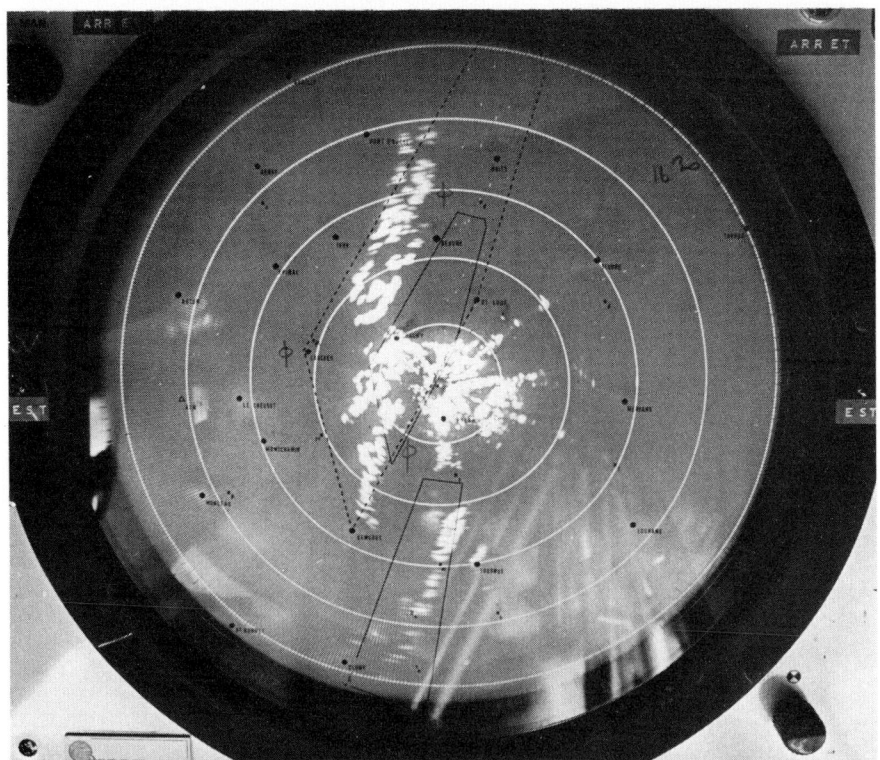

From the first blossoming of the vines until the *vendange* a constant storm watch is maintained over all the Burgundy vineyards between Dijon and Mâcon. Radar equipment in the control room of Champforgeuil airport at Châlon-sur-Saône gives early warning of the approach of cloud formations bearing the hail which can destroy a year's crop in minutes.

The Pilatus monoplane of Air Alpes is on 24-hour standby to spray the clouds to precipitate the fall 'safely' as rain rather than hail.

An island of people in the sea of vines. A view of Chénas, one of the nine named *crus* of the Beaujolais, from the hill of vineyards above it. The flat, Provençal-type pantile roofs mark the southward progress towards high sunshine.

a result the wines of Morey more frequently appeared under the names of Chambolle and Gevrey. Thus the village fell far behind in the league of reputations and even as recently as ten years ago it was safe to say that the underestimated wines of Morey represented the best value for money on the Côte de Nuits. Writer after writer said just that, with the result that, over the past few years, prices have risen faster than those of other villages and now a village wine from Morey will sell at about the same price as one from Gevrey-Chambertin.

Of the many *premier cru* vineyards, Clos des Lambrays historically enjoys a high reputation, though the quality of the wine probably has fallen over the past few years. Like Clos de Tart, it is in the hands of a single owner, but just over a hundred years ago it was split between no less than seventy-four different proprietors. At that time it was divided into two separate vineyards, one called Bouchots and the other Larrets (indeed Clos des Larrets is an alternative name still sometimes used for the whole vineyard).

The upper part of the Monts Luisants vineyard produces a white wine that is more interesting for its novelty than its intrinsic merit.

1er cru vineyards: Clos des Lambrays (or les Larrets), les Ruchots, les Sorbés, le Clos Sorbés, les Millandes, le Clos des Ormes (part), Meix Rentiers, Monts Luisants, les Bouchots, Clos Bussière, aux Charmes, les Charrières, Côte Rotie, Calouère, Maison Brulée, Chabiots, les Mochamps, les Froichots, les Fremières, les Genevrières, les Chaffots, les Chénevery (part), la Riotte, le Clos Baulet, les Gruanchers, les Façonnières.

Possible declassification: Bourgogne and Bourgogne Grand Ordinaire.

The next village on the Route des Grands Crus after Morey-Saint-Denis is Gevrey-Chambertin, but for two kilometres between them the road is lined on either side by a splendid succession of *grand cru* vineyards – Latricières and Mazoyères, Charmes, Griotte and Chapelle, Chambertin and Chambertin Clos de Bèze, Mazis and Ruchottes: of all these the twin glories are Chambertin and Clos de Bèze.

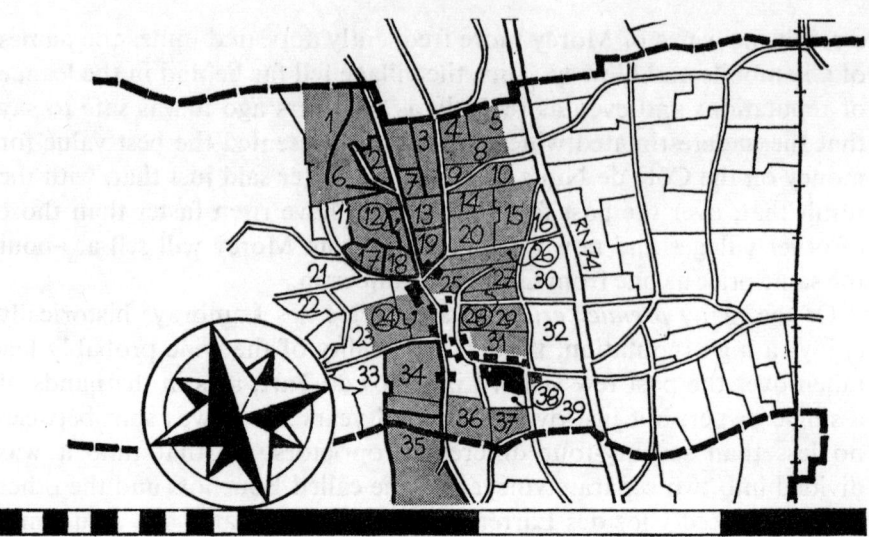

MOREY-SAINT-DENIS

Shaded areas indicate *premier cru* vineyards, except those bordered with a heavy boundary line, which are *grand cru*. The names of *grand cru* vineyards are shown in bold type in the legends, asterisks indicating that only a part of the vineyard is *grand cru*

1	**Monts Luisants***	Bas Chénevery	16
2	**Clos de la Roche**	les Blanchards	27
3	**les Mochamps**	**les Bonnes Mares**	35
4	aux Charmes	les Bouchots	22
5	aux Chezaux	**Calouère**	17
6	**les Genevrières***	les Chabiots	19
7	**les Froichots**	**les Chaffots**	11
8	Clos des Ormes	aux Charmes	4
9	les Charrières	les Charrières	9
10	les Herbuottes	les Chénevery	15
11	**les Chaffots**	aux Chezaux	5
12	**Clos Saint-Denis**	Clos Baulet	28
13	**les Frémières**	Clos Bussière	37
14	Façonnières	Clos des Lambrays	23
15	les Chénevery	Clos des Ormes	8
16	Bas Chénevery	**Clos de la Roche**	2
17	**Calouère**	**Clos Saint-Denis**	12
18	**Maison Brulée**	Clos Sorbés	29
19	**les Chabiots**	Clos Solon	30
20	les Millandes	**Clos de Tart**	34
21	Côte Rotie	Côte Rotie	21

CÔTE DE NUITS

Chambertin
Chambertin Clos de Bèze
Colour: red
Average production (joint declaration): 744 hl.
Minimum degree: 11·5°
Area: 28 ha.

In a narrow strip between the road and the woods at the top of the hill lie the two vineyards which many believe produce the greatest red wine in the world; Chambertin and Chambertin Clos de Bèze. They are generally considered together, for the wine of Clos de Bèze can always be sold as Chambertin (though the wine of Chambertin cannot be sold as Chambertin Clos de Bèze).

Historically, the Clos de Bèze is the senior. In 630, Amalgaire, Duke of Lower Burgundy, gave the Abbey of Bèze, near Dijon – which he had founded sixteen years earlier – a plot of land at Gevrey. The monks cleared much of the surrounding scrub and planted a vineyard there. In 1219 the Abbey of Bèze sold their vineyards to the Chapter of Langres, who remained nominal proprietors until the French Revolution. The diocese also purchased several other plots of vines in the

22	les Bouchots	Façonnières	14
23	Clos des Lambrays	les Financières	38
24	Meix Rentiers	**les Frémières**	13
25	les Gruanchers	**les Froichots**	7
26	la Riotte	**les Genevrières***	6
27	les Blanchards	les Gruanchers	25
28	Clos Baulet	les Herbuottes	10
29	Clos Sorbés	**Maison Brulée**	18
30	Clos Solon	Meix Rentiers	24
31	Les Sorbés	les Millandes	20
32	Très Girard	**les Mochamps**	3
33	en la Rue de Vergey	**Monts Luisants***	1
34	**Clos de Tart**	les Porroux	39
35	**les Bonnes Mares**	la Riotte	26
36	les Ruchots	les Ruchots	36
37	Clos Bussière	en la Rue de Vergey	33
38	les Financières	les Sorbés	31
39	les Porroux	Très Girard	32

neighbourhood, but seems to have lost interest in the vineyards at the beginning of the seventeenth century when they leased out the property. Shortly afterwards the lessor was able to negotiate better terms because the land and vines had been run down. In 1731 the lease passed to Claude Jobert, who was able to promote the wine well through his connections at court. In due course he became official supplier not only to the Imperial court but also to that of the Palatinate. His influence probably ensured that the only Burgundy served at the 'Dinner of the Three Emperors' in 1867 was a Chambertin of the 1846 vintage. (The meal is reputed to have cost 400 francs a person, but perhaps the wines of Bordeaux were expensive in those days too, for the menu included wines of Chateaux Yquem, Margaux, Latour and Lafite, as well as sherry and Madeira.)

M. Jobert was so successful that by 1781 the wine was selling twenty-five times more expensively than in the century before. The Bishop of Langres soon realized that, although the value of his property had increased considerably, he was making no more profit, and in a series of lawsuits he sought to regain full possession of Clos de Bèze. He was unsuccessful and, quite exceptionally, at the time of the Revolution the vineyard did not come up for auction, but passed straight to the heirs of the Jobert family.

There is no record of the date of planting the vineyard of Chambertin; but documents of 1219 mention the wood of '*campo Bertwyn*'. Tradition has it that a far-sighted peasant called Bertin recognized the success of the monks of Bèze, purchased the adjoining plot of land to their vineyard, and planted it in vines. This came to be known as the Champ de Bertin, on his death as Champ Bertin and, finally, Chambertin.

The fact that Chambertin was the favourite wine of Napoleon did nothing to harm its popularity. He ensured that his baggage train was always equipped with several cases: he took it on his Russian campaign and celebrated the fall of Moscow by consuming a half bottle in the Kremlin. During his disastrous retreat, his catering staff claimed that all the wine was carried off by Cossacks. They must have put themselves in the export business for the market was soon flooded with Chambertin 'returned from Russia'. Indeed, so much of this wine was offered that it would have accounted for the total production of several vintages – and for his defeat, since there can have been little but bottles of wine in his army's ammunition wagons. His further commercial success – posthumous though it might be – in the brandy trade should ensure that wine merchants owe a deep debt of gratitude to the Emperor Napoleon Bonaparte I.

Professor Saintsbury was no admirer of Chambertin, nor of Napoleon and the two facts are not unconnected. As he says of the wine, 'It was Napoleon's favourite and the fact rather "speaks" its qualities, good and not so good.'

Chambertin is considered by most writers on Burgundy as being the king of those wines. Gaston Roupnel, a son of Gevrey himself and, therefore, probably not without a little prejudice, describes it as the perfect Burgundy, 'Solid and full-bodied, like the greatest Cortons, it has the delicacy of a Musigny, the velvet of a Romanée, the perfume of the highest of Clos Vougeots.' Alexandre Dumas claimed that nothing made the future appear more rosy than a glass of Chambertin.

For the visitor who is more familiar with the grand *châteaux* of Bordeaux coming to Burgundy for the first time, the workaday appearance of even a great vineyard must come as a surprise. Indeed, the most that marks its limits is a signboard at each end and even that might be considered ostentatious in Burgundy; there is nothing at all to mark the vineyard of Romanée-Conti. As Orizet says, 'The king we seek appears magnanimous in his simplicity, a vineyard among other vineyards, a glorious plot with nothing to distinguish it; humble even like its origins "the field of Bertin".'

The two vineyards are shared between twenty-five owners. As might be expected, some are more '*sérieux*' than others and the *appellation* suffers from the same problem as Clos de Vougeot – too much variation of quality. Some growers, seeking the easy way out, have pushed their vines to produce the maximum possible quantity, knowing that the system of declassification *en cascade* would always give them an outlet for their wines. The system introduced for the 1974 vintage should limit such excesses and encourage quality rather than quantity. At its best, its rich fullness places Chambertin high in the hierarchy of the world's wines.

Due to its outstanding popularity, Chambertin has often suffered from imitation which led the growers of the twin vineyards to take steps to protect their property in law. Two decisions given by the court of Dijon in 1931 and 1932 were the forerunners of much of the *appellation contrôlée* legislation in Burgundy.

Most of the better shippers offer a Chambertin under their label, and among the well-known *domaines* with holdings are: Dr Marion, Rousseau Père et Fils, Louis Jadot, Louis Latour, Drouhin-Laroze, Joseph Drouhin, Camus and Trapet.

Possible declassification: Gevrey-Chambertin *1er cru*, Gevrey-Chambertin, Bourgogne and Bourgogne Grand Ordinaire.

Charmes-Chambertin (or Mazoyères-Chambertin)
Colour: red
Average production: 867 hl.
Minimum degree: 11·5°
Area: 31·61 ha.

The first vineyard in Gevrey on the way from Morey is the *grand cru* of Mazoyères-Chambertin, which lies on the slope on the right of the road. For some reason, which does not appear to have been documented, it was joined with its neighbour towards Gevrey, Charmes-Chambertin, to form one vineyard. Wine produced from any part of the combined area (and, indeed, from a portion of vines called aux Charmes) can be sold under either name. This may provide the largest *grand cru* in Gevrey-Chambertin but by a somewhat illogical arrangement. The wine lacks the complete greatness of le Chambertin but provides an excellent bottle at about two-thirds the price of its more illustrious neighbour.

The growers include Rousseau (who, having vines in both halves, sells under both names), Seguin, Camus and Pierre Ponnelle; but, once again, the wine is sold under the labels of many shippers.

Possible declassification: as for le Chambertin.

Latricières-Chambertin
Colour: red
Average production: 201 hl.
Minimum degree: 11·5°
Area: 6·93 ha.

Lying on the same level of the slope, and beside, le Chambertin,

Latricières is generally considered to come directly after it in quality and Gaston Roupnel says that 'because of its exquisite finesse, it is worthy of following Chambertin and even of completing it'.

An interesting feature of these lesser *grands crus* of Gevrey-Chambertin is that although they have the full status, the old *A.C.* maximum figure gave them the right to produce about ten cases to the acre more than any other *grands crus* in Burgundy. Perhaps because of this Hugh Johnson suggested that they are not true *grands crus*, but have an in-between status. As he says, 'French wine law sometimes becomes more subtle than theology'. Nevertheless they *do* have the full rank, though there seems no adequate reason for such preferential treatment.
Drouhin-Laroze, Camus and Trapet are again amongst the growers.

Possible declassification: as for le Chambertin.

Griotte-Chambertin
Colour: red
Average production: 78 hl.
Minimum degree: 11·5°
Area: 5·49 ha.

Lying below the road and facing Clos de Bèze, the vineyard of Griotte-Chambertin produces a small quantity of a wine rarely seen abroad. Whether the name originates from *griotte*, the wild cherry, which might have grown on the site, or from the expression *criot* – stony ground – is uncertain.

Locally-based shippers Thomas-Bassot are one of the more important owners in the vineyard.

Possible declassification: as for le Chambertin.

Mazys (or Mazis or Mazy)-Chambertin
Colour: red
Average production: 270 hl.
Minimum degree: 11·5°
Area: 12·59 ha.

An important vineyard situated between Clos de Bèze and the village of Gevrey, Mazys is frequently found on wine-lists, though there is little doubt that in earlier times, it, like the other vineyards with Chambertin as a suffix, often masqueraded under the name of Chambertin itself. When it is well-produced in a good year it can almost be worthy of such a deception; and Louis Orizet describes it as 'a courtier worthy of his king'.

Possible declassification: as for le Chambertin.

Chapelle-Chambertin
Colour: red
Average production: 163 hl.
Minimum degree: 11·5°
Area: 5·39 ha.

The monks of Bèze and the representatives of the Bishop of Langres became so well established during their time as owners in Gevrey, that they constructed a series of buildings for their spiritual and temporal needs. The building attached to the Clos du Chapitre that was used as lodgings for the vineyard workers, the cellars and press-house, still remain though the property is now privately owned. The oldest surviving part is a door from the fourteenth century. The Chapel of Notre Dame, built to the south of the village in 1155 is older still. It was extended in 1547 and at one period boasted its own resident hermit. Unfortunately, it – the chapel, not the hermit – was razed to the ground during the French Revolution; its name survives in that of a *grand cru* surrounding the former site.

Damoy and Trapet are two of the owners producing wine there.

Possible declassification: as for le Chambertin.

Ruchottes-Chambertin
Colour: red
Average production: 87 hl.
Minimum degree: 11·5°
Area: 3·10 ha.

The last and smallest of the *grands crus* of Gevrey, Ruchottes, stands highest of all up the slope where the Montagne de la Combe Grisard begins to curve round to the narrow valley of the Combe Lavaux. The rocky nature of its soil has given it its name and a certain finesse.

Thomas-Bassot and Magnien are among the owners.

Possible declassification: as for le Chambertin.

Gevrey-Chambertin
Colour: red
Average production: 11,475 hl.
Minimum degree: 10·5°, *1er crus* 11°
Area: 430 ha.

Though its vineyard area is second to that of Beaune, Gevrey-Chambertin has the largest production of any village on the Côte d'Or. This, and the outstanding quality of its wines give it a considerable reputation. Exceptionally its vineyards stretch away so far across the plain on the other side of the N74 that some of the wine produced from those vines may not be worthy of such an exalted name. The vineyards also overlap into Brochon, the next village to the north, though on the further side of that village their best *appellation* is Côte de Nuits Villages. Though a few of its wines may be unworthy, two *premier cru* vineyards, Clos Saint-Jacques and les Véroilles, fully deserve *grand cru* status and it is not unusual for the former to sell as expensively as le Chambertin itself.

These two vineyards stand apart from the east-facing slope, south of the village, where all the *grand crus* lie. They are to the north on the Combe au Moine facing south-east. The slope is steeper, which gives it extra shelter from the wind and rain from the west. Moreover the soil is different, with ridges of sandstone and chalk.

In the nineteen-thirties the Clos Saint-Jacques belonged to one owner, but it has since been split up. According to Camille Rodier, it matches le Chambertin in every way, during the early part of its life, but lacks the great staying-power of the other. It takes its name from a chapel dedicated to Saint James which once stood there.

Les Véroilles, or les Varoilles, as it is now more generally called, was planted before the twelfth century and passed into the hands of the ubiquitous clergy of Langres during the thirteenth and fourteenth centuries. It remained under their ownership until the Revolution, when

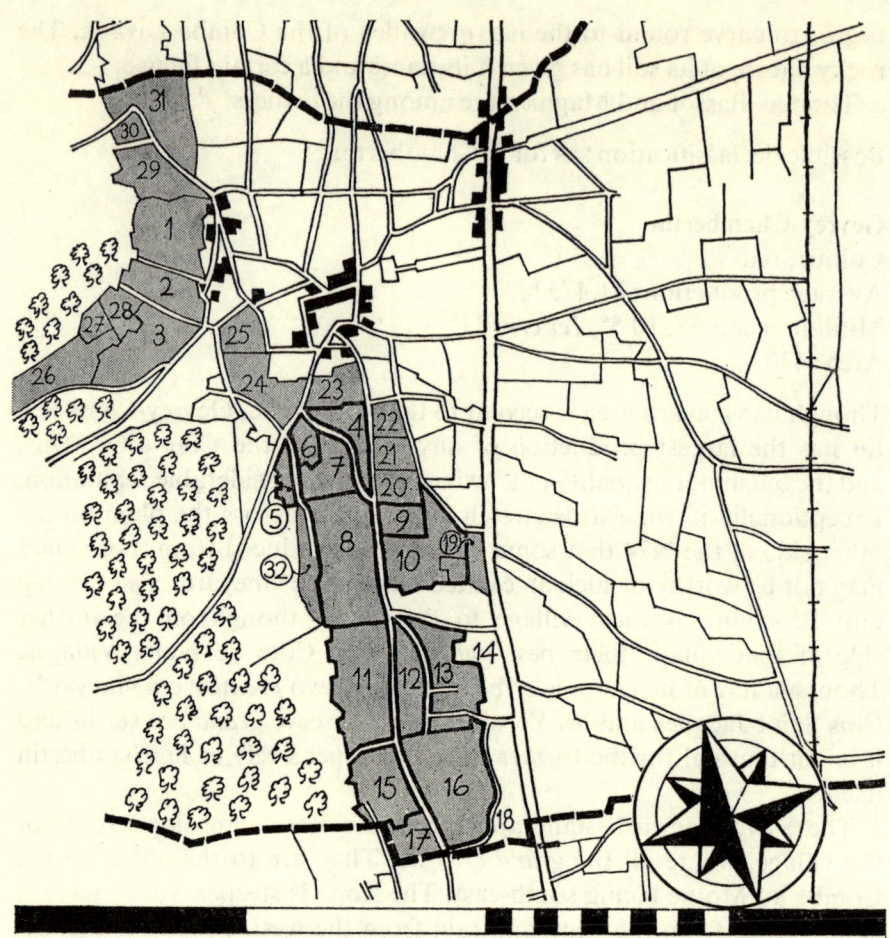

GEVREY-CHAMBERTIN

Shaded areas indicate *premier cru* vineyards, except those bordered with a heavy boundary line, which are *grand cru*. The names of *grand cru* vineyards are shown in bold type in the legends

1	Gazetiers	Bel Air	32
2	Saint-Jacques	**Chambertin**	11
3	Lavaux	**Chambertin Clos de Bèze**	8
4	**Mazys Bas**	les Champeaux	31
5	Ruchottes du Dessus	Champonnets	25
6	**Ruchottes du Bas**	Champs Chenys	14

it was divided between several buyers. It has since been reconstituted and is now again under a single proprietor, which makes for consistency of quality. Two other vineyards on the same slope, Etournelles and Gazetiers, also can be recommended, whilst la Petite Chapelle, to the south of the village, also produces a good wine.

Gevrey-Chambertin, however, does not rely solely on wine for its prosperity. Its nearness to Dijon has enabled it to attract a broad range of industries including a jam factory, a tar distillery and a manufacturer of electrical equipment. In competition with local produce, Ricard constructed a production centre for their apéritifs just to the north of the

7	Mazys-Chambertin (Hauts)	Chapelle-Chambertin	9
8	**Chambertin Clos de Bèze**	**aux Charmes**	13
9	**Chapelle-Chambertin**	**Charmes-Chambertin**	12
10	**Griotte-Chambertin**	Cherbaudes	21
11	**Chambertin**	Clos Prieur	22
12	**Charmes-Chambertin**	Combe aux Moines	29
13	**aux Charmes**	Combottes	17
14	Champs Chenys	les Corbeaux	23
15	**Latricières-Chambertin**	aux Echezeaux	18
16	**Mazoyères-Chambertin**	Etournelles	28
17	Combottes	le Fonteny	24
18	aux Echezeaux	Gazetiers	1
19	la Petite Chapelle ou Championtonnois	Gemeaux	20
20	Gemeaux	les Goulots	30
21	Cherbaudes	**Griotte-Chambertin**	10
22	Clos Prieur	**Latricières-Chambertin**	15
23	les Corbeaux	Lavaux	3
24	le Fonteny	**Mazys Bas**	4
25	Champonnets	**Mazys-Chambertin (Hauts)**	7
26	Véroilles	**Mazoyères-Chambertin**	16
27	le Poissenot	la Petite Chapelle ou Championtonnois	19
28	Etournelles	le Poissenot	27
29	Combe aux Moines	**Ruchottes du Bas**	6
30	les Goulots	**Ruchottes du Dessus**	5
31	les Champeaux	Saint-Jacques	2
32	Bel Air	Véroilles	26

village in 1965. Gevrey-Chambertin has, too, one of the largest railway marshalling yards in France.

Before these modern developments, Gevrey had a past rich in history. It is first mentioned as Gabriacus in documents dated 640, but the construction of the village did not really begin until 895, when Richard, Duke of Burgundy, gave some land there to the Abbey of Saint Benigne. Its form as a community began to take shape with the construction of a church dedicated to Saint Aignan at the beginning of the twelfth century and a castle – on the orders of the Abbot of Cluny – at the end of the thirteenth. (The church is still standing, though there was a move in 1840 to demolish it and replace it with something more imposing. Among the tombs is one from the fifteenth century depicting a vineyard worker holding a pruning knife.) During the religious wars of the sixteenth century the village was captured and sacked on several occasions and the population fell from 400 families to no more than eighty. Gevrey was a centre for the region – as is shown by the fact that the inhabitants of Brochon had to borrow its scaffold to hang a sow that had taken a child out of its cradle and eaten it alive. The sentence had been imposed by the Carthusian Abbot of Dijon who was then titular lord of Brochon.

A 1789 census of the village showed a population of 1,156. The Revolution was widely welcomed: those who did not show sufficient enthusiasm were branded as aristocrats and made to pay homage to the Republic at the foot of the tree of Liberty. More sadly, most of the documents recording the history of the village were burnt in the main square.

A hospital was built in the village in 1895, but, perhaps because of the health-giving properties of the local wine, it was closed for lack of patients. Recently, perhaps because of the inflammatory properties of the local wine, it has taken on a new lease of life as a police station.

Alexis Lichine claims that it is difficult to find a bottle of wine from one of the great vineyards in the local restaurants. They certainly are present on the wine-list of the best of them, 'La Rôtisserie de Chambertin', but the excellence of the food does not fully compensate for the condescending – or perhaps xenophobic – attitude of the wine-waiter. Attached to this restaurant, in some most attractively furnished cellars, is a small museum of wine and cooperage.

1er cru vineyards: to the south of the village: aux Combottes, Bel Air, Issarts, les Corbeaux, les Gemeaux, Cherbaudes, la Perrière, Clos Prieur (but *not* Clos Prieur Bas), le Fonteny, au Closeau, Craipillot, Champitonnois (or Petite Chapelle), Ergots, Clos du Chapitre (part).
To the north of the village: Les Véroilles (or les Varoilles), Clos Saint-Jacques (or Village Saint-Jacques), Gazetiers, Combe aux Moines, Éternelles (or Etournelles), Lavaux, Poissenot, les Champeaux, les Goulots, Champonnets.

Possible declassification: Bourgogne and Bourgogne Grand Ordinaire.

Brochon, two kilometres to the north of Gevrey, does not have its own *appellation* and no longer has any classified growths. Two vineyards – Queue de Hareng (an unlikely name to appear on a label) and Crébillon – used to enjoy a certain reputation. Indeed, the latter was adopted as a pen-name by local resident Prosper Jolyot, who achieved some fame as a tragedian during the first half of the eighteenth century.

Fixin
Colour: red (though white is theoretically possible)
Average production: 1,677 hl.
Minimum degree: 10·5°, *1er cru* 11°
Area: 128·04 ha.

Fixin is the last village *appellation* of the Côte d'Or and, although the vineyards continue to Couchey, Marsannay and Chenove, the last is almost overwhelmed by the urban sprawl of Dijon. It does, however, manage to hold up its head with the two vineyards of Clos du Chapitre and Clos du Roy. Fixin has a history dating back to Roman times and a viticultural tradition almost certainly as old. Its fame now rests on the most ardent of Napoleonophiles, M. Noisot; formerly commander of the Imperial Grenadier Guards, he was one of the few present at Napoleon's final farewell at Fontainebleau. In 1837 he purchased some land at Fixin, which he determined should be a continuing memorial to his beloved Emperor and opened it to the public as a park. The main attraction is a statue of 'The Awakening of Napoleon' (to immortality) by François Rude, a fashionable sculptor of the time. While it may appeal to the patriotic instincts of many Frenchmen, to others it seems

BURGUNDY

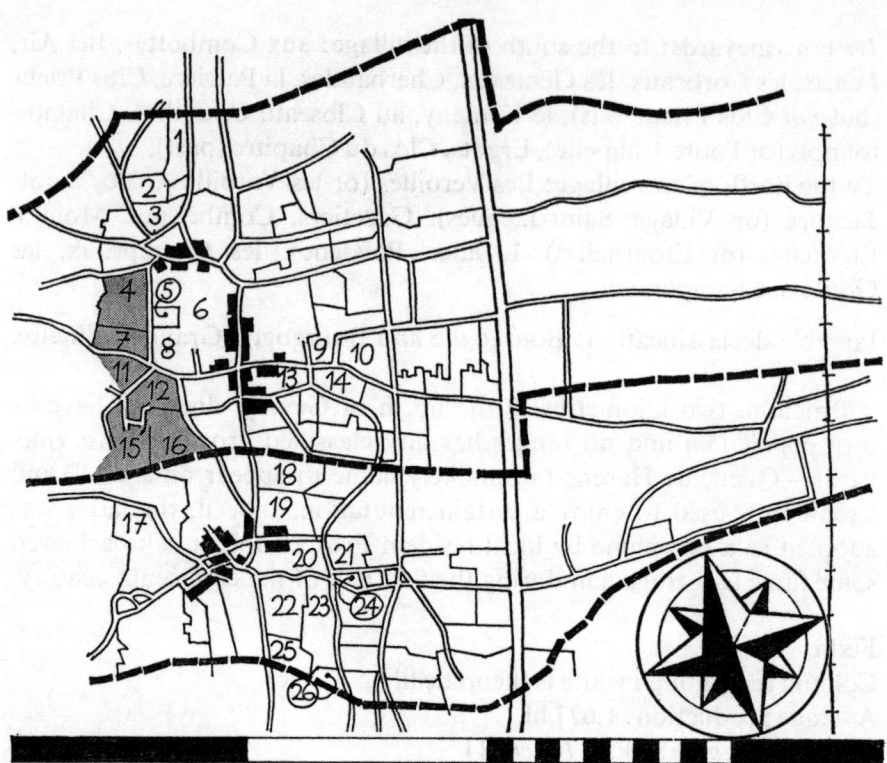

FIXIN and BROCHON

Shaded areas indicate *premier cru* vineyards

FIXIN		FIXIN	
1	les Mogottes	les Arvelets	4
2	les Champs Pennebaud	les Boudières	8
3	le Resier	les Champs Pennebaud	2
4	les Arvelets	au Cheusots	12
5	en Combe Roy	Clos du Chapitre	16
6	les Entre-Deux Velles	en Colmée	10
7	les Hervelets	en Combe Roy	5
8	les Boudières	aux Crais	14
9	Croix Blanche	Croix Blanche	9
10	en Colmée	les Entre-Deux Velles	6
11	les Meix Bas	les Hervelets	7
12	au Cheusots	les Meix Bas	11
13	les Ormeaux	les Mogottes	1
14	aux Crais	les Ormeaux	13

220

more like a corpse hurriedly abandoned by bodysnatchers. To complete the facilities of the park, M. Noisot arranged to be buried there, vertically, sabre in hand, standing guard over his old commander and Emperor.

Rights granted to Fixin by its overlords the Bishops of Langres ensured that it escaped most of the horrors of war until 1589, when it was captured by the Huguenots, who partly destroyed the church and the Manor of Perrières, belonging to the Cistercian order. Worse followed four years later, when a roving band of German soldiers burnt all they could and then raped 'all the girls and women they could catch.'

The outstanding vineyard of Fixin is the Clos de la Perrière, which surrounds the old manor-house on the hillside behind the village. It was presented to the Cistercians at the beginning of the twelfth century by Hugues II, whose brother was a monk in the order. It remained in their possession until 1622, when it was sold to Jean Bouhier of Dijon and, in due course, to the Marquis de Montfort, who created such a demand for its wine that he was able to sell it at the same price as le Chambertin. Alexis Lichine rates it as superior to both Charmes- and Chapelle-Chambertin. Slightly lower down the slope, and only slightly lower in quality, is the Clos du Chapitre, yet another vineyard that belonged to the Bishops of Langres. A third *premier cru* vineyard is aux Cheusots, now more generally sold as Les Chéseaux or Clos Napoleon. An excellent wine, though not a *premier cru*, is produced

15	la Perrière	la Perrière	15
16	Clos du Chapitre	le Resier	3
BROCHON		BROCHON	
17	Queue de Hareng	Carre Rougeaud	26
18	la Créole	Crébillon	20
19	Croix Violette	la Créole	18
20	Crébillon	le Créot	23
21	Crête Vents	Crête Vents	21
22	les Jeunes Rois	Croisette	25
23	le Créot	Croix Violette	19
24	les Journaux	les Jeunes Rois	22
25	Croisette	les Journaux	24
26	Carre Rougeaud	Queue de Hareng	17

from la Mazière by the *domaine* of Dr Marion. The Domaine Pierre Gelin et Fils are also local growers of repute.

It used to be said that, because of the small production, the wines of Fixin were little-known and could be bought at low prices, but they are not behind the other wines of the Côte in this matter. Fixin is the only village *appellation* that can be declassified into Côte de Nuits Villages.

1er cru vineyards: la Perrière (part), le Clos du Chapitre (part), Cheusots (part), les Meix Bas (part), les Arvelets (part), les Hervelets (part).

Possible declassification: Côte de Nuits Villages, Bourgogne and Bourgogne Grand Ordinaire.

11 CHABLIS AND THE YONNE

Chablis is separate and distinct from Burgundy, not only as a vineyard area, but also as a district. It is over a hundred kilometres from the most northerly part of the nearest, central-vineyards of Burgundy, while the vineyards of the Aube *département*, which produce champagne, lie only twenty-five kilometres away. Indeed, viticulturally speaking it is very closely related to champagne and it is only because it formed part of the Duchy of Burgundy that it has always been considered a wine of that region. The grapes of Chablis are ideal for making sparkling wines for, like those of Champagne, they are grown on a basically chalky soil.

Though the region of Chablis is so far separated from the Côte d'Or, the majority of its production passes through the hands of the shippers of Beaune and Nuits: it is represented in Paris and the world by the Comité Interprofessionel de la Côte d'Or et de l'Yonne pour les Vins d'Appellation Contrôlée de Bourgogne, which is based in Beaune. The main reason for the great shippers of the Côte d'Or opposing the compulsory bottling of wine in the area of production – as has happened in Alsace – is their fear that it would ultimately mean that they were not permitted to bottle the wines of Chablis (nor, for that matter, those of the Beaujolais).

Chablis is part of Burgundy, but it maintains its own traditions. The wine is not offered for sale in the *pièce*, or hogshead, as on the Côte d'Or, but in the *feuillette*, which is half the size. Also some grape varieties are permitted in the Yonne for wines with the *appellation* Bourgogne (not for Chablis) which are unknown on the Côte d'Or. Thus for red

BURGUNDY

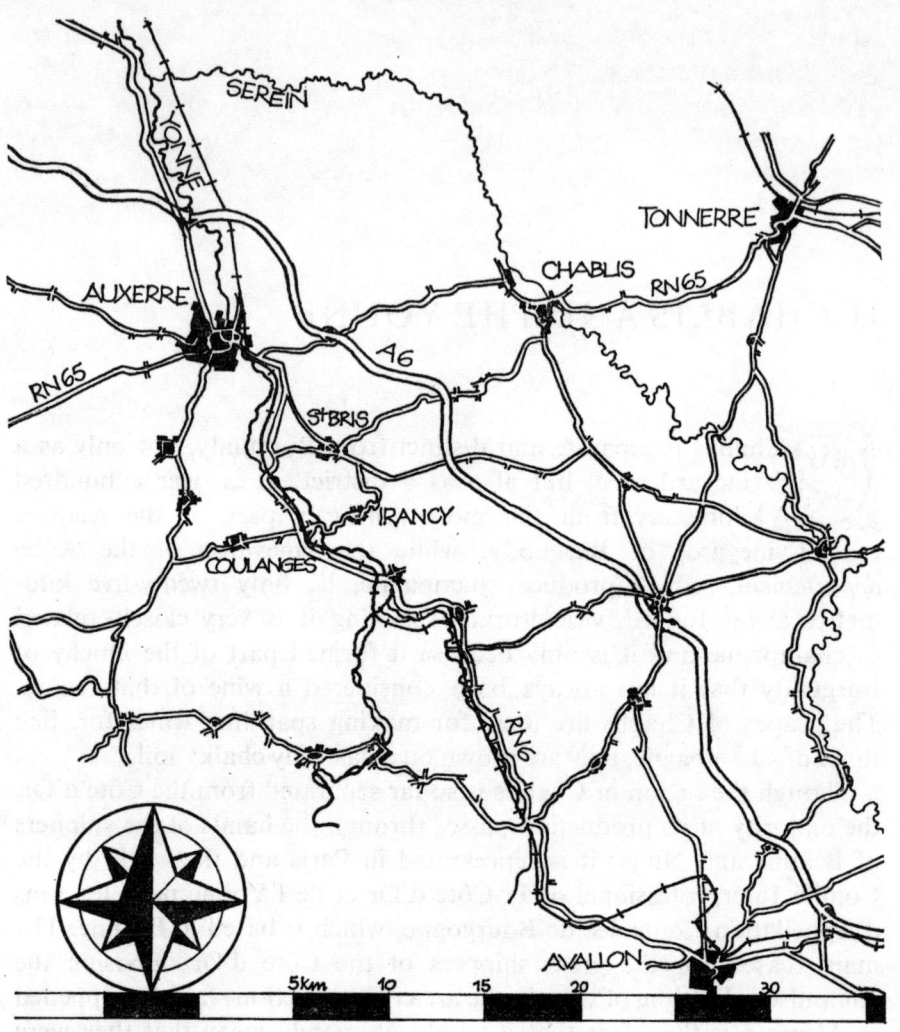

THE YONNE

wines, we find the *césar* and the *tressot* and, for the white Bourgogne Grand Ordinaire, the *sacy*.

As the Autoroute du Sud sweeps over the crest of a hill near Joigny, the character of the countryside changes. Heavily wooded slopes give way to clearer, more rounded, amiable agricultural land. For many years the vineyards and wine production of this part of France have been in decline for simple, and all but inescapable, economic reasons. At one time during the last century two-thirds of the total production of the wines of Burgundy came from the Yonne department. A considerable area was under vines in the five districts of Chablis, Avallon, Auxerre, Joigny and Tonnerre; but now only Chablis is of any importance in markets outside the immediate area – and although it has grown in stature, its output has declined in quantity.

In the first case Chablis has suffered from the fact that it is only 170 kilometres from Paris and, particularly at the time of the industrial revolution, the capital proved a powerful attraction to the young people of the Yonne, drawing heavily on the reservoir of labour necessary to a flourishing wine industry. That drain might never have occurred if viticulture had continually prospered in Chablis. The growing of grapes, however, is by no means simple or certain in these vineyards which, apart from those of Alsace and Champagne, are the most northerly in France. The vines are exposed to a harsh climate: May frosts can – and all too often do – destroy a vintage at the outset, as largely happened in 1945, 1951, 1953 and 1957. Since 1959, after a series of experiments, all the better vineyards are equipped with propane or oil-fired heating systems to protect the vines against the frosts. These are expensive both to install and maintain.

Even by the most exaggerated vineyard standards this soil is infertile. The rich greyish subsoil, a bituminous clay known as kimmeridgian (after the village of Kimmeridge in Dorset) affords only a thin covering to the bare rock and ploughing turns the vineyards into fields of sharp-edged stones. Since the vines are planted on steep slopes, the soil and fertiliser are often washed down to the bottom and all has to be carried up again manually and reinstated on the middle slopes where the best grapes grow.

Traditionally, when a vineyard in Chablis was rooted up, it was left fallow for up to twenty years to reconstitute itself. Modern chemical treatments have considerably reduced the period, but the vineyards of the area have a singular patchwork aspect, since a considerable proportion of them are always resting, planted with a secondary crop. Leaving land thus largely unproductive for a period of seven or eight years adds to the overall capital requirements of the local growers.

The most serious blow to the growers of Chablis was the arrival of phylloxera. When they were faced with the choice of having to replant completely all their holdings or give up producing wine, the majority took the second course. This problem finally demonstrated that Chablis was the most difficult of wines to produce economically. At the same time the industries of Paris, hungry for labour, offered a certain wage each week: the labour-drain continued.

Ironically, as output has fallen, the reputation of the wine has increased until it is now probably the most imitated white wine in the world. True Chablis can only be produced from the *chardonnay* grape (not even the *pinot blanc*) within the strictly delimited, almost circular area, barely six kilometres in radius, with the small town of Chablis at its centre.

In recent years, the great increase in demand for wine has led to much replanting in the area, for the possibilities of increasing production in the *appellation* are considerable. Much of the new planting has been done by such local growers as Vocoret; and some by shippers in Beaune, with or without the support of foreign capital. Sadly some has been purely speculative, with Parisian investors – including, it is rumoured, Brigitte Bardot – buying up vast acreages of land for replanting. If the slopes faced the wrong way, earthmoving equipment has altered their contours. Where there was not enough soil, it has been carted in by the lorry-load. Such tampering with nature has come in for much local criticism, particularly from an occasional satirical newspaper called *Le Chablis Republicain*.

The origins of the vineyards in Lower Burgundy (or is it Upper Burgundy? – the vineyards of the Yonne seem to appear under both titles) date back to Roman times, but it was under the medieval church that expansion really began. Auxerre was the centre of the trade, because it was the seat of the local bishopric and also because its position on the River Yonne made it an ideal port for the dispatch of the wines to

Paris. The sixth Bishop of the see, Saint Germain, particularly encouraged the plantation of vineyards and the distribution of wines. As early as 1212, King John of England was a customer, buying twenty-six casks; and in later years Henry VIII purchased some. Henry IV of France drank them as his daily wines (what wines did he not drink?) and they were much appreciated throughout Europe.

The area under vines was important, as can be judged by the writings of Fra Salimbene, a monk who left Italy for France in 1247. 'I remember how, when I dwelt at Cremona, Brother Gabriel, who was a learned and holy man, told me that Auxerre had more plenty of vineyards and wine than Cremona and Parma and Reggio and Modena together, whereat I marvelled and thought it incredible. But when I dwelt myself at Auxerre I saw he had said the truth; for not only are the hillsides covered with vineyards, but the level plain also, as I have seen with my own eyes. For the men of that land sow not, nor do they reap, neither have they storehouse nor barn; but they send wine to Paris by the river which flows hard by; and there they sell it at a noble price.' As to the qualities of the wine, he continued, 'Note also that the red wines are held in but poor esteem for they are not equal to the wines of Italy. Note also that the wines of Auxerre are white, and sometimes golden, and fragrant and comforting and of excellent taste, and they turn all who drink them to cheerfulness and merriment ... And know that the wines are so strong that, when they have stood awhile, tears gather on the outer surface of the jar.' (Without wishing to doubt the credibility of this excellent monk, surely this phenomenon can be no more than condensation on a jar brought from a cool cellar to a warm refectory.)

By the seventeenth century as many as 150 merchants used to bring their wine by boat to Paris and offer it for sale at the Porte Saint-Bernard. At about the same time, as on the Côte d'Or, there was much planting of inferior grape-varieties such as the *sacy* and the *essert*, which produced larger quantities of coarser wine. The growers of Chablis, however, held out against this tendency and continued to plant the *chardonnay*, or *beaunois* as it is called in the region. Their present-day reputation stems from that integrity. Until then it had just been one wine-producing village amongst many others; a village, though, that had already a proud tradition. As long ago as 1118 the monks of Pontigny, a daughter-house of Citeaux, had established a *domaine* of fifty acres there that was said to rival Clos de Vougeot.

Nowadays Chablis is the outstanding wine of the Auxerrois, for while Irancy, Saint-Bris, Joigny and Auxerre may have admirers, Chablis has a world-wide reputation. The road to it from Auxerre passes between low rounded hills quilted with cornfields, cherry-orchards and occasional vines. It is quiet and narrow, as often lined with sycamores as poplars; the villages are small, dusty and apparently introverted. After fifteen kilometres along the modest N65 lies Chablis. For no apparent reason it was bombed by Italian aircraft during the war, and some of the wounds, though patched, still have an angry look. Yet there remain some splendid houses and courtyards, often mirrored in the placid, and aptly named, river, the Serein. The town is calm and unhurried, scarcely seeming aware or interested that any wine-lover should want to make a pilgrimage to it.

The centre of the old town is the church of Saint Martin, which dates back to the thirteenth century and is one of the best preserved specimens of its type in France. The southern doorway is decorated with a remarkable selection of wrought-ironwork and horseshoes, thanks-offerings to Saint Martin, the patron saint of horsemen. Surrounding the church are a number of attractive ivy-clad houses of the fifteenth and sixteenth centuries.

A few yards away, the Hôtel-Restaurant l'Etoile is well-known for its cooking under the direction of M. Bergerand and its menu and wine-list well reflect the produce of the area. Another small restaurant, just across the square, 'Au Vrai Chablis' is also justifiably popular. The *escalope de veau 'Tante Nini'* is piquantly flavoured with sorrel, and the wines, from the carafe to the best, are good, for the owners are the Testut brothers, owners of both a *grand* and a *premier cru* of Chablis. For the more casual drinker, the ideal accompaniment is that speciality of Burgundy, the *gougère*, a bun of *choux* pastry lightly flavoured with cheese.

If anything the vineyards of Chablis are even more fragmented than those of the Côte d'Or and growers tend to have holdings in several small parcels. This can help to minimize the crippling effect of frost damage. An important co-operative cellar, La Chablisienne, founded in

1923, accounts for between 30 and 40 per cent of the total production of the area.

It has already been said that much of the production passes through the hands of the Beaune shippers, but some local companies specializing in the wines of the Chablis region have now built up extensive commercial contacts in France and abroad. In England, the best known of these is probably J. Moreau et Fils, who also have extensive holdings in *grand* and *premier cru* vineyards. Other shippers include Simonnet-Febvre, Long-Depaquit (which now belongs to the Beaune shippers, Bichot), A. Régnard et Fils, and Laroche. Amongst the better-known growers are Robert Vocoret, Louis Pinson, Testut Frères and Droin-Beaudoin.

Chablis Grand Cru
Colour: white
Average production: 1,548 hl.
Minimum degree: 11°
Area: 99·30 ha.

From the main square of Chablis you have but to look north, across the Serein, to see – on a single slope facing south and south-west – all eight of the *grands crus* of Chablis: Bougros, les Preuses, Vaudésir, Grenouille, Valmur, les Clos, Blanchots and the newest of all, la Moutonne. Until 1951, la Moutonne was a brand-name used by Long-Depaquit, for wines produced from their vines in les Preuses and Vaudésir. In that year a court decision confirmed the name as that of a *grand cru* vineyard in its own right. It has had a reputation for many years. Warner Allen says that in great years it used to sell at a price not less than that of le Montrachet or Château d'Yquem. Walter Berry also considered that the 1881 vintage Moutonne was one of his most successful purchases.

Of the eight vineyards, les Clos is the largest and, in the opinion of many people in Chablis itself, produces the finest wine; certainly it takes the longest time to develop. A *grand cru* Chablis should be left in bottle, and in no circumstances drunk under three years old. Indeed, it often does not begin to show its real merits until it is eight years old. Valmur and Vaudésir both have admirers, but it is interesting to note that small

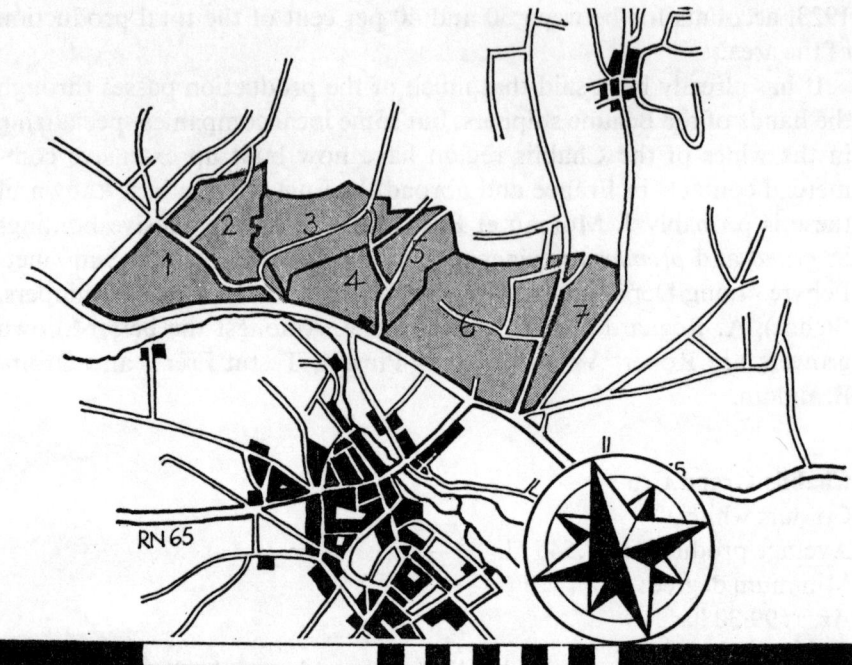

CHABLIS *GRANDS CRUS*

Shaded areas indicate *grand cru* vineyards

1	Bougros	Blanchots	7
2	les Preuses	Bougros	1
3	Vaudésir	les Clos	6
4	Grenouille	Grenouille	4
5	Valmur	les Preuses	2
6	les Clos	Valmur	5
7	Blanchots	Vaudésir	3

portions of both those vineyards face in a different direction to the main slope. As wines from these plots are distinctly inferior, they are not fully planted, but there must be much temptation to profit from their *grand cru* status.

One of the owners in the Vaudésir vineyard is the London wine-importer Peter Reynier, whose excellent wine is made for him by local shipper Régnard. Many of the local growers vinify similarly for other absentee landlords.

Each writer and connoisseur has his own particular favourite amongst the *grand crus* of Chablis, but only a rare expert can recognize the nuances of difference between them. All are immaculate wines; light gold, with a hint of green; delicate, yet positive in bouquet; utterly dry, yet never tart and in good years with a majestic depth of flavour. As Hugh Johnson says, '*Grand cru* Chablis tastes important, strong and almost immortal'. Even at its most pedestrian it is a splendid accompaniment to all shellfish – especially oysters – and most fish. At its best, flinty, but never metallic like many of its imitations, it is as big as any red wine drunk with a well-cooked fowl, veal or pork. While it will support cream sauces, the addition of brandy – as for a lobster thermidor – proves too much. Chablis is always shown off to its best by simple, and good, cooking.

As with all the wines of Chablis, imitation and even passing-off are common and it has been suggested that 'round the world, every day, as much wine is drunk under its name as it often produces in a whole harvest'. Chablis, and least of all a *grand cru*, is not a cheap wine and it is always worth spending rather more to have a guarantee of authenticity.

Grand cru vineyards: in Chablis: Bougros, les Preuses, Vaudésir, la Moutonne, Grenouille, Valmur, les Clos.
In Fyé: Blanchots.

Possible declassification: Chablis *1er cru*, Chablis, Bourgogne and Bourgogne Grand Ordinaire.

Chablis Premier Cru
Colour: white
Average production: 9,859 hl.
Minimum degree: 10·5°

On both sides of the valley of the Serein lie a number of small villages with a proud viticultural tradition and these, together with Chablis itself, produce the *premier cru* wines of the area. To the north of the river are Fyé and Fleys and to the south, la Chapelle-Vaupelteigne, Poinchy, Fontenay, Maligny, Milly, Beine and Chichée.

When the original classification was drawn up there were no less than twenty-four different *premier cru* vineyards, but, as in Germany, there has been a concentration of names to reduce them to eleven. The main reason for this course was that a grower's holdings were divided between so many small parcels of vines no one of which produced enough to make it worthwhile to commercialize it separately. In such a case he often blended it with his other wines and sold it, without the benefit of a vineyard name, as either Chablis *premier cru* or Chablis. Moreover some of the vineyard names were little known. As nothing is simple in Burgundy, the grower, at present, has the choice of using either the old name or the new. Thus in Troesmes he can call his wine Chablis Troesmes or Chablis Beauroy, or even Chablis *premier cru*. If this movement towards the ultimate simplification of names spreads as far as the Côte d'Or, it will make the buying of fine wine much easier for the majority of consumers.

Of the *premier cru* vineyards, Vaillons often equals some of the *grand cru* wines, particularly when it is young. Of the other vineyards, the most generally seen are Montée de Tonnerre and Fourchaume.

1er cru vineyards, with the old vineyard names in brackets:
To the north of the Serein: Fourchaume (Fourchaume, Vaupulent, Côte de Fontenay, Vaulorent, l'Homme Mort), Montée de Tonnerre (Montée de Tonnerre, Chapelot, Pied d'Aloup), Monts de Milieu, Vaucoupin, Les Fourneaux (les Fourneaux, Morein, Côte des Prés-Girots).
To the south of the Serein: Beauroy (Beauroy, Troesmes), Côte de Léchet, Vaillons (Vaillons, Châtains, Séché, Beugnons, les Lys), Méli-

nots (Mélinots, Roncières, les Epinottes), Montmains (Montmains, Forêts, Butteaux), Vosgros (Vosgros, Vaugiraut).

Possible declassification: Chablis, Bourgogne and Bourgogne Grand Ordinaire.

Chablis
Colour: white
Average production: 11,512 hl.
Minimum degree: 10°
Area: 5,000 ha. approx.

Surprisingly, the production of wine with the simple *appellation* Chablis is often less than that of the *grands* and *premiers crus* together, but it is far more commonly seen on the label and in most vintages it is probable that a lot of *premier cru* wine is declassified into Chablis. Much of the wine comes from the neighbouring villages of Beine, on the road to Auxerre, Chemilly, six kilometres up the Serein, and Béru which lies behind Fleys. Though there are several vineyard names, these may not be used for this quality of wine.

Like the other peripheral white wine of Burgundy, Pouilly-Fuissé, Chablis has been subject to violent fluctuations of price. Indeed the situation became so alarming that a joint committee of the growers of Chablis and their major French customers met to agree a maximum price to the grower for the wine of the 1972 vintage. Unfortunately, the price fixed turned out to be unrealistic, but even after it had been increased by mutual consent, many of the producers preferred to hold on to their wine and sell it directly to foreign customers – who were not bound by the agreement – for higher prices. Thus the shippers of Beaune found themselves forbidden to compete for wines they wished to purchase. Happily the situation now seems to have regularized itself as a result of a fall in the number of customers – and in prices. Similarly, some growers who had insisted on selling their wine only in bottle, are now happy to sell it in cask again.

An ordinary Chablis is often rather greener on the palate – and even to the eye – than one from a classified vineyard and many drinkers appreciate its crisp freshness. As a French friend of Stephen Gwynn described it, 'J'aime ce Chablis; il est si dur, presque brutal'. Sadly

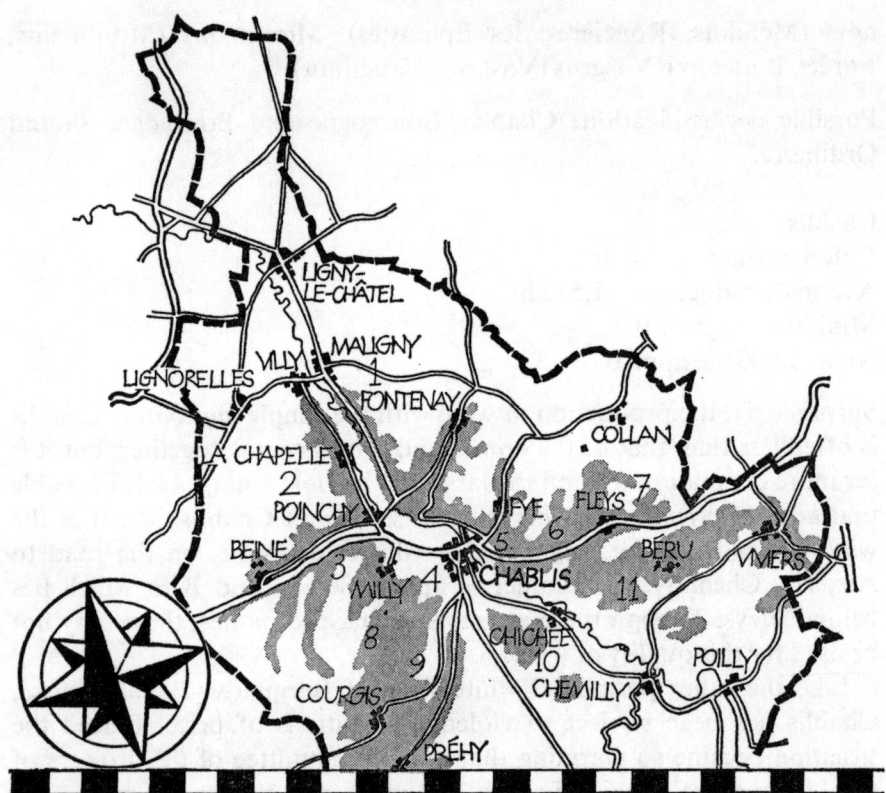

CHABLIS

Shaded areas indicate *premier cru* vineyards

1	Monts de Milieus	Beauroy	8
2	Montée de Tonnerre	Côte de Léchet	7
3	Fourchaume	Fourchaume	3
4	Vaillons	les Fourneaux	11
5	Montmains	Mélinots	6
6	Mélinots	Montée de Tonnerre	2
7	Côte de Léchet	Montmains	5
8	Beauroy	Monts de Milieus	1
9	Vaucoupin	Vaillons	4
10	Vosgros	Vaucoupin	9
11	les Fourneaux	Vosgros	10

some growers, by over-chaptalizing their wines, are producing something altogether too near the style of the white wines of the Côte d'Or. Chablis is a distinct wine with its own attractions and it cannot hope to be successful – and, indeed, would betray its own greatness – if it took on its rivals on their home ground.

An interesting fact claimed by certain Chablisiens is that it is difficult to find bad vintages so far as quality is concerned; for, while several years produced wines high in acidity, after some years in bottle they developed a bouquet and delicacy not always to be found in those great *finages* heavy in alcohol.

Chablis has its own wine fraternity, Les Piliers Chablisiens, whose banquets have the reputation of being even more uninhibited than those of the other Burgundian orders. They hold several banquets during the year but their main festivities are centred on the last weekend of November, when a full range of the recent vintage is on show.

Possible declassification: Bourgogne (if the wine has 10·5° or more) and Bourgogne Grand Ordinaire.

Petit Chablis
Colour: white
Average production: 4,609 hl.
Minimum degree: 9·5°

In terms of quantity, Petit Chablis is not an important *appellation*. It is largely produced in the areas where the vineyards were not replanted at the time of phylloxera, and almost entirely in the smallest of smallholdings. Though it, too, is made solely from the *chardonnay*, the subsoil differs from that of Chablis itself. Three villages which have built up a certain reputation for their Petit Chablis are Maligny (which has a fine castle, with a twelfth century keep), Villy and Lignorelles.

A Petit Chablis is best drunk young, even when it is only six months old; and for that reason it is an admirable carafe wine. There is a move amongst certain growers to upgrade the status of their Petit Chablis by resurrecting the *appellation* Chablis Villages which has now been forbidden for several years. They consider the title would have a greater – and valuable – prestige.

Possible declassification: Bourgogne (if the wine has 10·5° or more), Bourgogne Grand Ordinaire.

While Chablis is, in both quantity and quality, the major wine of the area, many of the *climats* also produce excellent *aligotés*. Perhaps, though, the most interesting wine in the area, if only for its complete difference, is:

Sauvignon de Saint-Bris
Colour: white
Average production: 3,947 hl.

The village of Saint-Bris-le-Vineux, nine kilometres south-east of Auxerre, has traditionally grown the *sauvignon* grape. This was not officially recognized until it was granted VDQS status for the first time at the 1974 vintage. About thirty growers from Saint-Bris and the neighbouring villages make this wine, though little of it appears in the trade. John Harvey of Bristol, have however, featured the wine for some years and it may be more widely known in England than in France.

As one might expect, a wine made from the *sauvignon* grape tastes like no other from Burgundy (it is also the first VDQS wine in Burgundy) but rather resembles a Loire *sauvignon*. Indeed, it is in many ways like the wines of Sancerre, though lacking to a certain degree their finesse, and hardly competing with their price.

Some of the local growers who have had difficulty in selling their wine have grouped together for the production of sparkling wine dealt with in a later chapter. It is interesting that the *aligoté* wines of Saint-Bris and Chitry are ideal for champenization and some local growers have always waited for the visit of the buyers from the German *sekt* companies, before selling their wines on the French market.

Little remains of the rest of the vineyards of the Auxerrois. Even as lately as 1950 there were many vineyards at Auxerre itself, but now there is only one; the three-hectare Clos de Chainette, for long the property of the Monastery of Saint Germain. Now it belongs to the Hôpital Psychiatrique de l'Yonne whose patients work in the vines. Twenty years ago its white and rosé wines were sold in cask at public auction. The quality of the wine can be gauged from the fact that, in 1970, its Bourgogne Rosé won a major prize in open competition at the Concours Agricole in Paris. A few years ago, however, the vines were grubbed up and replanted and the new wine awaits their maturity.

The best reputed red wines of this area comes from the steep slopes behind the village of Irancy. A typical grower is Robert Colinot, who has deep vaulted cellars just off the main street. In all he has ten acres of vineyards and as much again of cherry-orchards. Part of his vines are in the reputed *cru* of Palote, and he produces not only red wines, but also rosé – for which the village is well-known – and some *aligoté*. Though he seems content to chat endlessly to visitors, he is also a successful *vigneron* for his whole crop is sold within weeks of being bottled, at fifteen months old. Most of his customers are private individuals from Paris. A Bourgogne rouge from Irancy demands long in bottle before it shows its full charm; but the wait is well-rewarded. On the other side of the River Yonne, the village of Coulanges-la-Vineuse supports a handful of growers, who make a red wine similar to that of Irancy.

The best wines of Avallon, from along the valleys of the Cure and the Cousin, are burly, alcoholic reds from the *pinot*, and rather subtler whites, but little is now made there for other than purely local consumption. Joigny still produces a small quantity of an acceptable *vin gris* from a variety of *cépages*. Apart from Chablis, the healthiest survivor in the Auxerrois is Tonnerre, where, in the Armançon valley, some big, slow-maturing red wines are made from the *pinot noir*: and – notably in the Vaumorillon vineyards – a sound white from the *chardonnay*; while Epineuil has a good reputation for its *vin gris*. Some undistinguished wines, marginally the best of which are red, come from Sens.

There are indications, slight but positive, that the ancient winelands of the Yonne may be stirred again by the current rise in the tide of wine sales.

12 APÉRITIFS AND DIGESTIFS

The huge increase in the sales of sparkling wine over the past few years has not passed unnoticed in Burgundy. Since, however, Bourgogne Mousseux (or Sparkling Burgundy) is made by exactly the same process as champagne, involving fermentation in the bottle, it will never be a cheap product. Indeed merchants in Burgundy were the first to realize the possibilities of producing sparkling wines outside Champagne itself: and thirty-two companies are now involved in the business, from all parts of Burgundy, from Belleville-sur-Saône in the Beaujolais to Chablis in the north. The main centres are still the first – Nuits Saint-Georges and Rully, with Savigny probably third in importance.

The annual output is now in excess of six million bottles a year, or about 20 per cent of French production of champagne-method sparkling wines, excluding champagne itself. The majority of this production does not as a rule appear under the label of the producer himself, for most of it is sold to shippers for re-sale under their own labels. Only recently the sparkling wine companies, realizing that the majority of their turnover was in the hands of other shippers, have made serious efforts to introduce their wines under their own brand names. Certain growers send their wine to be treated by the *mousseux* companies, but this practice is becoming rarer.

For a good sparkling wine a base with a fair amount of acidity is needed, and the *aligoté* is ideal for this purpose. Most of this comes from the Hautes-Côtes of Nuits and Beaune, the Région de Mercurey

The smallholdings of the Hautes Côtes de Beaune; vines, fruit and cattle make up the mixed farming about Meloisey, the quiet, closely stone-built village, dominated by its fourteenth-century church.

Egrappillage – collecting the grapes missed by the pickers – at le Montrachet. The price that this – arguably the finest of all white wines – fetches is adequate economic justification for sending two people into every row of vines to make a second gathering.

The professional Burgundian, *tastevin* (the tasting cup of Burgundy) in hand, samples the new wines before the Hospices de Beaune sale.

Clos de Vougeot, the heart of the Burgundy winefield. The former *cuverie*, château and 80-acre vineyard; and beyond, the village of Vougeot.

and the fringe vineyards of Chablis. By law, though, there must be in the blend at least 30 per cent of wine made from the noble grape varieties; from the Côte d'Or the *chardonnay* and the *pinot*: from the Yonne the *chardonnay*, *césar* or *tressot*: and from the Beaujolais and the Mâconnais the *pinot* and the *chardonnay*, with *gamay* only from the area of the nine great *crus* of the Beaujolais. This means that a large proportion of the blend, if it were a still wine, would be eligible for the superior *appellation* of Bourgogne: that the blend consists of wine from the viticultural area of Burgundy; and would have the right to an *appellation* of the region. While the method of production is the same as for Champagne, with the *rémuage*, disgorging and dosage of cane sugar syrup, there is a main difference in that Bourgogne Mousseux has only to age in bottle for nine months, as opposed to the two years for champagne.

Of the producers, perhaps the best known are Labouré-Gontard (which belongs to that charming anglophile, Mme de Loisy), Bouillot and Moingeon-Guéneau in Nuits Saint-Georges; Ambal and André Delorme in Rully; and Parigot-Richard in Savigny. More recently in the field is the Société d'Intérêt Collectif Agricole du Vignoble Auxerrois, which is a group of vineyard owners in the Chablis area. They have purchased a three-hectare cave originally dug out of the hillside at Saint-Bris, to provide rock for the construction of the Panthéon at Paris. After a period as a mushroom farm, this cave is now serving as maturation cellar for their wine which is sold under the name of Bailli des Meurgis. Most shippers have a sparkling wine under their own label and, as with other wines, a reliable shipper is likely to have a reliable Bourgogne Mousseux.

Of the three colours of Sparkling Burgundy there is little doubt that the white is the best. Whilst it has never sought to rival champagne, its merits give its makers justification for pride. A good sparkling white Burgundy will more than outclass an inferior champagne. Denzil Batchelor says of it, 'It is a wine made for people who don't like wine: a wine for people who like deb dances, garden fêtes, lawn-tennis parties, lolling in punts on hot summer evenings.' Fortunately the wine is neither so Edwardian – nor so upper class – as Mr Batchelor would have us believe; nor is it so decadent. It is the most enjoyable of apéritifs and is perhaps Burgundy's best answer to a Moselle, to be taken chilled on a hot summer afternoon, the most agreeable of wine-drinking sensations.

No-one in the wine-trade seems to take sparkling red Burgundy seriously: yet vast quantities of it are consumed, presumably with pleasure, in the north of England and the United States. Indeed, the American reputation of one major shipping company of Nuits depends almost solely on its sparkling red Burgundy. It is by no means as bad a wine as many people would like to believe, though it is doubtful whether its reputation as an aphrodisiac has any justification in fact. To the Frenchman the idea of a sparkling red wine is abhorrent: to the Anglo-Saxon it is just slightly risqué – and this may be based on its reputation in history. Of this Denzil Batchelor again says 'in the old days before World War I, it was a particular favourite of ladies of easy virtue and also of young girls who were inclined to wish that their own virtue was not quite so difficult'. If sparkling white Burgundy makes an ideal apéritif, it may be that the red makes the ideal nightcap. The sparkling rosé, or *œil de perdrix* as it is sometimes called, seems to have disappeared completely from the scene.

A vast amount of sparkling wine without the *appellation* is also made within the area. Some is made by the champagne method, but from wines from outside the area; whilst some is produced by the *cuve close*, or tank method. The fact that a sparkling wine bears the name of a producer of Rully or Beaune or Nuits is no guarantee that it is a sparkling Burgundy; the only authentication lies in the words 'Appellation Bourgogne Contrôlée' on the label.

As many producers consider that the word *mousseux* has a low quality image in the eyes of the public, they now sell their wine as Crémant de Bourgogne. A wine that is so described must be made by the *méthode champenoise* and be *appellation contrôlée* according to a government decree of early 1975.

Perhaps the most popular apéritif in Burgundy is the *vin blanc cassis* (or *kir*, as it is often called). This is a glass of dry, white wine, ideally an *aligoté*, with a dash of blackcurrant liqueur in it. (Most recipes seem to give a wine to liqueur proportion of four to one, but this makes far too sweet a drink. The ideal formula is just enough *cassis* to counteract the acidity of the wine). The Côte d'Or is the largest blackcurrant producing *département* in France: fields of the bushes are often to be seen

APÉRITIFS AND DIGESTIFS

amongst the vineyards, particularly on the plain and in the *arrière-côtes*. While many families make their own *cassis* liqueur, there are also several commercial brands of which l'Héritier-Guyot, Boudier and Lejay-Lagoute of Dijon and Vedrenn of Nuits Saint-Georges are among the best-known.

A bottle of *cassis* is always useful in the kitchen for it can be used as an ingredient in many desserts and goes well with ice-cream. Many people to whom *kir* does not appeal prefer to substitute a red wine for the white, when it becomes a *cardinal*.

The other fruit liqueurs produced locally in any quantity are Crème de Prunelle, which is made from sloes; and Framboise, which has a raspberry base. Both fruits grow widely in the *arrière-côtes*, the former wild and the latter on a commercial basis. Both liqueurs are rather sweet to drink by themselves, but a Prunelle 'on the rocks' is most agreeable and Chez les Anges – perhaps the best Burgundian restaurant in Paris – serves as its speciality apéritif a glass of sparkling wine from Rully, with a dash of Framboise.

A rarer apéritif in Burgundy, now made almost solely on a family basis, is *ratafia*. More widely seen in Champagne, it is made by the addition of brandy to unfermented grape-juice. To the English palate, which is trained to dry apéritifs, it seems over sweet, but to a Frenchman, used to a glass of port before his meal, it comes as no surprise.

Within the framework of the *appellation contrôlée* regulations, Burgundy also produces two brandies; Marc de Bourgogne and Fine Bourgogne. After the pressing of the grapes at vintage time, the grower puts on one side the cake of skins and pips called *gennes* in Burgundy and the *marc* elsewhere. This is left to ferment slowly, in a cask or an airtight vat, for the next month or two. During the months of November, December and January, mobile stills, looking rather like supercharged steam traction-engines, visit every wine village to distill the *marc*. These stills are privately owned and work for the growers. By law, the distillation must take place in a public place. Thus they can be found by the side of the road or on the village square. Normally the distiller is only too pleased to show visitors round and to give a glass of the spirit hot from the still to the unwary. Generally it comes off at about 52 per cent alcohol, or 91° British proof.

The best *marc* comes from *gennes* that have not been pressed too heavily and which are distilled slowly. Certain distillers have a better reputation for their spirits than others. Nowadays it seems fashionable to ask for a *marc égrappé*, that is, a *marc* from a base with no stalks left in it during fermentation and distillation. Theoretically this gives a smoother spirit; but since it is general practice nowadays to vinify with the minimum amount of stalks, most *marc* is *égrappé*, whether it claims it or not.

Marc is a very highly flavoured brandy, which comes as a shock to many who try it for the first time. Unfortunately many growers do not let it age (in oak casks) long enough. In a period favouring neutral spirits, it is not very successful outside the area of Burgundy itself; though its warming capacity has gained it some favour in the winter sports resorts and it seems to appeal to the Italians.

The Marc de la Cloche of Jules Belin is perhaps the best-known brand, and the *marc* of the Hospices de Beaune is widely appreciated. Most of the major shippers offer a *marc*, and Bouchard Père et Fils are reputed to age theirs longer than the majority. Whilst *marc* is generally sold at about 78° British proof, it cannot, by law, be sold at less than 70°.

The second brandy of Burgundy is the Fine Bourgogne, which is generally regarded as a more agreeable spirit. In theory it can be distilled from Burgundy wine: but that is too expensive a raw material for the production of a commercial spirit and in practice it is distilled almost entirely from the *lie*, or lees, the deposit left in the cask after racking. The lees are collected during the year and then sent to be distilled by the ambulant distiller. Fine Bourgogne, when it is aged, can rival a good cognac; but the production is, unfortunately, very limited and it is not often seen outside the homes of the growers.

13 SOME TASTING NOTES

Burgundy has an undeserved reputation for not keeping, though certainly it is rare to find such venerable bottles of it as one associates with Bordeaux. The explanation probably is that wines from the *pinot* develop more quickly than those of the *cabernet*. Perhaps, too, vinification that employs less time in the vat and incorporates a smaller proportion of *rafle* (grape-stalks), gives a wine which is not slow to show its qualities.

As in all quality vineyard areas of France, the difference between vintages is considerable and an outstanding year in Bordeaux is sometimes no more than average in Burgundy, and the reverse, also, is often the case. There are few more misleading beliefs than that one vintage assessment is valid for all the wines of France – or, indeed, for all the wines of Burgundy. The vintage chart has its value so long as it is kept in perspective. Even in a bad vintage there are always some fine bottles and occasionally some great ones; though, for good and obvious reasons, the reverse is virtually never the case. The following notes about vintages, though based on fairly extensive tastings, must be accepted as generalizations to which there will always be exceptions.

1975: After a good spring and early summer, expectations for this vintage were quite high at the beginning of August. The trouble began in the middle of August when severe hail-storms over the south of the Beaujolais and also on the Côte d'Or damaged a belt of vineyards in the villages of Pommard, Volnay, Monthélie, Auxey-Duresses and Saint Romain.

Continuous rain from the last week in August until the vintage, combined with simultaneous warm weather in conditions which inevitably produced *pourriture*, which was widespread, and severely restricted the total production. The average, on some *domaines* of the Côte de Beaune, was as little as fifteen hectolitres to the hectare. Generally speaking the crop was better on the Côte de Nuits, particularly in those vineyards composed of old vines.

The quality of red wines will be mixed, depending on the care taken by growers at the time of vinification. The wines of the Hospices de Beaune, tasted just before the Sale, suggest they may have more depth than those of 1974, but rather less colour. On the other hand, it is considered an excellent vintage for white wines, so far as quality is concerned, and some great wines will be seen.

Chablis did not suffer from the same surplus of rain as the Côte d'Or: indeed, it had an exceptionally dry summer. The quantity of the crop is normal and the quality excellent.

Beaujolais produced about half its normal vintage and the quality is mediocre. Over 20 per cent of the total was declared in Beaujolais Nouveau and prices were about half as much again as the year before. The small quantity available for the rest of the year will cause prices to remain high.

1974: This promised, summer-long, to be one of the finest vintages of the century. After a very hot August the grapes were one to two weeks in advance, but three weeks rain during the *vendange* reduced the quality to good instead of outstanding. The red wines have a surprisingly deep colour, but will be ready for drinking early, apart from certain picked early which will have more body and potential; the white have considerable finesse and some of them will make outstanding bottles.

As a result of spring frosts on the Côte d'Or the crop was small, particularly in the villages of Chassagne- and Puligny-Montrachet and, to a lesser extent, Meursault.

The Beaujolais Nouveau was difficult: a lot of it was thin. The prospect is of quick developing red wines and some white wines of high quality but limited quantity. The fact that it was the sixth successful vintage in succession was unprecedented in the recent history of Burgundy and gave a certain imbalance to the trade which relies on a proportion of off-vintages to maintain an equilibrium.

1973: This was one of the record crops of the century. The grapes showed very well at the beginning of September but then they absorbed a fortnight's continuous rain with the result that the quantity was much larger than anyone had anticipated. The popular story that a grower in Meursault vinified in his swimming pool may or may not be true, but certainly many had difficulty in finding vat space for the fermentation of all their crop. The heavy rain before the vintage made for a light character and there was a serious tendency on the part of many growers to chaptalize beyond the legal limits.

The Côte d'Or red production is fairly light with some finesse; but early maturing. Some wines, however, are taking on colour and firmness with age and will develop better than at first anticipated. The white is likely to be of superior quality with some even excellent. Chablis, too, has high expectations. In the Beaujolais the wines are fruity and agreeable.

1972: Early on this large crop had an excess of acidity. This posed certain vinification problems and fermentation was exceptionally vigorous. From the Côte d'Or, and particularly the Côte de Nuits some outstanding red wines, with plenty of body, promise a fine and long future.

Among the whites the acidity has been more slow to disappear and most will be fairly good but not better than that. One Chablis shipper decided to sell none of his 1972 wines under his own label; a decision he has probably since regretted. The Beaujolais Nouveau proved to be ungenerous and its reputation suffered as a result. With more maturity, some of the Beaujolais wines are showing well but the vintage was not a happy one: prices were extremely high for wines generally difficult to appreciate when young. The vintage in the Région de Mercurey was held to be disappointing.

1971: A vintage of outstanding quality, but sadly small quantity. Apart from limited damage by hail which imparted a *gout de grêle* to a small proportion of the *récolte*, particularly from the village of Pommard, the vintage is of uniformly fine quality. The great red wines have a potential of thirty or more years, and the whites are also excellent.

1970: An important quantity of quick developing wine was made. Whilst certain have still some years to go the majority are now ready and make enjoyable drinking. As the prices for this vintage were reasonable the wines are an attractive proposition, particularly for restaurateurs. Surprisingly, the red wines have taken on colour and firmness with aging and the general estimation of them is improving.

1969: Produced a sub-average quantity harvest of excellent wines. At present (early 1976) the whites show exceptionally well, but the *grands crus* reds are still rather tight. They should develop over several years.

1968: A large crop of poor wines: 1968 is not to be seen as an estimable vintage for red wines, while some typical, sound, but not outstanding whites were produced.

1967: This was a strange vintage which came in for almost universal criticism at its inception. Since then, however, it has developed well. Certain lesser reds reached a peak in about 1972, but subsequently lost much of their colour and body while retaining a certain amount of finesse. Others, however, are still improving – though they have taken on a particularly 'black' tinge. It is characterized by a dry finish.

1966: An important, high quality vintage which shows well at present. One can generally be sure of satisfaction with a genuine bottle of this year.

1965: Not often discussed in Burgundy wine circles.

1964: In an average-sized production of generally excellent wines one finds some bottles already slightly past their best. Anyone with stocks of this vintage in his cellar should study development regularly.

1963: A poor year for red wines and for most whites, though certain of the latter still show surprisingly well. A Meursault Cuvée Goureau of the Hospices de Beaune of this vintage, recently tasted, was unquestionably a fine white Burgundy.

1962: On the Côte d'Or a large harvest produced some good wines still worth drinking. The crop in the Beaujolais was the smallest since 1957.

1961: Not a large crop but the wines were outstanding and will improve for many years to come. Considered by many to be the outstanding Burgundies of the past twenty-five years. Only those of the 1971 vintage present a serious challenge to that ranking.

SOME TASTING NOTES

1960: A large crop of disappointing, light wines.

1959: These wines were popularly acclaimed at their first appearance as 'the vintage of the century' (as happens all too frequently nowadays). The better wines are showing very well at the moment, but not many of them have a long future.

1958: Rarely seen nowadays, the white wines were considered better than the red. The crop was very important in size but luck or inside knowledge is needed to find a great bottle.

1957: A small vintage which produced some outstanding, full-bodied wines with some *grands crus* now perhaps at their peak. Virtually nothing was produced in Chablis.

1956: A late crop of light-bodied wines which have not lasted. It is too late now for all but the few freaks of the vintage.

1955: An important crop of fine quality wines which will still benefit for keeping: much depth and tannin.

1954: An over-average production of average to good wines. It is doubtful whether any wine of this vintage still exists in the trade.

1953: Some very good wines, both red and white which have held well. The crop was no more than average in size.

1952: Good wines which should not be left but drunk soon. A cool vintage time prevented this from being an exceptional year.

1951: A small crop of poor wines.

1950: An important quantity of variable wines. A Clos de la Roche tasted recently showed very well but with a dryish finish, disappearing slowly with aeration. The vintage was never fashionable but some of the white wines, particularly, were outstanding.

1949: Excellent wines after a dry summer. The whites are now probably past their peak, though the reds show well.

1948: Very good wines, saved by sun at the beginning of September after a disappointing summer. Some great wines.

1947: A very hot summer caused some problems with the fermentation of the musts. A few wines tasted 'burnt' because the grapes shrivelled on the vines. Generally, though, the quality is excellent, apart from a small proportion having disappointing keeping qualities.

1946: A little-known vintage of quick maturing wines, now mostly gone. Any remaining should be drunk now – which may already be too late.

1945: A small vintage because of frost damage but it contained an impressively large proportion of fine wines.

Of older vintages tasted recently the 1937 has a great reputation, though some of that year are still not ready for drinking because of excessive tannin. The oldest vintage from the Côte d'Or that can generally be relied on to produce an outstanding wine is 1929. Anyone lucky enough to find a bottle should profit from it. The 1923 was another great vintage: Edmund Penning-Rowsell said that a Beaune Clos des Fèves of that year tasted in early 1974 had plenty of flavour, was 'fruity but not sweet; rich, but not enriched', with surprisingly deep colour for its age. Certain bottles of 1915 continue to show well and 1904 still offers some excellent quality. It is difficult to find an enjoyable – as opposed to interesting – Burgundy from the nineteenth century – though both a Pommard 1885 and a Musigny 1865 opened recently in Beaune had a certain amount of charm.

Any discussion of old vintage Burgundies must devote appreciable attention to the remarkable collection amassed by Dr Barolet, the eccentric physician who lived on the Faubourg Saint Nicholas in Beaune. As well as vinifying wines from his own vineyard he used regularly to purchase grapes from other growers and make wines for his own cellars. At the time of his death in 1968 he had amassed a collection of over 100,000 bottles, which was in due course purchased by the Swiss-owned company, Schenk. Many of these wines have since reached the United States and Britain, giving people there the rare opportunity of buying bottles from most of the best Burgundy vintages of this century.

Where do the wines of Burgundy stand in relation to food? Has the fine reputation of the cooking of the area followed the wines or have the two grown up interdependent, like Siamese twins? What Burgundies should be drunk with which dishes? As opposed to the wines of some other areas those of Burgundy are made to be drunk with food. With the possible exceptions of Beaujolais and Bourgogne Mousseux, every wine from the region is enhanced by being served with a meal and often one which, tasted alone in a sample room, seems austere reveals its full splendour on the dinner table.

While the combinations of Chablis and oysters and Chambertin and pheasant may be classical, it is pedantic to lay down fixed lines as to which wine accompanies which food. Smoked salmon is the only dish that seems to kill a Burgundy completely, though recently the Elysée Palace partnered it on a menu with a Montrachet. Similarly, a full Beaujolais could be drunk with a curry, though a glass of beer would probably provide a better accompaniment.

The Burgundian disdains the decanter for the service of wine. He believes his wines have less need of aeration than those of Bordeaux, so the bottle is often served from a basket. Another practice that some find strange is that of serving red Burgundy – often – and Beaujolais – always – cellar cool. A village wine from the Côte de Beaune does not suffer from being brought straight from the cellar to the table. Even though it may not show itself immediately, the full flavours are swiftly released when the bowl of the glass is warmed in the palm of the hand. It is disappointing, though, to be offered a bottle of red Burgundy that has been lying in the dining room of a restaurant for a month or more, until the sustained warmth has neutered the wine. A bottle of great red Burgundy is best brought up to the room twelve hours or so before the meal. The time the cork should be drawn varies from bottle to bottle. For a wine ten years old or less an hour before the meal is reasonable. Anything older is safest opened immediately before it is drunk.

Too many restaurateurs serve their fine Burgundies in glasses that could hold the better part of a bottle. So a normal serving seems lost, wallowing anaemically at the bottom. There may be that good commercial justification for these glasses. They must encourage the customer to order the second bottle more quickly, but they are both unwieldy and destructive. The ideal glass probably is tulip-shaped and capable of holding comfortably a sixth of a bottle in its bottom third. Such a glass cannot fail to enhance any wine.

The wines of Burgundy reflect the province itself. They are happy, welcoming and made for enjoyment – by people who enjoy them. A visit to Burgundy is rewarding; neither the area nor the wine ever loses its converts once they are made. There is a saying in the trade that a wine drinker progresses from sweet white wine to dry white wine, from red Burgundy to claret. This may be true for a few: but for many, red Burgundy is the ultimate in wine and anyone who has ever experienced a great Burgundy will always appreciate its value. The wines of Burgundy are easy to know, but difficult to know well. The effort is rewarded at all stages and, if this book should persuade someone to set off in quest of that rewarding knowledge, it will have justified its making.

BIBLIOGRAPHY

BAYNES, J. M.: *The Vineyards of France*, London, Hodder & Stoughton, 1950
BEARDMORE, Septimus: *Quarterly Review*, 1877
BELLOC, Hilaire: *Advice*, London, Harvill Press, 1960
BERRY, C. W.: *A Miscellany of Wine*, London, Constable, 1932
BESPALOFF, Alexis: *The Signet Book of Wine*, New York, New American Library, 1971
BREJOUX, Pierre: *Les Vins de Bourgogne*, Revue du Vin de France, Paris, 1967
BRERETON, Geoffrey: *A Short History of French Literature*, London, Cassell, 1962
BRILLAT-SAVARIN, Jean-Anthelme: *The Physiology of Taste*, tr. J. C. Nimmo and Bain, New York, Boni and Liveright, 1926
CHANCRIN, E. and LONG, J.: *Viticulture Moderne*, Paris, Hachette, 1966
CLOS-JOUVE, Henri and BENOIT, Félix: *Le Beaujolais Secret et Gourmand*, Solar, 1973
DOROZYNSKI, Alexander and BELL, Bibiane: *The Wine Book*, Manchester, Cliveden Press, 1969
ENGEL, René: *Propos sur l'Art du Bien Boire*, Nuits Saint-Georges, Confrérie des Chevaliers du Tastevin, 1971
FOILLARD, Léon and DAVID, Tony: *Le Pays et le Vin Beaujolais*, Villefranche-sur-Saône, Jean Guillermot, 1929
FORGEOT, Pierre: *Pélerinage aux Sources du Bourgogne*, Colmar, SAEP, 1971
—: *Origines du Vignoble Bourguignon*, Paris, Presses Universitaires de France, 1972
GROSSMAN, Harold J.: *Grossman's Guide to Wines and Spirits* (3rd ed.), New York, Charles Scribner's Sons, 1955
GUILLAUME, André: *La Côte d'Or* (2nd ed.), Dijon, 1963
GWYNN, Stephen: *Burgundy*, London, Constable, 1934

BURGUNDY

HATCH, Evelyn M.: *Burgundy Past and Present*, London, Methuen, 1927
JOHNSON, Hugh: *The World Atlas of Wine*, London, Mitchell Beazley, 1971
—: *Wine* (rev. ed.), London, Mitchell Beazley, 1974
LARMAT, L.: *Atlas de la France Viticole – Les Vins de Bourgogne*, Paris, L. Larmat, 1952
LAVEDAN, Pierre: *French Architecture*, London, Penguin, 1956
LAYTON, T. A.: *Choose Your Wine*, London, Duckworth, 1949
LEGLISE, M.: *Principes de Vinification*, Beaune, CIB, 1974
—: *Elévage et Conservation du Vin en Cave*, Beaune, CIB, 1974
LICHINE, Alexis: *The Wines of France* (3rd ed.), London, Cassell, 1956
MARION, Maurice: *Illustration et Défense du Vin de Beaune*, Beaune, Syndicat de Défense des Interêts Viticoles de Beaune, 1939
MARRES, Paul: *La Vigne et le Vin en France*, Paris, Armand Colin, 1950
MARRISON, L. W.: *Wines and Spirits* (3rd ed.), London, Penguin, 1973
MONTAGNE, Prosper and GOTTSCHALK, Dr (eds.): *Larousse Gastronomique* (English ed.), London, Paul Hamlyn, 1961
MORTON SHAND, P.: *A Book of French Wines* (revised and edited by Cyril Ray), London, Penguin, 1964
ORIZET, Louis: *Fragrances*, Mâcon, Editions de la Grisière, 1964
PENNING-ROWSELL, Edmund: *The Wines of Bordeaux*, London, International Wine and Food Society, 1969
POSTGATE, Raymond: *The Plain Man's Guide to Wine* (rev. ed.), London, Michael Joseph, 1957
POUPON, Pierre and FORGEOT, Pierre: *A Book of Burgundy*, London, Lund Humphries, 1958
—: *Les Vins de Bourgogne* (6th ed.), Paris, Presses Universitaires de France, 1972
—: *The Wines of Burgundy* (4th ed.), tr. Ott, Paris, Presses Universitaires de France, 1974
RODIER, Camille: *Le Vin de Bourgogne – La Côte d'Or*, Dijon, L. Damidot, n.d.
—: (Preface to) *Clos de Vougeot*, Dijon, M. Venot, n.d.
SAINTSBURY, George: *Notes on a Cellar Book*, London, Macmillan, 1920
SIMON, André: *The Supply, The Care and The Sale of Wine*, London, Duckworth, 1923
—: *Guide to Good Food and Wine* (rev. ed.), London, Collins, 1960
—: *A Wine Primer* (rev. ed.), London, Penguin, 1973
WARNER ALLEN, H.: *The Wines of France*, New York, Brentano's, n.d.
—: *Natural Red Wines*, London, Constable, 1951
—: *White Wines and Cognac*, London, Constable, 1952
—: *Through the Wine Glass*, London, Michael Joseph, 1954
WINE TRADE CLUB: *The Wine Trade of England, Past and Present* (text of lecture given in the Vintners' Hall), London, Wine Trade Club, 1911

BIBLIOGRAPHY

YOXALL, H. W.: *The Wines of Burgundy*, London, International Wine and Food Society, 1968

Articles which have appeared in:
Le Chablis Républicain, La Revue du Vin de France, Wine Mine, The Compleat Imbiber, Wine and Spirit and *Augustus Barnett News.*
Material supplied by 'Food from France' and by the Comités Interprofessionels of Villefranche-sur-Saône, Mâcon and Beaune.

GENERAL INDEX
Compiled by Susan M. Lawes with assistance from John Grant

Aedui, the, tribe, 20, 78
Ain, *département*, 2
Algeria, wines from, 7
Aligoté, grape, 13, 55, 56, 58, 61, 65, 116, 170, 173, 236, 237, 238, 240
Allen, H. Warner, 48, 56, 97, 190, 204, 206, 229
Aloxe-Corton, district; 176, also 129, 171; village of, 4, 47, 120, 128, 176, 204; early vinification, 22; vineyards of, 176
Alsace, wines compared, 39; trade with, 25
America, United States of, trade with, 50, 51, 53, 68, 72, 74, 75, 83, 92, 95, 149, 188, 248; taste in wine, 27, 40, 240; wines from, 7, 90, 92; vine stocks from, 28, 34, 187
Angerville, Marquis d', Domaine, 52, 148
Anse-Lachassagne, district, 77
Appellation Contrôlée, 10–18; Regulations, 10; legislation, 14, 15, 30, 54; classification, 10–12; declassification, 14–18, 59; effects of, 57, 60; introduction, 28 (see also individual districts and vineyards)
Ambal, firm of, 239
l'Arbesle, village of, 72
Arbuissonnas, village of, 76
Arcénant, village of, 65
Armand, Comte, 152
Arrières-Côtes, district of, 61–63, also 142, 241; wines of, 13, 55

Ausonius, 89
Australia, wines from, 7
Austria, trade with, 25
Autun, town of, 20, 138
Auxerre, town of, 21, 28, 226; district of, 223, 228
Auxey-Duresses, *appellation*, 141; vineyards, 141; *Domaines* in, 52; early cultivation, 20; village of, 120, 128, 141, 206
Avallon, district of, 225, 237
Avignon, Papal Court of, 23
Azé, village of, 93
Azergues, village of, 74

Bailli des Meurgis, brand, 239
Barolet, Dr., collection of, 169, 248
Bas-Beaujolais, district of, 72, 73
Batchelor, Denzil, 239, 240
Baubigny, village of, 61
Beardmore, Septimus, 27
Beaujeu, town of, 69, 76, 78
Beaujolais, district of, 67–87; villages of, 6, 11; geography, 6, 67, 70; production, 7; classification, 11; declassification, 15; pruning, 33, 69; *élevage*, 43; *négociants*, 46; grape varieties, 58; Route de, 68; early cultivation, 69; *vigneronnage*, 71; exports of, 72; vinification, 72; *appellation*, 73–76; *cuisine*, 79, 87; vintages in, 244
Beaujolais Nouveau, 46, 68, 74, 244

GENERAL INDEX

Beaujolais Supérieur, *appellation*, 76, also 74
Beaujolais-Villages, district of, 76–79; also 6, 73, 74
Beaujolais Blanc, 75, 82 (see also Saint Véran)
Beaune, *appellation*, 153–163, also 165; vineyards of, 11, 26, 48, 49, 157, 158, 163, 165; early wines of, 23; medicinal use, 24; early exports of, 24; Viticultural Congress, 28; production, 157; vintages in, 248; prices in 17th century, 23; 18th century, 48; 19th century, 26
Beaune, town of, 4, 21, 61, 119, 153; Château de Beaune, 48; Hôtel-Dieu, 4, 152, 158; Hospice de la Charité, 4, 158, 159 (see also Hospices de Beaune); wine museum, 49
Beaune Bastion, brand, 158
Beaune du Château, brand, 158
Beaunois, grape, 13, 222 (see also *Chardonnay*)
Beauvernais, Domaine de, 85
Beine, village of, 232, 233
Belgium, trade with, 24, 27, 50
Bélin, Jules, shipper, 184
Belloc, Hilaire, 130, 172, 190
Benedictine Order, 22, 89, 142
Béru, village of, 233
Bertagna, *Domaine*, 52, 200
Berry, Walter, 229
Bespaloff, Alexis, 76
Bétault, Hugues, 25
Beurot, grape, 13 (see also *Pinot gris*)
Bévy, village of, 65
Bichot, Albert, firm of, 49, 190, 229
Blacé, village of, 76
Blagny, *appellation*, 135; vineyards of, 135, 139; hamlet of, 133
Blending of wines, 120; with Algerian, 7
Blondeau, *cuvée*, 148
Boillot, *cuvée*, 141
Boillot, Henri, 148
le Bois d'Oingt, town of, 73, 77
Bois de la Salle, Château du, 84
Boisseaux Estivant, firm of, 59

Boisseaux, M., 138 (see also Patriarche, Père et Fils)
Bordeaux, wines compared, 6, 11, 53, 75, 243; mixture, 35
Bottles, 71, 79
Bottling, 44, *domaine*, 50
Bouchard Ainé et Fils, firm of, 24, 49; *domaines*, 101, 113, 158
Bouchard, Père et Fils, firm of, 24, 263; *domaines*, 8, 47, 48, 63, 130, 131, 148, 158; wines of, 59, 242
Bourgneuf Val d'Or, village of, 112
Bourgogne, *appellation*, 57–60, also 10, 53, 142, 223, 239
Bourgogne Aligoté, *appellation*, 55, also 10, 13, 53, 65, 88
Bourgogne Blanc, 58, 88, 105
Bourgogne Grande Ordinaire, *appellation*, 54, also 10, 53, 57, 105
Bourgogne, Marc de, 241 (see also Distillation)
Bourgogne Mousseux, 238, also 116, 169
Bourgogne Passetoutgrain, *appellation*, 56, also 10, 13, 53, 65, 105
Bourgogne Rosé, 58, 116, 236, 180
Bourgogne Rouge, 58, 88, 105, 237
Bouze-les-Beaune, village of, 13, 61, 156
Bouzeron, village of, 116
Brand names, 59, 158
Brochon, village of, 180, 215, 219
Brokers (*courtiers*) 44, (*commissionaires*), 71
Brosse, Claude, 90
Brouilly, district of, 79, also 58, 77; villages of, 79
Brouilly, *appellation*, 6, 79
Bugey, wines of, 2
Bureaux, Marcel, 112
Burgundy, viticultural area, 2; *départements*, 2; cuisine, 1, 3, 55, 93, 138, 162, 248; geography of, 3; holdings, 8; production, 6; comparison with other wines, 6, 39; vintage in, 37; misusage of name, 58; historical survey, 19–30; early cultivation, 20; Dukes of, 3, 4, 22, 23, 49, 67, 142, 145,

GENERAL INDEX

149, 152, 158, 162, 165, 171, 177, 194, 209, 218; Kings of, 21; Margaret of, 3; Marie of, 127; Hugues of, 138; medicinal usage, 24, 91, 189
Buxy, village of, 55, 105

Cabernet, grape, 243
Caesar, Julius, 20, 78, 85
Calvet, *domaine*, 139, 162
Camus, *domaine*, 212, 213
Canada, trade with, 49; as owners, 81
Casks, wines drunk from, 26, 73, 147; ageing in, 43, 242; types, xvi, 42, 71, 92, 116, 223
Cassis, 3, 240
Cercié, village of, 76, 79, 81
César, grape, 54, 58, 225, 239
Chabert, Marguèrite, 83
Chablis, *appellation*, 223–237; vineyards of, 3, 26, 229, 232; production, 7; compared to Bordeaux, 6, Mâcon, 88, 96, Rully, 101; holdings, 8; phylloxera, 28; classification, 11; viticulture, 32, 35; cuisine, 228; wines of, 97
Chablis Grand Cru, *appellation*, 229; vineyards, 231
Chablis Premier Cru, *appellation*, 232
Chablis, town of, 228, 232
Le Chablis Republicain, 226
la Chablisienne, co-operative, 228
Chagny, town of, 5, 99, 117
Chaintré, village of, 95
Châlet de Saint Jean des Vignes, tasting-room, 74
Chalon-sur-Saône, town of, 61, 99
Chalons, Jean de, Prince of Orange, 127
Chambolle-Musigny, district of, 203–204; village of, 4, 128, 201, 204; vineyards of, 52, 204; compared to Volnay, 148, Beaune, 157
Champagne, compared to Chablis, 223, Bourgogne Mousseux, 239, 240
Champy, père et fils, firm of, 24, 258; *domaines*, 167, 195
Chandesais, firm of, 101
Chandon de Briailles, *domaine*, 170
Chânes, village of, 76, 77, 94

Changes, village of, 61
Chanson, Père et Fils, family and firm, 24, 48, 163, 159; *domaines*, 8, 47, 49, 143, 157, 167, 170; branded wines, 60, 158
Chantovent, firm, 139
Chapaize, village of, 89, 90
la Chapelle de Guinchay, village of, 69, 76, 85
Chapelle des Minimes, 78
la Chapelle-Vaupelteigne, village of, 323
Chaptalization, 41, 235
Chardonnay, grape, 4, 5, 13, 36, 55, 56, 58, 61, 75, 86, 88, 92, 95, 104, 116, 125, 142, 147, 198, 226, 227, 235, 237, 239
Chardonnay, village of, 93
Charentay, village of, 76, 79
Charlemagne, *appellation*, 173
Charlemagne, Emperor, 22, 171, 173
Charny-les Mâcon, village of, 90
Chassagne-Montrachet, *appellation*, 125–9; village of, 4, 13, 120, 125; vineyards of, 52, 129
Chasselas, village of, 94
Chassey-le-Camonce, village of, 116
Chatillon d'Azergues, Château de, 73
Chauvenet, firm of, 181
Chaux, village of, 65
Cheilley-les-Maranges, *appellation*, 121; village of, 61, 120
Chemilly, village of, 233
Chénas, *appellation*, 85; village of, 6, 58, 69, 76, 84
Chenove, village of, 219
Chevallier, Gabriel, 68, 71, 77
Chévannes, village of, 65
la Chêvre Noir, brand, 59
Chichée, village of, 232
Chiroubles, *appellation*, 82; village of, 6, 58, 76, 82; vineyards of, 83
Chitry, village of, 236
Chorey-les-Beaune, *appellation*, 164; village of, 120, 164; classification, 11; Château de Chorey, 164
Church, as vineyard owners, 21, 22, 25, 48, 65, 86, 128, 153, 158, 180, 187, 189, 194, 195, 200, 209, 214, 215, 218, 221,

257

GENERAL INDEX

Church, as vineyard owners—*continued*
  227, 236; trade with, 24, 25
Cirey-les-Nolay, village of, 61
Citeaux, Abbey of, 22, 180, 197, 200;
  Abbots of, 23, 24, 152, 171, 194, 197
C.I.V.B., 223
Clair-Däu, *domaine*, 8, 52, 61, 200
Clairet (see Bourgogne Rosé)
Clerget, Raoul, grower, 123
Clessé, village of, 93
Clevner, grape, 13 (see also *Pinot gris*)
Cloche of Jules Bélin, marc de la, 242
Clochemerle, 6, 68, 77
Clos de la Roche, *appellation*, 206, also
  191, 205, 247
Clos de Vougeot (monograph), 2
Cluny, town of, 5, 88, 89; Abbey of, 22,
  89, 218
Cochylis, vine pest, 34
Colinot, Robert, 237
Collonges-les-Bévy, village of, 65
Columella, 21
Comblanchien, village of, 180, 181
Commissionaire, 71
Common Market, effect of, 42
Compagnons du Beaujolais, 76
Compagnons du Gosier Sec, 78
Concours Agricole in Paris, 15, 237
Condemine, François, 86
Confrérie des Chevaliers du Tastevin, 32,
  198
Confrérie de Vignerons de Saint
  Vincent, 90
Cooperages, 143
Co-operative Cellars, 8, 38, 39, 54, 55,
  61, 63, 65, 70, 74, 79, 83, 86, 89,
  92, 93, 98, 185, 228
Corgoloin, village of, 180, 181
Cormot, village of, 61
Corton, *appellation*, 171, also 170;
  vineyards, 26, 49, 171
Corton Charlemagne, *appellation*, 172,
  also 170; vineyards of, 14, 25, 173
Corton-Grancey, Château de, 48, 172
Côte de Beaune, district of, 118–177,
  also 4; villages of, 5; *domaines*, 52;
  brokers, 44; *pourriture*, 244;
  appellation, 163–164; compared to

Côte de Nuits, 179
Côte de Beaune Villages, *appellation*,
  120–121; classification, 10; compared
  to Côte de Nuits Villages, 180
Côte de Brouilly, *appellation*, 81, also 6,
  58
Côte de Buxy, 105
Côte Chalonnaise, district, 5, 55, 88,
  99–117 (see also Région de Mercurey)
Côte Dijonnaise, 3, 59, 60
Côte de Nuits, district of, 178–222, also
  4; villages of, 3, 4; compared to
  Mercurey, 112, Santenay, 124, Côte
  de Beaune, 179; vinification, 38;
  domaines, 49; brokers, 44; *pourriture*,
  244
Côte de Nuits Villages, *appellation*, 180–
  181, also 61; classification, 11;
  compared to Côte de Beaune Villages,
  180
Côte d'Or, district of, 118–222, also 3, 4;
  département, 2; production, 7;
  négociants, 46–47; *domaines*, 47–48, 52;
  compared to Bordeaux, 6, Mâcon, 88;
  holdings, 8, 11; *en primeur*, 47; grape
  varieties, 13, 54, 56; Bourgogne
  production, 58, 59; phylloxera, 28;
  casks, 71; viticulture, 32–38, 70;
  Bourgogne Mousseux, 239;
  vinification, 38; *cassis*, 240–241;
  élevage, 43; early prices, 26
Côtes du Rhône, comparison with, 75
Couchey, village of, 60, 180, 219
Coulanges-la-Vineuse, village of, 237
Coulure, vine disease, 35
Courtier, 44
Court noué, vine disease, 35
Cousinerie de Bourgogne, 165
Crémant de Bourgogne, 65, 240 (see also
  Bourgogne Mousseux and Sparkling
  Burgundy)
Crème de Prunelle, 241
Créot, village of, 61
Crimea, vines from, 23
Croonenburg, family of, 24
Cruse, firm of, 152
Curtil-Vérgy, village of, 65
Cuvée Elizabeth, brand, 60

258

GENERAL INDEX

Cuvée Voltaire, brand, 60

Dagobert, 21
Damoy, *domaine*, 214
Darviot, *domaine*, 158
Davayé, village of, 94
David, Tony, 68, 77
Delagrange-Bachelet, *domaine*, 132, 148
Delorme, André, firm of, 101, 116, 239
Delorme, Jean-François, *domaine*, 116
Denicé, village of, 76
Dépagneux, firm of, 93
Deschamps, tasting cellar, 84
Dezizes-les-Maranges, *appellation*, 121; village of, 61, 120; vineyards of, 121
Dijon, town of, 3, 21, 57, 58, 60, 61; vine growers of, 41; Bishop of, 23
Diseases and pests of the vine (see *cochylis*, *coulure*, *court noué*, *eudemis*, mildew, *millérandage*, oïdium, *phylloxera*, *pourriture*, *pyralis*, red spider); remedies against, 23, 27–29, 34–36
Distillation of wine, 44; legislation, 162, 241
Domitian, Emperor, 21
Doudet-Naudin, shippers, 167
Droin-Beaudoin, growers, 229
Drouhin, Joseph, family and firm, 49, 50, 130, 156, 159, 162; *domaines*, 49, 167, 200, 212, 163
Drouhin-Laroze, *domaine*, 195, 212, 213
Duboeuf, Georges, firm of, 71
Dubreuil-Fontaine, *domaine*, 170
Dufouleur, firm, 181
Dumas, Alexander, 130, 211
Dumay, Charlotte, 171
Durand-Blochet, M., 187 (see also Domaine Romanée-Conti)
Duret, M., grower, 181
Durette, village of, 76
Duty on French wines, effect of, 26

Échevronne, village of, 61, 63, 176
les Echézeaux, *appellation*, 191–192, also 187; vineyards of, 11, 18, 191–192
Égrappage, 39
Élevage, 43, 162

Émeringes, village of, 76
Emperors of France, Napoleon I, 25, 197, 210, 219; Napoleon III, 27
Engel, René, *domaine*, 191, 195
England, trade with, 49, 50, 53, 57, 69, 72, 74, 75, 83, 95, 205, 236, 240, 248; 18th century, 24, 25; 19th century, 26, 27; ownership, 71, 231; English taste, 40; English army, effect of, 184–185; English Kings, 222
Epertully, village of, 61
Epineuil, village of, 237
l'Etang-Vérgy, village of, 65
Etruscans, early trade with, 19
Eudemis, vine pest, 34

Fargues, village of, 90
Faiveley, J., family and firm of, 181, 198; *domaines*, 8, 47, 49, 101, 112, 157, 184, 185, 195
Fermentation, 39, 40, malo-lactic 42, 74
Fêtes de la Vigne, 153
Feuillette, xvi, 223
Finage, 135, 235
Fine de Bourgogne, 241, 242
Fixin, *appellation*, 219–222; village of, 4, 181; vineyards of, 222
Flagey-Echézeaux, village of, 128, 187, 191, 194
Flanders, trade with, 23
Fleurie, *appellation*, 83, also 77; village of, 6, 58, 69, 76; classification, 11; vineyards of, 83
Fleurot-Larose, *domaine*, 122, 130
Fleys, village of, 232
Foillard, Leon, 68, 77
Folie, Domaine de la, 116
Fontenay, village of, 232
Foreign ownership, 47, 71, 82, 231
Forgeot, Pierre, xv, 1, 20, 171
Fouloir-égrappoir, 39
Framboise, 241
France, Kings of, 23, 49, 171; (Philippe de Valois) 145; (Henri IV) 48, 107, 145, 152, 222; (Louis XI) 127, 145, 167; (Louis XIV) 79, 81, 90, 113, 145, 198; (Louis XV) 152
French laws of inheritance, 25

259

GENERAL INDEX

French Revolution, effects of, 25, 89, 187, 205, 209, 214, 215, 218
Fuissé, village of, 95
Fussey, village of, 61
Fyé, village of, 232

Gaboureau et Verry, firm of, 24 (see also Chanson, Père et Fils)
Gaidon, Pierre, 82
Gamay, grape, 5, 13, 22, 54, 56, 57, 58, 60, 61, 65, 69, 70, 84, 88, 90, 239
Gamay, village of, 13, 123
Gauvin, Cuvée, 148
Geisweiler, firm of, 181
Gelin, Pierre et fils, *domaine*, 222
Gennes (*marc*), 24
Geoffray, Claude, 81
Germain, Jacques, 164
Germany, trade with, 23, 24, 25, 50, 72, 236
Gevrey-Chambertin, *appellation*, 215–219; village of, 4, 128, 204, 215; classification, 11; vineyards of, 50, 52, 219
Gilly-les-Vougeot, village of, 197, 204
Givry, district of, 107–111, also 101; village of, 5; vineyards of, 111
Glantenays, family of, 25
Gouges, Henri, *domaine*, 52, 185
Goureau, *cuvée*, 148
Gout de grêle, 245
grafting, 34
Grange Chartron at Régnié, 78
Grape varieties (see *aligoté, beaunois, beurot, cabernet, césar, chardonnay, clevner, gamay, pinot blanc, pinot gris, pinot Liébault, pinot noir, sacy, sauvignon, tressot, melon de Bourgogne*); early varieties, 21, 227
Greffe anglaise, 34
Grillet, Château (Côtes de Rhône), 188
Gros, *domaine*, 190
Grossman, Harold, 157
Guillemard-Dupont, *domaine*, 58
Gwynn, Stephen, 69, 172

Hail, fight against, 36
Harvey, John, & Son Ltd, 122, 236

Haut Beaujolais, district of, 72
Hautes-Côtes de Beaune, district of, 61–63, also 54, 57, 58, 238, 61; classification, 11
Hautes-Côtes de Nuits, district of, 63–65, also 57, 238; classification, 11
Healy, Maurice, 190
Hectare, xvi
Hectolitre, xvi
Herbert, Bridget, 130
L'Héritier Guyot, firm of, 199, 241
Holland, trade with, 23, 24, 74
Hôpital de Meursault, 138
Hospices de Beaune, 158–162, also 139; vineyards of, 8, 139, 157, 158, 170, 172; wines of, 244; *cuvées*, 25, 49, 141, 143, 148, 152, 160, 246; Sale, 153, 159, 198; price comparison, 160
Hospices de Nuits, 185
Hospices, *marc des*, 162, 242
Huguenots, trade with, 23, 147

Igé, village of, 93
Illustration et Défense du Vin de Beaune, 157
Irancy, village of, 3, 58, 228, 237
Italy, early viticulture, 20; trade with, 25

Jaboulet-Vercherre, firm and family of, 149, 152
Jacob, Louis, *domaine*, 63
Jadot, Louis, firm of, 163, 212; *domaines*, 49, 158, 173
Japan, trade with, 50
Jéhan de Massol, *cuvée*, 148
Jobert, Claude, 210
Johnson, Hugh, 55, 213, 231
Joigny, district of, 225, 228, 237
Juliénas, *appellation*, 85, also 77; village of, 6, 58, 69, 76, 78, 85
Jullié, village of, 76, 78
Jullien, 26, 69, 195
Jully-les-Buxy, village of, 99, 105
Jus de goutte, 43
Jus de presse, 43

Kir, 55, 240; Canon, 55

GENERAL INDEX

Labaume Ainé, firm of, 25
Labet, Emile, firm and family of, 143, 241
Labouré-Gontard, firm of, 239
Lacenas, village of, 76
Ladoix-Serrigny, *appellation*, 177, also 176; village of, 120, 171; classification, 11
Lafon, Comte, 139, 157
Laguiche, Marquis de, *domaine*, 50, 130
Lamarche, *domaine*, 194
Lamartine, Alphonse de, 95
Lancié, village of, 76, 77
Lantignié, village of, 76
Laplanche, M., 151
Laroche, shippers, 229
Latour, Louis, firm of, 163; *domaines*, 8, 47, 93, 101, 105, 152, 158, 170, 172, 173, 189, 212
Lausseure, Jules, 27
Lavirotte, Affre, firm of, 25
Lebelin, *cuvée*, 143
Leflaive, *domaine*, 132, 135
Leroy, shippers, 141, 187
Létra, village of, 78
Leynes, village of, 76, 94, 95
Lichine, Alexis, 29, 50, 138, 169, 179, 218, 221
Lie (lees), 242
Liger-Belair, shippers, 188
Lignorelles, village of, 235
Liqueurs, 181
Loché, village of, 5; wines of, 5
Loisy, Mme de, 239
London, trade with, 24
Long-Depaquit, shippers, 229
Lugny, village of, 93
Lupé-Cholet, firm of, 181
Lyons, Seneschal of, 73

Mâcon, town of, 71, 87, 90, 93; *appellation*, 91
Mâconnais, district of, 88–98; wines of, 5, 6, 58, 75; geography, 87; viticulture, 33; production, 7
Mâcon Supérieur, *appellation*, 92
Mâcon Villages, *appellation*, 93

Magenta, Duc de, *domaine*, 52, 128; wine of, 128
Magnien, firm of, 215
Magny-les-Villiers, village of, 61, 65
Maison du Beaujolais, 79
Maison des Hautes-Côtes, 65
Maligny, village of, 232, 235
Mancey, village of, 89
Marc, 42, 241
Marc égrappé, 242
de Marcilly, shipper, 128
Marey, family of, 25, 181, 189, 190, 205
Marey-les-Fussey, village of, 56, 65
Marey-Monge, Domaine de, 52, 188, 189
Marion, Dr, *domaine*, 212, 222
Marion, Maurice, 157
Marsannay, *appellation*, 60, also 3, 58
Marsannay-la-Côte, village of, 3, 52, 60, 180, 181, 219
Maufoux, Pierre, 122
Mavilly-Mandelot, village of, 61, 63
Max, Louis, grower, 59, 164
Meloisey, village of, 58, 61, 63, 149
Melon de Bourgogne, grape, 55
Mémoires d'un Touriste, 197
Mercurey, *appellation*, 112–113, also 49, 101; vineyards of, 49, 112
Mercurey, Région de, 99–117, also 5, 56, 238; geography, 99; production, 7; villages of, 5, 99 (see also Côte Chalonnaise)
Messanges, village of, 65
Méthode ancienne, 39
Meuilley, village of, 65
Meursault, district of, 135–141, also 26, 97, 148, 246; village of, 4, 120, 135; vineyards of, 97, 139; classification, 11; Château de Meursault, 138, 139
Meursault-Blagny, district of, 120, 139
Mildew, vine disease, 34, 35, 36
Millérandage, vine disease, 35
Milly, village of, 232
Moillard, firm of, 181, 185
Moines, Cuvée des, 197
Moingeon-Guéneau, firm of, 239
Mommessin, firm and family of, 71, 206
Monassier, Armand, 116

261

GENERAL INDEX

Montagny, *appellation*, 105–107, also 97, 101; village of, 5; vineyards of, 105
Montauzan, Chateau de, 76
Monthélie, *appellation*, 143; village of, 120, 143, 206; vineyards of, 20, 143; Château de Monthélie, 143
Montjeu, Rézerolle de, 148
Montmélas, village of, 76
Montmerle, village of, 78
Moreau, J. et Fils, shippers, 229
Morelot, Dr., 158, 176, 197
Morey-Saint-Denis, *appellation*, 206–207; village of, 4, 128, 191, 201, 205, 206; vineyards of, 207
Morgeot, hamlet of, 128
Morgon, *appellation*, 81–2; village of, 6, 58, 69, 77
Morin, Père et Fils, firm of, 195
Morot, Albert, 158
Moucheron, Comte de, 138, 139
Moulin-à-Vent, *appellation*, 83–4, also village of, 6, 58, 69, 77
Muteau, General, *cuvée*, 148

Nantoux, village of, 61, 63
Négociants, 8, 38, 43, 45, 46; origin, 24
Neustadt-an-der-Weinstrasse, 90
New Zealand, wines of, 7
Nicolas, firm of, 101
Nierstein, Rhine, 204
Nièvre, *département*, 2
Noëllat, *domaine*, 190, 195
Noisot, M., 219
Nolay, village of, 5, 61, 63
Notre Dame du Raisin, Chapel of, 81
Nuits Saint-Georges, *appellation*, 181–185, also 26, 49, 52; village of, 4, 128, 181; classification, 11; vineyards of, 185; *mousseux*, 238

Odénas, village of, 76, 79, 81
Oïdium, vine disease, 27, 36
Orches, village of, 5, 54
Origines du Vignoble Bourguignon, 20
Orizet, Louis, 69, 97, 211, 214
Ouillage, 44
Ouvrard, Jules, 198
Ouvrée, xvi, 169

Papes, Cuvée des, 197
Parigot-Richard, firm of, 239
Paris l'Hôpital, village of, 61
pasteurization, 44
Patriarche, Père et Fils, firm and family of, 55, 60, 138, 161, 162, 163; *domaines*, 158
La Paulée de Meursault, 138
Le Pays et le Vin Beaujolais, 68
Pèlérinage aux Sources du Bourgogne, xv
Penning-Rowsell, Edmund, 248
Pernand-Vergelesses, *appellation*, 169–170, also 55, 56, 176; village of, 120, 128, 169, 171; vineyards of, 170; Pernand Blanc, 170
le Pérreon, village of, 76
Perret, Denis, retailers, 163
Pétasse, Joseph, *cuvée*, 159
Petit Chablis, district, 235; classification, 11
Petitjean, M., 169
Peyrat, Victor, 85
Phoenicians, early trade with, 19
Phylloxera vastatrix, vine pest, 27, 34, 82, 226, 235; effect on prices, 26; effect on production, 28, 61, 99, 113, 187
Piat, firm of, 50, 71, 93
Picard-Stockel, *domaine*, 128
Pièce, xvi, 223, 71
Pigeage, 42
les Piliers Chablisiens, 235
Pinot blanc, grape, 13, 54, 58, 92
Pinot gris, grape, 13, 58, 198
Pinot Liébault, grape, 13
Pinot noir, grape, 4, 13, 21, 22, 54, 55, 56, 57, 58, 60, 61, 65, 88, 105, 116, 125, 142, 237, 239, 243
les Pierres Dorées, 73
Pinson, Louis, firm of, 229
les Plessis, village of, 94
Poinchy, village of, 232
Pommard, *appellation*, 149–152, also 26, 37, 157; village of, 4, 120, 149, 181; vineyards of, 152; Château de Pommard, 151
Ponnelle, Pierre, *domaine*, 158, 200, 212

GENERAL INDEX

Pontaneveux, 71
Postgate, Raymond, 84, 190
Pot, xvi, 71
Pouilly, village of, 95
Pouilly-Fuissé, *appellation*, 95, also 5, 75, 93
Pouilly-Loché, *appellation*, 98
Pouilly-Vinzelles, *appellation*, 98
Poulet, Père et Fils, firm of, 24
Poupon, *domaine*, 139
Poupon, Pierre, 50
Pourriture, vine disease, 13, 244
Pousse d'Or, *domaine*, 52, 148
Prémeaux, village of, 180, 184
Prices, 17th century, 23; 19th century, 26; Hospices de Beaune Sales, 160–161; fluctuations, 39, 185, 233 (see also 'wine explosion')
Prieur, Jean, firm and family, 50, 138; *domaine*, 139, 200
Prieuré, Domaine du, 200
En primeur, 47, 57, 75
Prissé, village of, 94
Prissy, village of, 180
Probus, 21
Protheau, firm of, 112
Provignage, system of, 28
Prudhon, Ramonet, *domaine*, 128
Pruning, 33, 70, 95, 165
Pruzilly, village of, 76, 85, 94
Puligny-Montrachet, *appellation*, 133–135; village of, 4, 120, 125, 128, 130, 133; vineyards of, 133; Château de Puligny, 52, 135
Puligny-Montrachet-Blagny, *appellation*, 133
Pyralis, vine pest, 34, 79

Quartaut, xvi
Quarterly Review, 27
les Quatre Journaux, 189
Quincié, village of, 76, 77, 79, 81

Raclet, Bernard, 79
Ramain, Dr., 188
Ratafia, 241
Ray, M. François, 25

Rebourseau, General, *domaine*, 50
Red spider, vine pest, 34
Régnard, A. et fils, shippers, 229, 231
Régnié, village, 76
La Reine-Pédauque, *domaines*, 47, 176, 180, 195
Remoissenet, Père et Fils, firm of, 101, 158
Remontage, 42
Renarde, Domaine de la, 116
Reulle-Vérgy, village of, 65
Reynier, Peter, firm of, 231
Rhône, *département*, 67, 76, 84, 85
Rivolet, village of, 76
la Rochepot, village of, 5, 61, 63
Roche-pourrie, 82
la Roche Vineuse, village of, 93
Rodet, Antonin, firm of, 101, 112
Rodier, Camille, 2, 3, 22, 38, 148, 181, 184, 195, 198, 201, 215
Rois, Cuvée des, 197
Romanèche-Thorins, village of, 69, 71, 76, 79, 84
Romanée-Conti, *domaine*, 52, 130, 141, 187, 189, 191
Ronsard, poet, 152
Ropiteau Frères, shippers, 139, 143
Rosey, village of, 105
Roumier, Père et Fils, *domaine*, 52, 201
Roupnel, Gaston, 2, 19, 200, 211, 213
Rousseau, *domaine*, 52, 212
Rully, *appellation*, 113–116, also 97, 101, 238; village of, 5, 99; vineyards of, 116

Sacy, grape, 55, 225, 227
Saint-Amour, *appellation*, 86, also 6, 58, 94, 95
Saint-Amour-Bellevue, village of, 76
Saint Aubin, *appellation*, 124–125; village of, 120, 123; vineyards of, 125; classification, 11
Saint Bris, *appellation*, 228, 236
Saint-Bris-le-Vineux, village of, 3
Saint Étienne d'Ouillères, village of, 76
Saint Étienne la Varenne, village of, 76, 79
Saint Julien, village of, 76, 77

263

Saint Lager, village of, 76, 77, 79, 81
Saint Martin-sous-Montaigu, village of, 112
Saint Romain, *appellation*, 142, also 20, 52; village of, 120, 142
Saint Syphorien d'Ancelles, village of, 76
Saint Vallérin, village of, 105
Saint Véran, *appellation*, 94, also 75, 77
Saint Vérand, village of, 76, 94
Saint Vincent, patron saint of wine growers, 32, 198
Saintsbury, Professor George, 24, 69, 130, 171, 211
Salimbene, Fra, 227
Salles, village, 76
Sampigny-les-Maranges, *appellation*, 121; village of, 61, 120
Sancerre (Loire), 236
Saône et Loire, *département*, 2; viticultural area, 5, 59, 61, 67, 76, 84, 86, 95, 101, 121; holdings, 8; production, 7; growers of, 56
Santenay, *appellation*, 122–123, also 26; village of, 4, 120, 122; vineyards of, 11, 52, 123
Sauvignon, grape, 236
Sauvignon de Saint-Bris, *appellation*, 236
Sauzet, Étienne, 132, 135
Savigny, *appellation*, 165–169, also 26, 54, 63, 238; village of, 4, 120; vineyards, 169
Scandinavia, trade with, 88, 181
Seagram, firm of, 82
Seguin, firm of, 212
Selkirk, Alexander, 145
Sens, village of, 237
Shand, P. Morton, 97, 101
Simon, André, 149, 188
Simonnet-Febvre, firm of, 229
Société d'Élevage et de Diffusion des Grands Vins (see La Reine-Pédauque)
Société d'Intérêt Collectif Agricole du Vignoble Auxerrois, 239
Soil, for wine growing, 2, 32, 70, 82, 88, 95, 128, 131, 133, 143, 152, 173, 179, 213, 215, 223, 225, 235
Solutré, rock of, 5, 97; village of, 94, 95
Sombernon, village of, 59

Sonoma, California, 204
Sous-marques, 47
Spain, trade with, 25
Sparkling Burgundy, 27, 113, 181, 236 (see also Bourgogne Mousseux and Crémant de Bourgogne)
Stendhal, 197
Sulphur, 27, 36, 39, 44
Suremain, family of, 143
Sur lie, 56
Switzerland, trade with, 23, 24, 25, 50, 72

Tastevin, 43, 199
Taxes, effect of, 46
Testut Frères, *domaine*, 229
Thénard, Baron, *domaine*, 107, 130
Thévenin, Roland, *domaine*, 52, 131, 135, 141, 142
Thévenot-le-Brun, *domaine*, 56
Thomas-Bassot, 213, 215
Thorin, *domaine*, 71
Tollot-Beaut, *domaine*, 164
Tonnerre, district, 225, 237
Topographie des Vignobles, 26
Tournus, town of, 5, 89
Trapet, *domaine*, 212, 213, 214
Treatise on Agriculture, 21
Tressot, grape, 54, 58, 225, 239

Uchizy, village of, 90

Vauchignon, village of, 61
Vaux, village of, 76, 77
Vedrenne, firm and family of, 162, 184, 241
Vergisson, village of, 95
Verzé, village of, 93
Vienot, Charles, 184
La Vignée, brand, 59
Villamont, Henri de, *domaine*, 63, 169
Villars-Fontaine, village of, 65
Villefranche, town of, 67, 70, 73, 78
Villers-la-Faye, village of, 65
Ville sur Jarnioux, 73
Villié-Morgon, village of, 76, 82
Villy, village of, 235
Vin blanc cassis, 240; *vin de comptoir par*

GENERAL INDEX

excellence, 73; *vins de garde*, 73, 170; *vin de goutte*, 42; *vin gris*, 237; *vin de négoce*, 50; *vin de presse*, 42
Vine stocks, 34
Vin Fin de la Côte de Nuits, 181
Vinification, 39
Vintages, 243–249; (19th century), 23; (1881) 229; (1904) 170, 206; (1906) 48; (1915) 188; (1923) 172; (1928) 190; (1929) 84; (1945) 225; (1951) 225; (1953) 225; (1957) 225; (1959) 116; (1968) 159; (1970) 236; (1971) 15, 37; (1972) 38, 39, 40, 55, 59, 74, 116, 133, 233; (1973) 37, 38, 74, 88, 116; (1974) 37, 211
Vinzelles, village of, 5, 98
Viré, village of, 93
Viticulture, 31–37
Voarick, *domaine*, 165
Vocoret, Robert, 226, 229
Vogüé, Comte Georges de, 200, 201
Volnay, *appellation*, 145–148, also 52; village of, 4, 120, 145; vineyards of, 25, 26, 143, 148
Volnay-Santenots, *appellation*, 139
Voltaire, 24, 171
Vosne-Romanée, *appellation*, 193, also 49; village of, 4, 128, 187; vineyards of, 26, 193
Vougeot, *appellation*, 199; village of, 4, 52

'Wine explosion', 30, 45, 72, 101, 133, 161, 195, 226
Wines of France, 29, 50
World Atlas of Wine, 55
World Wars, effects of, 99, 107, 113, 187, 228

Yonne, *département*, 2; viticultural area, 8, 54, 55, 58, 59, 223 (see also Chablis)
Yoxall, Harry, 201

Zell, Moselle, 204

INDIVIDUAL VINEYARDS

les Amoureuses, Chambolle, 204
les Angles, Volnay, 148
les Arvelets, Pommard, 152

les Basses-Vergelesses, Pernand, 170
Bâtard Montrachet, 131–132, also 125
Beaumonts, Vosne, 194
Bellevue, Château de, Morgon, 82
en Bessay, Juliénas, 86
Bienvenues-Bâtard-Montrachet, 132
Blanchefleurs, Beaune, 49
Blanchots, Chablis, 229
Bonnes-Mares, 201
Bonnet, Château, Chénas, 85
Bouchots, Morey, 207
aux Boudots, Nuits, 184
la Boudriotte, Chassagne, 128
Bougros, Chablis, 229
les Bressandes, Beaune, 158
les Bressandes, Corton, 171
Brouilly-Pisse-Vielle, 78

Cailleret-Dessus, Volnay, 148
en Cailleret, Chassagne, 128
le Cailleret, Puligny, 133
en Cailleret, Volnay, 148
les Cailles, Volnay, 184
Calouère, Morey, 205
Capitans, Château des, Juliénas, 85
Caradeux, Pernand, 170
les Carquelins, Moulin-à-Vent, 84
Cazetiers, Gevrey, 217

le Cellier aux Moines, Givry, 111
les Chabiots, Morey, 206
les Chaffots, Morey, 205
Chaize, Château de la Brouilly, 79
les Chalumeaux, Puligny, 133
Chambertin, 209, also 26, 49, 157;
   sparkling, 27
Chamirey, Château de, Mercurey, 112
la Champagne de Savigny, Beaune, 157
en Champans, Volnay, 148
Champ Canet, Puligny, 133
Champs-Fulliot, Monthélie, 143
la Chapelle des Bois, Fleurie, 83
Chapelle Chambertin, 212
les Charmes, Chambolle, 204
les Charmes, Meursault, 139
Charmes-Chambertin, 212
les Chataigniers, St Vérand, 94
Chatelard, Château de, Beaujolais, 75
les Chères, Juliénas, 86
les Chéseaux, Fixin, 221
aux Cheusots, Fixin, 221
Chevalier Montrachet, 131
en Chevret, Volnay, 148
les Chilènes, Beaune, 157
Clavoillons, Puligny, 133
Climat de la Forge, Morey, 205
les Clos, Chablis, 229
Clos Arlots, Nuits, 185
Clos des Avaux, Beaune, 157
Clos Barrault, Mercurey, 113
Clos de Bèze, 209

INDIVIDUAL VINEYARDS

Clos Blanc de Vougeot, 199
Clos de la Bousse d'Or, Volnay, 145, 148
Clos de Chainette, Auxerre, 236
Clos du Chapitre, Fixin, 219, 221
Clos du Chapitre, Lugny, 93
Clos de Chênes, Volnay, 143, 148
Clos de la Commaraine, Pommard, 152
Clos de Corton, 157
Clos des Épeneaux, Pommard, 157
Clos de Fèves, Beaune, 26, 49, 248 (see also Fèves)
Clos Frantin, Vosne, 49
Clos des Lambrays, Morey, 207
Clos des Langres, Corgoloin, 180
Clos des Larrets (see Clos des Lambrays)
Clos de la Marche, Mercurey, 113
Clos des Marconnets, 49 (see also Les Marconnets, Beaune)
Clos de la Maréchale, Nuits, 49, 184
Clos de Mouches, Beaune, 49, 157, 158
Clos du Moulin des Moines, Auxey, 141
Clos de la Mousse, Beaune, 158
Clos des Myglands, Mercurey, 49, 112
Clos Napoléon, Fixin, 221
Clos de la Perrière, Fixin, 221
Clos des Pierres Blanches, Côte de Beaune, 164 (see also Pierres Blanches)
Clos du Roi, Beaune, 26, 49
Clos du Roi, Corton, 171
Clos du Roy, Fixin, 219
Clos Saint Denis, 205, also 191
Clos Saint Jacques, Gevrey, 215
Clos Saint Jean, Chassagne, 128
Clos Saint-Pierre, Givry, 111
Clos Saint-Paul, Givry, 111
Clos Salomon, Givry, 111
Clos de Tart, 205, also 25
Clos de Tavannes, Santenay, 11, 123
Clos de Topes-Bizot, Bourgogne, 59
Clos des Ursules, Beaune, 158
Clos Vignon, Marey les Fussey, 65
Clos de Vougeot, 194–199; hectarage, 11; holdings, 49, 50; sparkling, 27; history, 22, 24, 25, 26; Confrérie des Chevaliers du Tastevin, 33; Château de la Tour de Clos Vougeot, 195
les Combettes, Puligny, 133

le Combe d'Orveau, Chambolle, 200
la Comme, Santenay, 123
le Corton, 171, also 26, 49
Côte-Rôtie, Chiroubles, 83
aux Crais, Marsannay, 61
Crébillon, Brochon, 219
Criots-Bâtard-Montrachet, 132, also 125
les Cras, Volnay, 148

Dessus des Marconnets, Côte de Beaune, 164
Dominode, Savigny, 165
les Duresses, Auxey, 141, 143

les Echézeaux du Dessus, 191
les Épeneaux (see Épenots)
les Épenots, Pommard, 152
Éternelles, Gevrey, 217
d'Etroyes Château, Mercurey, 112
d'Etroyes-Juillet, Château de, Mercurey, 112

aux Favière, Marsannay, 61
Fer-Meulin, Marsannay, 61
Fèves, Beaune, 157
les Folatières, Puligny, 133
Fourchaume, Chablis, 232
les Fremières, Morey, 206
Fremiet, Volnay, 148
les Froischots, Morey, 206

Gaillard, Château, St Véran, 94
les Genevrières, Meursault, 139
les Gouttes d'Or, Meursault, 139
la Grande Châtelaine, Côte de Beaune, 64
la Grand'rue, Vosne, 194
Grands Echézeaux, 190–191, also 52, 187
les Gravières, Santenay, 123
Grenouille, Chablis, 229
Grèves, Beaune, 11, 48, 158
Grille-Midi, Chiroubles, 83
Griottes-Chambertin, 213

Hameau de Blagny, Blagny, 133

INDIVIDUAL VINEYARDS

Île de Vergelesses, Pernand, 170

Jacques, Château des, Moulin-à-Vent, 84
Juliénas, Château de, 86

Larrets, 207
Latricières-Chambertin, 212
Lavières, Savigny, 167
Loyse, Château de, Beaujolais, 75

Maison Brulée, Morey, 205
les Malconsorts, Vosne, 189
la Maltroie, Chassagne, 128
Mandelot, Château de, Mandelot, 63
les Marconnets, Beaune, 157, 158
les Marconnets, Savigny, 158, 165
les Maréchaudes, Corton, 171
les Mauchamps, Morey, 206
la Mazière, Fixin, 222
Mazoyères-Chambertin, 212
Mazys (or Mazis or Mazy)-Chambertin, 213
Mondes-Rondes, Côte de Beaune, 164
Montée de Tonnerre, Chablis, 232
le Montrachet, 129–131, also 26, 48, 50, 52, 107, 122, 125, 173, 188
les Monts-Luisants, Morey, 206
Morgeot, Abbaye de, Chassagne, 128
les Mouilles, Juliénas, 85
la Moutonne, Chablis, 229
aux Murgers, Nuits, 184
le Musigny, 200, also 49, 50

Palote, Irancy, 237
la Perrière, Fixin, 185
les Perrières, Corton, 47
les Perrières, Meursault, 139
la Petite Chapelle, Gevrey, 217
Pièce-sous-le-Bois, Meursault, 139
Pétures, Volnay, 148
Pierres Blanches, Côte de Beaune, 164
Pizay, Château de, Morgon, 82
la Platière, Pommard, 152

Portier, Château, Moulin-à-Vent, 84
Poruzot, Meursault, 139
les Preuses, Chablis, 229
les Pucelles, Puligny, 133

aux Quatre Vents, Fleurie, 83
Queue de Hareng, Brochon, 219

Redrescul, Savigny, 167
Richebourg, 190, also 24, 26, 52, 84, 157, 187
la Romanée, 188, also 26, 128, 187
Romanée-Conti, 187, also 24, 52
Romanée Saint-Vivant, 189, also 22, 24, 25, 52, 91, 187, 188
Ruchottes, Chassagne, 128
Ruchottes-Chambertin, 214
les Rugiens Bas, Pommard, 152
les Rugiens Haut, Pommard, 152

Saint-Armour, Château de, 86
les Saint-Georges, Nuits, 26, 184, 185
Santenots, Volnay, 148
Santenot-Volnay, 26
Sous-le-Dos-d'Âne, Meursault, 139
Sous-le-Puits, Puligny, 133
Suchot, Vosne, 194

la Tâche, 189, also 52, 187
les Thévenins, St Amour, 86
Thivin, Château, Côte de Brouilly, 81
les Thorins, Moulin-à-Vent, 84
la Tour du Bief, Moulin-à-Vent, 84

Vaillons, Chablis, 232
Valmur, Chablis, 229
les Vaucrains, Nuits, 184
Vaudésir, Chablis, 229
Vaumorillon, Tonnerre, 237
les Véroilles, Gevrey, 215
les Vergelesses, Pernand, 167, 170
la Vierge Romaine, Chassey, 116
Vigne de l'Enfant Jésus, Beaune, 48, 158